Target Markets

North Korea's Military Customers in the Sanctions Era

Andrea Berger

www.rusi.org

Royal United Services Institute for Defence and Security Studies

Target Markets: North Korea's Military Customers in the Sanctions Era
Andrea Berger
First published 2015

Whitehall Papers series

Series Editor: Professor Malcolm Chalmers
Editors: Adrian Johnson and Ashlee Godwin

RUSI is a Registered Charity (No. 210639)
ISBN 978-1-138-65493-8

Published on behalf of the Royal United Services Institute for Defence
and Security Studies
by
Routledge Journals, an imprint of Taylor & Francis, 4 Park Square,
Milton Park, Abingdon OX14 4RN

SUBSCRIPTIONS
Please send subscription orders to:

USA/Canada: Taylor & Francis Inc., Journals Department, 530 Walnut Street, Suite 850,
Philadelphia, PA 19106, USA

UK/Rest of World: Routledge Journals, T&F Customer Services, T&F Informa UK Ltd,
Sheepen Place, Colchester, Essex CO3 3LP, UK

Contents

About the Author   v
Acknowledgements   vi
Acronyms and Abbreviations   vii
Note on Sources   viii

Introduction   1

I. North Korea in the Global Arms Market   12

II. North Korea's Contemporary Defence-Export Industry   35

III. Resilient Customers   63

    Syria   64

    Iran   70

    Uganda   80

    Democratic Republic of the Congo   85

    Burma   89

    Cuba   97

    Armed Palestinian Organisations and Hizbullah   104

    Liberation Tigers of Tamil Eelam   108

IV. Reluctant Customers   113

    Ethiopia   114

    Yemen   122

V. Ad Hoc Customers   129

    Republic of the Congo   131

    Tanzania   134

    Eritrea   135

VI. Know Your Customer   139

Conclusion: Remaining Seized of the Matter   152

Appendix A: North Korean Brochure for AT-4 Anti-Tank Missile   155

Appendix B: Brochure for Gafat Armament Industry   159

About the Author

Andrea Berger is the Deputy Director of the Proliferation and Nuclear Policy programme at the Royal United Services Institute, where she is also a Senior Research Fellow. Her research focuses on non-proliferation, arms control and sanctions policy, and she takes special interest in the operations of proliferation networks. Andrea has worked extensively on North Korean nuclear issues, having led RUSI's engagement with the Korean Workers' Party, Korean People's Army, and the DPRK Ministry of Foreign Affairs over a number of years, both in London and Pyongyang. Prior to joining RUSI, Andrea worked in non-proliferation research at the International Centre for Security Analysis. She has also worked for the Government of Canada in a number of analytical capacities, latterly in the Department of Foreign Affairs, Trade and Development.

Acknowledgements

I am immensely fortunate to have benefited from the insights and expertise of many officials and experts over the course of researching and writing this Whitehall Paper. Foremost amongst them is Malcolm Chalmers, who gave me the opportunity to pursue this longstanding interest, unaware that he would have to endure animated, near-daily accounts of my findings in the months that followed. His constant guidance was indispensable to this study. Caroline Cottet and Michele Capeleto generously provided assistance with my early research. Joshua Pollack, Thomas Plant and Adrian Johnson offered thoughtful and detailed feedback on initial drafts of the manuscript, for which I am endlessly grateful. Many others also contributed their insights through private conversations or interviews, helping to shed light on a subject about which information is so sparse.

Sincerest gratitude is similarly owed to Ashlee Godwin, who tirelessly managed an often intercontinental editorial process to prepare this manuscript for print. My final thank you is reserved for the first person who read this paper, whose input was invaluable.

Acronyms and Abbreviations

CIA	Central Intelligence Agency
CNC	Computer numerically controlled
DDI	Directorate of Defence Industries (Burma)
DPRK	Democratic People's Republic of Korea
DRC	Democratic Republic of the Congo
FDLR	Democratic Forces for the Liberation of Rwanda
FNLA	National Front for the Liberation of Angola
IRGC	Iran Revolutionary Guard Corps
ITAR	International Traffic in Arms Regulation
KCNA	Korean Central News Agency
KOMID	Korea Mining Development Trading Corporation
KPA	Korean People's Army
MANPADS	Man-portable air-defence systems
MaRV	Maneuverable re-entry vehicle
MLRS	Multiple-launch rocket system
MTCR	Missile Technology Control Regime
NPT	Nuclear Non-Proliferation Treaty
ONI	Office of Naval Intelligence (United States)
P5	Permanent five members of the UN Security Council
PLO	Palestine Liberation Organization
PSI	Proliferation Security Initiative
R&D	Research and development
RoC	Republic of the Congo
SBIG	Shahid Bagheri Industrial Group (Iran)
SIPRI	Stockholm International Peace Research Institute
SSRC	Scientific Studies and Research Centre (Syria)
UAE	United Arab Emirates
UK	United Kingdom
UN	United Nations
US	United States
WMD	Weapons of mass destruction

Note on Sources

This Whitehall Paper draws upon an array of sources. Information on contemporary North Korean activity is not easy to obtain, particularly regarding military relationships and arms sales since 2006, with both customer and supplier eager to hide the existence of a contract or delivery. The DPRK and its customers have adapted to the UN arms embargo imposed against North Korea in 2006 and strengthened in 2009. To circumvent sanctions, they rely upon complex logistical and financial networks. Amongst other tactics, they lengthen the chain of brokers and intermediaries involved in a transaction to mask North Korean involvement, conceal illicit goods in containerised shipping, and engage in barter deals that evade due-diligence procedures in the global financial system. While sanctions have undoubtedly made life more difficult for North Korea's arms exporters and their clientele, their responses have complicated the international community's ability to detect sanctions-busting activity.

As a consequence, relevant information is scattered between media reports, declassified or leaked documents, government statements, UN reports, defector testimony and open-source imagery. This study brings that disparate information together, and makes every attempt to corroborate it. Substantiation is not always possible and subjectivity is therefore often unavoidable. As a result, this author makes clear where a particular assessment rests on a single source or where subjectivity as to the reliability of the information is used. Where an allegation appears particularly questionable, it is either introduced as such or omitted entirely.[1]

A disproportionate amount of the information used to support the claims in this paper is of Western origin. Few governments see countering North Korea's arms trade as a top priority. The US devotes by far the most resources and attention to this issue, as it is largely seen as a response to

---

[1] Reports that Zimbabwe has struck a deal with North Korea to trade uranium for arms is one example, though it is widely believed that Zimbabwe under Robert Mugabe is a customer of weaponry from Pyongyang. See Itai Mushekwe, 'Zimbabwe in "Arms for Uranium" Pact with North Korea', *Nehanda Radio,* 19 September 2013, <http://nehandaradio.com/2013/09/19/zimbabwe-in-arms-for-uranium-pact-with-north-korea/>, accessed 23 October 2015.

the North Korean nuclear problem. This is in line with the US's activeness within the non-proliferation arena generally. Other Western nations as well as countries like South Korea and Japan recognise it as important and actively engage with the issue where and to the extent possible, but are ultimately unable to devote comparable resources to addressing it. Elsewhere, few governments give attention to countering North Korean arms sales at all. Credible information on sanctions-relevant activity is thus primarily offered in US and Western sources. The author's limited access to translation resources has expanded this study's reliance on English-language material (though not necessarily from Western nations). As a result, it is hoped that future scholarship on the issue of the North Korean arms trade will be forthcoming from experts with access to a wider range of foreign-language resources.

In an effort to counteract any inherent bias and corroborate the disparate information presented in this study, the author has conducted extensive interviews with former and serving officials, military officers in countries of concern, experts around the world, and a businessman who has engaged in arms trade with North Korea. These interviews and conversations were conducted on a strictly not-for-attribution basis. While all of the conversations and interviews conducted by the author contributed to the thinking and analysis within the study, only some are directly cited in the text. Given the sensitivity of the subject and the small size of the community working on North Korean weapons sales and sanctions policy, the author has taken extra care to anonymise any interviewees that are directly referred to. Their affiliations and locations are described in general terms below, and each interviewee has been assigned a letter that is used for reference throughout the study:

- Interviewee A is an expert specialising in the former Soviet Union
- Interviewee B is an expert specialising in the defence industry in Russia
- Interviewee C is an arms dealer with experience in trading with North Korea
- Interviewee D is a former official working on North Korea for a Western government
- Interviewee E is a serving official working on North Korea for a Western government
- Interviewee F is a foreign official working in Yemen
- Interviewee G is a military officer in Yemen
- Interviewee H is an expert specialising in Yemen's security policy
- Interviewee I is an expert specialising in Yemen's security policy
- Interviewee J is an Asian former official specialising in North Korea.

INTRODUCTION

North Korea's first nuclear test in October 2006 confirmed the fears of those who had watched it withdraw from the Treaty on the Non-Proliferation of Nuclear Weapons three years earlier: Pyongyang was steaming ahead on a quest for a deliverable nuclear-weapons capability. The UN Security Council reacted swiftly to the development, acknowledging that other approaches – including the so-called 'Six-Party Talks' between North Korea, South Korea, Japan, the US, China and Russia – had not succeeded in preventing it. 'All of us find ourselves in an extraordinary situation, which requires the adoption of extraordinary measures', Russia's representative on the Security Council noted.[1] The US agreed that it constituted 'one of the gravest threats to international peace and security that [the Security] Council has ever had to confront'.[2] China called the move 'brazen', a term it reserves for its harshest condemnations.[3]

Amongst the extraordinary measures enacted by the Security Council in Resolution 1718 (2006) was an arms embargo. Member states were prohibited from importing from the Democratic People's Republic of Korea (DPRK), the official name for North Korea,[4] any weapons of mass destruction (WMD) or related materiel, or major conventional weapons systems.[5] The Resolution also set out that member states should prevent any transfer 'from the DPRK by its nationals or from its territory, of

---

[1]   UN Security Council, 'Security Council Condemns Nuclear Test by Democratic People's Republic of Korea, Unanimously Adopting Resolution 1718 (2006)', 14 October 2006, <http://www.un.org/press/en/2006/sc8853.doc.htm>, accessed 20 October 2015.

[2]   *Ibid.*

[3]   Joseph Khan, 'Angry China is Likely to Toughen its Stand on North Korea', *New York Times*, 10 October 2006.

[4]   This paper will use the two names interchangeably.

[5]   Major conventional weapons systems were defined as including: 'any battle tanks, armoured combat vehicles, large calibre artillery systems, combat aircraft, attack helicopters, warships, missiles or missile systems as defined for the purpose of the United Nations Register on Conventional Arms, or related materiel including spare parts, or items as determined by the Security Council' or by the Sanctions

technical training, advice, services or assistance related to the provision, manufacture, maintenance or use' of the weapons mentioned above. In a similar vein, member states were forbidden from selling *to* the DPRK any of these same weapons, or their related materiel or services.[6]

When North Korea unsuccessfully attempted to launch a satellite using long-range ballistic-missile technology in April 2009 and tested a second nuclear device in May 2009, the UN Security Council tightened the arms embargo against the country. Resolution 1874 (2009) extended the embargo to include all arms and related materiel and services, though an exception was made for sales of small arms and light weapons *to* North Korea.[7] Nevertheless, weapons-related exports by Pyongyang were henceforth prohibited by international law.

Conventional arms trade was targeted by the UN Security Council in response to successive North Korean nuclear tests for a number of reasons. In part, an arms embargo was simply one of the available tools for punishment, alongside restrictions on luxury goods, travel bans for North Korean officials and asset freezes. To a larger extent, however, the arms embargo was a means of achieving two things: first, reducing revenue sources for the regime, particularly for its nuclear and missile programmes; and second, disrupting North Korea's broader proliferation network.

France's representative to the Security Council highlighted the first objective during his remarks on the passage of Resolution 1874 (2009). The resolution, he said, is designed to:[8]

Committee established pursuant to the resolution. UN Security Council Resolution 1718 (2006), S/Res/1718 (2006), 14 October 2006, para. 8(a).

[6] *Ibid.*, para. 8(a)(i). 'Related materiel and services' is a term that has yet to be defined by the relevant UN Sanctions Committee. Instead, it has been subject to interpretation by UN member states, and by the UN Panel of Experts established pursuant to the resolution. Some points of clarity have emerged as a result of specific incidents, and a more general consensus appears to be emerging that items or services can be categorised as 'weapons-related' if they contribute directly to the use or manufacture of lethal armaments. Machine tools used in weapons production lines would therefore be considered 'weapons-related', for example.

[7] Circumstances underpinning the decision to exempt small arms and light weapons are not entirely clear. In most of the author's informal conversations on the subject, it has been asserted that China insisted on the provision. Two claims have been made in particular: that the exemption was inserted because North Korea should be allowed access to these weapons for self-defence, and that the comparatively small revenue generated by the export of these weapons means they are not relevant to efforts to inhibit Pyongyang's nuclear and missile programmes. UN Security Council Resolution 1874 (2009), S/Res/1874 (2009), 12 June 2009, para. 10.

[8] Statement by Ambassador Ripert of France to the UN Security Council, S/PV.6141, 64th year, 6141st meeting Friday, 12 June 2009.

[L]imit North Korea's capacity to advance its banned programmes, in particular by cutting off the financial resources originating from another destabilizing activity – the spread of weapons throughout the world – by blocking the financial networks that fuel those programmes, by extending the embargo to products that feed it, and by adopting sanctions against the persons and entities involved.

His assertion, and that of the Security Council as a whole, is premised on the fact that North Korea's nuclear and missile programmes draw to some degree upon those domestic coffers that are filled by overseas arms sales. Some North Korean entities, such as the Second Economic Committee, are actively involved in both activities. In addition to being 'responsible for overseeing the production of North Korea's ballistic missiles', the Second Economic Committee also directs the activities of the nation's primary arms dealer overseas, the Korea Mining Development Trading Corporation (KOMID).[9] Curbing defence-export revenue streams can thus limit the resources available to entities responsible for pursuing nuclear- and missile-related procurement and production. In this sense, the volume of revenue that North Korea generates through weapons-related sales overseas is an important metric for the sanctions regime's success.

Inhibiting conventional arms sales can also help disrupt and undermine the North Korean weapons-export apparatus itself – a second objective of the arms embargo. In an era where foreign revenue generation has been prioritised by the North Korean regime, smaller multi-role entities may wither without overseas arms sales to sustain themselves. In addition, most of Pyongyang's military customers allow representatives or offices of North Korea's key arms-dealing entities to operate from their territories. Eroding the networks that North Korea draws upon to facilitate arms sales to foreign customers, and reducing the number of territories from which those individuals and entities are able to easily operate, could similarly increase Pyongyang's difficulties in sourcing goods and components for its nuclear and missile activities. The number of North Korean clients – regardless of the value of their custom – is therefore a significant metric of success for the sanctions regime as well.

Sanctions create other undesirable complications for North Korea and its customers, such as additional financial costs, especially at the transport stage of a transaction. Above all, the risk of being caught red-handed in violation of international law can involve political costs – more so for a would-be customer than for North Korea. As a result, it is believed that

---

9 US Department of the Treasury, 'United States Designates North Korean Entities and Individuals for Activities Related to North Korea's Weapons of Mass Destruction Program', 30 August 2010, <http://www.treasury.gov/press-center/press-releases/Pages/tg840.aspx>, accessed 20 October 2015.

sanctions might change the cost-benefit calculus behind some of the demand for North Korean goods and services.

The arms embargo offers a presumed third benefit not directly mentioned in official UN Security Council discussions: preventing undesirable military developments by the DPRK's foreign partners, particularly those which might seek their own WMD capabilities, whose actions pose a threat to international peace and security, or whose military might is used against their own populations. For example, sanctions might be expected to stem the flow of North Korean weapons to Syria, Burma and non-state militias in the Middle East.

The Security Council action helped to cement a longstanding downward trend in North Korea's defence-export industry, which was already troubled. As this study will demonstrate, the country's customer base for arms and related materiel and services had been steadily shrinking since the end of the Cold War. Before 1990, North Korea's military exports had formed an important part of its foreign-policy strategy and Pyongyang was gifting or selling discounted weapons to state and non-state customers, from Grenada to Malta to revolutionary groups across Africa.[10] In recent times, by contrast, those exports appear to have become less an expression of foreign-policy priorities than a means of generating revenue. Shifts in the international political climate and global defence market, North Korea's increasingly out-of-date technology, and strengthened international laws and norms against Pyongyang's military exports have all helped to undermine its prospects for success in this area.

Despite these changes and a robust sanctions regime after 2006, a host of countries continue to find North Korea an attractive partner. For example, a recent UN report identifies a number of countries – including Ethiopia, Tanzania and Uganda – that are suspected of recently being customers for its weapons-related goods or services.[11] In 2013, the US Treasury designated[12] new individuals and entities in Burma for allegedly doing the

---

[10] See *Malta Independent*, '1982 Labour Government "Secret" Agreement with North Korea – "Times Change" – Alex Sceberras Trigona', 7 February 2010, <http://www.independent.com.mt/articles/2010-02-07/news/1982-labour-government-secret-agreement-with-north-korea-times-change-alex-sceberras-trigona-270034/>, accessed 20 October 2015; US Department of State and Department of Defense, *Grenada: A Preliminary Report* (Washington, DC: Government Press Office, 1983), p. 24.
[11] UN Security Council, 'Report of the Panel of Experts Established Pursuant to Resolution 1874 (2009)', S/2014/147, 6 March 2014.
[12] The term 'designate' is used in this study to refer to a government's decision to sanction an individual or entity for carrying out activity counter to its laws. Designations ordinarily involve the freezing of assets, as well as prohibiting the nationals of the country taking the action from dealing with the sanctioned

same;[13] and over the past five years, numerous vessels containing illicit North Korean cargo destined for Syria have been seized.[14] North Korea's alleged dealings with non-state actors have also made headlines. The *Daily Telegraph* reported that Hamas's 2014 war against Israel had depleted its weapon stocks, and that as a result, the group was again turning to North Korea for replenishment.[15] An incident a few years earlier had highlighted Hamas as a North Korean customer: in 2009, Thailand seized a cache of North Korean weapons which the White House and Israel agreed was on its way to Hamas, and possibly Hizbullah.[16]

Demand perseveres and Pyongyang, for its part, is working to ensure supply. It is persistent in translating its arms-production capabilities and military expertise into financial gain, and, as this Whitehall Paper will show, is actively reaching out to new military markets. The job of governments and non-governmental experts working to improve the implementation of the sanctions regime is to develop a detailed understanding of the problem, to outline tailored, multilateral and creative solutions to counter it, and ultimately, to match North Korea's persistence.

Purposes of the Study

Recognising North Korea's continued ability to find markets for its weapons-related exports, this study's purpose is threefold: to fill in gaps in the existing scholarly literature on North Korean proliferation activity and foreign relations; to support sanctions implementation by providing detailed analysis of the recent demand for North Korean military products and services; and to advance ongoing discussions about the efficacy of the current UN sanctions regime.

In terms of the first aim, the majority of the analysis on Pyongyang's military endeavours focuses on the country's own nuclear and missile

---

individual or entity. In the US, those sanctioned by the Office of Foreign Assets Control are collectively referred to as 'Specially Designated Nationals'.

[13] US Department of the Treasury, 'Treasury Designates Burmese LT. General Thein Htay, Chief of Directorate of Defense Industries', 2 July 2013, <http://www.treasury. gov/press-center/press-releases/Pages/jl1998.aspx>, accessed 20 October 2015. See also US Department of the Treasury, 'Treasury Designates Burmese Companies and an Individual with Ties to the Directorate of Defense Industries', 17 December 2013, <http://www.treasury.gov/press-center/press-releases/Pages/jl2247.aspx>, accessed 20 October 2015.

[14] UN Security Council, 'Report of the Panel of Experts Submitted Pursuant to Resolution 1874 (2009)', S/2012/422, 14 June 2012.

[15] Con Coughlin, 'Hamas and North Korea in Secret Arms Deal', *Daily Telegraph*, 26 July 2014.

[16] Andrea Berger, 'North Korea, Hamas and Hezbollah: Arm in Arm?', 38 North, 5 August 2014, <http://38north.org/2014/08/aberger080514/>, accessed 20 October 2015.

programmes, rather than on its arms-related exports,[17] which have previously included WMD-relevant technology but today are believed to be largely conventional – both in terms of volume and revenue.[18] This is an understandable preoccupation, as it is precisely because of North Korea's national pursuit of WMD and delivery capabilities that UN restrictions on its arms trade were put in place. Yet, given Pyongyang's frequent use of conventional weapons-related exports as a means of generating revenue for its nuclear- and missile-development programme, and the importance of weapons sales in sustaining North Korea's proliferation apparatus as a whole, it is also essential that one activity is not discussed to the exclusion of the other.

Despite the overlap between the threat posed by North Korean WMD and that posed by its defence exports, analysis of the latter is thin. The valuable work that has been done in this area tends to be heavily supply-centric, and often focuses either on specific systems or individual bilateral military partnerships with Pyongyang.[19] Analyses of

---

[17] See, for example, Leon V Sigal, *Disarming Strangers: Nuclear Diplomacy with North Korea* (Princeton, NJ: Princeton University Press, 1998); Jonathan D Pollack, *No Exit: North Korea, Nuclear Weapons, and International Security*, Adelphi series 418–19 (Abingdon: Routledge for IISS, 2011); Su Hoon Lee (ed.), *Nuclear North Korea: Regional Dynamics, Failed Policies, and Ideas for Ending a Global Stalemate* (Boulder, CO: Lynne Rienner Publishers, 2012). Some work has been done on proliferation and North Korean illicit trade networks generally defined. See, for example, Sheena Chestnut, 'Illicit Activity and Proliferation: North Korean Smuggling Networks', *International Security* (Vol. 32, No. 1, Summer 2007).

[18] It is possible, and perhaps likely, that a single contract for large-ticket weapons, systems, or programmes such as ballistic missiles and weapons of mass destruction could account for more than the entire revenue from conventional-arms sales and services. However, as this paper will show, aside from those with Syria and possibly Iran, North Korea is today believed to have few such contracts.

[19] Examples of the valuable system-specific literature that has been produced, which encompasses analysis of North Korean exports, include Dinshaw Mistry, *Containing Missile Proliferation: Strategic Technology, Security Regimes, and International Cooperation in Arms Control* (Seattle, WA: University of Washington Press, 2003). Janne E Nolan's work on the missile market in the developing world remains relevant and is an exception to the supply-centric focus of the majority of the literature. Janne E Nolan, *Trappings of Power: Ballistic Missiles in the Third World* (Washington, DC: Brookings Institution, 1991). Similarly, while Joshua Pollack's analysis focuses on North Korea's ballistic-missile exports, his work importantly recognises the more recent comparative significance to Pyongyang of conventional-systems sales, particularly in light of the declining global demand for its missile products. Joshua Pollack, 'Ballistic Trajectory: The Evolution of North Korea's Ballistic Missile Market', *Nonproliferation Review* (Vol. 18, No. 2, July 2011). Among others, Balázs Szalontai of Kookmin University has produced quality analysis of North Korea's bilateral partnerships, including military partnerships, in regions such as the Middle East. Balázs Szalontai, 'Cracks in the

North Korean arms sales, particularly when presented by the media, consistently allude to the regime's quest to earn foreign currency through whatever means possible.[20] While there is truth to this claim, as Chapter II will demonstrate in relation to North Korea's arms-export catalogue, it is usually raised at the expense of robust demand-side analysis.

With regards to specific systems, Pyongyang's sale of ballistic missiles has undoubtedly received the most public attention,[21] not least due to their potential role as a delivery system for WMD. Together with other WMD-relevant technology, they represent the country's most troubling defence export. From the late 1980s until the early 2000s, they were believed to account for the bulk of North Korea's revenue from weapons sales, though it is possible that today the majority is generated through conventional weapons-related goods and services.[22]

Aside from weapons-systems-specific analysis, available literature on North Korea's arms sales largely examines individual bilateral relationships, such as the Iran–North Korea and Burma–North Korea connections. Literature that goes beyond bilateral ties usually only considers North Korea's foreign relations, broadly defined. Charles Armstrong's *Tyranny of the Weak* presents a comprehensive and detailed overview of the genesis of some of North Korea's longest-standing relationships, including those with a military component.[23] Exploring the contemporary practicalities of the DPRK's international dealings, John Park's 'North Korea, Inc.' offers

---

North Korea-Iran Axis', *NK News,* 5 August 2014, <http://www.nknews.org/2014/08/cracks-in-the-north-korea-iran-axis/>, accessed 20 October 2015. Outside of the Middle East, only a few of North Korea's bilateral military relationships have received attention. See, for example, Joost Oliemans and Stijn Mitzer, 'North Korea and Ethiopia, Brothers in Arms', *NK News,* 4 September 2014, <http://www.nknews.org/2014/09/north-korean-military-support-for-ethiopia/>, accessed 20 October 2015.

[20] See, for example, Claudia Rosett, 'North Korea's Middle East Webs and Nuclear Wares', *Forbes,* 13 February 2013.

[21] See footnote 19 for information on system-specific analysis, which is heavily concentrated on North Korea's ballistic-missile exports.

[22] In fact, in 1999 North Korea insisted that it would cease its sale of ballistic missiles if the US paid it $3 billion over three years – a proposal that was a non-starter in Washington. US Department of State Daily Press Briefing, DPB #40, 30 March 1999 at 2:50 pm, available at <http://fas.org/news/dprk/1999/990330db2.htm>, accessed 20 October 2015. See also Joseph S Bermudez, Jr, 'A History of Ballistic Missile Development in the DPRK', Center for Nonproliferation Studies Occasional Paper No. 2, 1999; Paul K Kerr, Steven A Hildreth and Mary Beth D Nikitin, 'Iran-North Korea-Syria Ballistic Missile and Nuclear Cooperation', Congressional Research Service, Report 7-5700, 16 April 2014.

[23] Charles K Armstrong, *Tyranny of the Weak: North Korea and the World, 1950–1992* (Ithaca, NY: Cornell University Press, 2013).

insights into the state trading companies operating abroad that bring life to some of the relations that Armstrong discusses and this paper presents.[24]

While this paper is informed by the supply-centric or system-specific analysis that exists in abundance in expert literature, its primary aim is to capture a broad picture of North Korea's military customers in the sanctions era, focusing particularly on what drives them. In doing so it updates the earlier literature and draws trends between known or suspected purchasing states. It is this understanding that enables a more concrete and nuanced discussion about the policy approaches that might successfully peel customers away from Pyongyang.

As a result, the second aim of this study is to support efforts to implement sanctions by analysing the demand for North Korean defence exports. Focusing on demand is crucial. Decades of scuppered negotiations have shown that when it comes to its military activity, Pyongyang is largely immune to external influence and pressure from those governments that are the most ardent supporters of the current sanctions regime. Arms-related exports appear to be no exception. As this Whitehall Paper will argue, concentrating efforts on making North Korea and its products less appealing from the perspective of potential consumers, rather than eroding North Korea's interest in supplying them, holds up the greatest prospect of success for the sanctions regime.

In analysing North Korea's military customers, this paper adheres to the scope of the extended arms embargo outlined in UN Security Council Resolution 1874 (2009): namely, 'all arms and related materiel, as well as financial transactions, technical training, advice, services or assistance related to the provision, manufacture, maintenance or use of such arms or materiel'.[25] It does not touch on the UN-mandated ban on luxury goods, which is designed to deny the North Korean regime its daily comforts, rather than directly inhibit military activity. Due to its focus on Pyongyang's customer base, this study also does not delve into detail about North Korean imports for its defence research-and-development programmes, though it does highlight the importance of denying North Korea access to advanced military technology. Instead, after briefly considering the evolution of North Korea's place in the global market (Chapter I) and the country's arms-manufacturing capabilities (Chapter II), this study identifies the state and non-state groups that form North Korea's sanctions-era clientele, and the items and services in Pyongyang's export catalogue that

---

[24] John S Park, 'North Korea, Inc.: Gaining Insights into North Korean Regime Stability from Recent Commercial Activity', United States Institute of Peace Working Paper, 22 April 2009, <http://www.usip.org/sites/default/files/North%20Korea,%20Inc.PDF>, accessed 20 October 2015.
[25] UN Security Council Resolution 1874 (2009), S/Res/1874 (2009), 12 June 2009.

they have found most attractive (Chapters III, IV and V). Together, these chapters will provide a rounded sense of the landscape of the market in which North Korea operates and the custom it enjoys.

This paper will also explore *why* countries turn to North Korea over other suppliers. Two common answers to this question are peppered throughout expert literature and public commentary: Pyongyang's offerings are inexpensive; and North Korea and its military customers are bonded by their shared pariah status.[26] While both these narratives carry some truth, the picture is more complex. North Korea is likely more competitive on price in certain categories of products and services – namely, conventional weaponry and related parts, and repair, maintenance and training services – a conclusion outlined in Chapter II. Furthermore, price and level of international isolation rarely offer a complete explanation for a customer's decision to purchase from North Korea. To effectively curtail demand, those wishing to improve sanctions implementation must first seek to fully understand the reasons that individual clients find Pyongyang an attractive supplier.

These perceived benefits vary widely between individual customers. Chapter III presents some of North Korea's recent 'resilient' customers: a group that is aware of the existence of sanctions, but defies them because of deep political and military ties to Pyongyang, North Korea's reliability as a supplier, shared international isolation and, to some extent, affordability. These include Syria, Iran, Burma and Uganda, amongst others. Chapter IV looks at the 'reluctant' customers: those who would probably prefer to purchase military goods elsewhere, but found that historical military aid and purchases from North Korea have created a degree of dependence upon their supply; those struggling to find other suppliers able and willing to replace or service Cold War-era weaponry; or those whose pockets are not deep enough to choose to buy elsewhere. These include Ethiopia and, until recent political turmoil, Yemen. Finally, Chapter V presents 'ad hoc' customers – states such as the Republic of the Congo (RoC) and possibly Tanzania – whose awareness of the sanctions regime is weaker than clients in other categories. For these countries, the need to extend the lives of their Cold War-era arsenals as inexpensively as possible made Pyongyang an attractive choice amongst limited options.

---

[26] See, for example, Oliemans and Mitzer, 'North Korea and Ethiopia, Brothers in Arms'. Bertil Lintner similarly focuses on price as the reason Burma started buying from North Korea. Bertil Lintner, 'Clouded Alliance: North Korea and Myanmar's Covert Ties', *Jane's Intelligence Review*, October 2009, p. 49, available at <http://www.asiapacificms.com/articles/pdf/clouded_alliance.pdf>, accessed 20 October 2015. See also 'Breaking the Iran, North Korea, Syria Nexus', Joint Hearing before the Committee on Foreign Affairs of the House of Representatives, 113th Congress, First Session, 11 April 2013, <http://docs.house.gov/meetings/FA/FA13/20130411/100636/HHRG-113-FA13-20130411-SD002.pdf>, accessed 20 October 2015.

In all three chapters examining the different categories of North Korea's customers, analysis focuses on the state and non-state groups that are known or strongly suspected to have purchased arms or related services from North Korea since the application of UN sanctions against the country in 2006. Two qualifications are necessary here. First, evidence of relevant contracts with North Korea during the sanctions era does not necessarily constitute a sanctions violation. Until UN Security Council Resolution 1874 (2009), North Korean sales of small arms, light weapons, and related materiel and services were not subject to UN arms embargoes. It was only in June 2009 that all arms and related materiel and services sold by Pyongyang were declared illegal, even if not North Korean-made.

Second, due to the nature of the activity in question, information on any given country's dealings with North Korea in this period is often inconsistent. Clusters of information appear in leaked US State Department cables dated up to 2010 or in annual UN reports, for example. As a result, while Chapters III, IV and V seek to bring together as many credible sources as possible to provide an outline of North Korea's *recent* customers, in many cases it is difficult to be certain that they are *current* customers at the time of writing. Information from before 2006 is included where relevant, particularly to demonstrate that a specific client's motivation for continually purchasing from Pyongyang either includes traditional political, military or personal friendships, or has notably changed over time.

The third and final purpose of this study is to advance ongoing discussions about the effect that UN sanctions have had in curbing North Korea's military sales, and thereby stemming the flow of profits into coffers that can fund nuclear and missile advancement. In particular, by providing the clearest and broadest picture of North Korea's defence-export markets to date, it highlights how, with the help of sanctions, the types of goods and services that North Korea markets most successfully are changing, with implications for the country's ability to maintain or expand these revenue streams.

In the process of painting this picture, the study draws several conclusions: that North Korea's customers vary greatly; that policy tools available to government and UN officials should be tailored to take account of those differences; and, as discussed in Chapter VI, that one of the long-term approaches with the greatest potential for success is to deny North Korea the technology that will allow it to remain relevant as a defence exporter.

Of the three broad types of customer identified – 'resilient', 'reluctant' and 'ad hoc' – this paper will demonstrate that the majority of known sanctions-era customers are of the most problematic, 'resilient' variety. They have longstanding military trade relationships with North Korea and defy pressure to cease them. Policy tools which might in other cases compel a country to stop dealings with North Korea are likely to have little effect towards 'resilient' clients, unless they form part of a broader political or military change in that country.

This is important to bear in mind when trying to curb demand from these customers, and this study highlights the importance of being aware of the reasons that a client chooses to buy from North Korea in the first place when selecting and applying policy tools. 'Reluctant' and 'ad hoc' clients have no particular affinity for North Korea itself as a supplier. As a result, they are in theory more easily dissuaded from continuing to do business with them than the 'resilient' customers are – a conclusion borne out by the recent RoC case (discussed in Chapter V). Interdictions and political pressure can have significant impact upon their procurement decisions, as can assistance (whether financial or procedural) in finding alternative supply.

Finally, this Whitehall Paper also explores one of the most significant, but unacknowledged, contributions of the UN sanctions regime: denying North Korea the ability to stay relevant as a defence exporter for the indefinite future, especially in the minds of customers who currently fall, or may in the future fall, into the 'reluctant' or 'ad hoc' categories. The arms embargo has been largely successful in mitigating Pyongyang's access to new, foreign weapons designs or production technology. North Korea has had to innovate on its own, often producing slight variations of its older weapons, as will be shown in Chapter II. Nevertheless, much of its arms-export catalogue now consists of base technology that is many decades old, and as a whole is sliding progressively farther out of date. Continuing to deny Pyongyang advanced weapons technology in the long term will undoubtedly make it more difficult for it to identify new markets for its conventional weapons.

Existing 'reluctant' or 'ad hoc' customers may fall by the wayside too. Life-extension programmes cannot go on indefinitely, and countries that currently possess Cold War-era weaponry will over time also have to withdraw them from service. Given that one of Pyongyang's current competitive advantages in these markets is its familiarity with repairing antique systems, if those deploying such weapons no longer require repair services and North Korea does not have newer wares to offer, Pyongyang may find itself more peripheral within the global defence market than ever.

I. NORTH KOREA IN THE GLOBAL ARMS MARKET

North Korea has been an important player in the global arms market for over fifty years, during which time it has exported military goods and services to clients around the world. During the Cold War, when arms trade with North Korea was not the politically poisonous and illegal endeavour that it is today, over sixty states and non-state groups are believed to have accepted military assistance from Pyongyang.[1] The country was merely one possible supplier amongst many in the communist bloc. Following the end of the Cold War, numerous structural and policy changes began to diminish North Korea's market reach and perceived legitimacy as a supplier. That trend was solidified with the advent of UN sanctions in 2006 and their subsequent strengthening in 2009. From that point forward, all states were required to prevent North Korea from buying or selling conventional weapons systems, missiles, weapons of mass destruction (WMD), and related goods and services.

This chapter describes these three periods: the Cold War; the post-Cold War period until October 2006, when UN Security Council Resolution 1718 was passed; and the ensuing era of international sanctions. In doing so it identifies and explains trends in North Korea's defence-export activity, including the volume of business and the most popular products and services. It also outlines the range of actors that have over time become involved in preventing and countering North Korean weapons-related trade. Lastly, it highlights the policy tools that those wishing to improve the implementation of sanctions have previously used, and continue to have available to them, in order to curb the number of North Korea's customers and the volume of illicit trade with each.

Together with Chapter II, which presents North Korea's contemporary defence-export catalogue and approach, this overview sets the stage for subsequent sections analysing Pyongyang's clients in the sanctions era,

---

[1] Andrea Matles Savada (ed.), *North Korea: A Country Study* (Washington, DC: GPO for Library of Congress, 1994), chapter on 'Relations with the Third World'.

the weapons and services they have recently selected from the North Korean catalogue, and their motivation for turning to North Korea over other suppliers.

Cold War, Hot Markets

North Korea's defence-industrial complex was conceived in the 1940s, immediately after the creation of the new state in 1948 and prior to the Korean War (1950–53). President Kim Il-sung was at the time eager to create an industrial base that would allow the country to equip its own armed forces. A photograph of Kim Il-sung firing the first North Korean-made rifle in 1948 is proudly displayed in the Korean Workers' Party Museum in Pyongyang.[2] Though not initially export-oriented, North Korea's defence production capability gained impetus during the Korean War and expanded further after it. In a plan adopted in late 1962, North Korea launched a sustained effort to seek self-sufficiency in military hardware and develop more sophisticated and diverse weaponry.[3]

Most of the equipment churned out by the first production lines was based on licensing agreements with fellow communist states, namely the Soviet Union and China, which also helped to establish arms factories in the country. In some cases, Pyongyang maintained the original designs, producing direct copies. In other cases it modified or improved them, an approach it would increasingly favour in coming decades. By the 1960s, it was able to manufacture an array of weapons systems, ranging from small arms and ammunition to light weapons, artillery, and tanks and other armoured vehicles. Because these weapons were based on then-current Soviet or Chinese designs, the technology was reasonably up-to-date.

North Korea's practice of exporting weapons and providing weapons-related services seems to have begun in earnest at this time, primarily as a contribution to the country's foreign-policy aims. Its main national objectives – reunification, the removal of US forces from the Korean Peninsula and securing economic investment – were more likely to be achieved with the broadest possible international support. North Korea saw opportunities to win such support during the period of decolonisation.[4] Independence movements were sweeping across Africa and Asia, in an attempt to cast off what Pyongyang agreed was imperialist oppression.[5]

---

[2] Author's visit to the Korean Workers' Party Museum, Pyongyang, June 2014.

[3] Translation of Republic of Korea National Intelligence Service, 'North Korean Military – Munitions Industry', January 1999, available at <http://fas.org/irp/world/rok/nis-docs/defense09.htm>, accessed 20 October 2015.

[4] Charles K Armstrong, *Tyranny of the Weak: North Korea and the World, 1950–1992* (Ithaca, NY: Cornell University Press, 2013), pp. 140–45, 168–204.

[5] *Ibid.*

Socialist forces were emerging across the globe as well, requiring support from ideological brethren if they were to grow stronger and successfully confront adversaries.[6]

North Korea did not discriminate ideologically, however, and it cast its net widely when searching for international political partners. This approach was motivated partly by competition with South Korea. 'Third World' countries in Africa, Southeast Asia and Latin America – neither Western-oriented nor part of the communist bloc – initially remained largely uncultivated diplomatic ground for the Koreas. In the 1960s and 1970s, Kim Il-sung raced to capture the loyalty of governments in these regions before Seoul could.[7]

To exploit this range of opportunities, Pyongyang offered various forms of support, including military assistance programmes, often for free, for dramatically reduced prices, or in exchange for political favours. During the Cold War period, Pyongyang is known to have exported: complete weapons systems (at this time only conventional); spare parts and munitions; repair and maintenance services; training services; and weapons production lines and technology. These categories of military assistance are consistent with the contemporary defence-export catalogue presented in Chapter II.

Some of this assistance, particularly to socialist movements or leaders overseas, was co-ordinated with the Soviet Union and/or China.[8] In these cases, Pyongyang may have felt that its active involvement would also demonstrate commitment to the communist cause and loyalty to one or both of its patrons, perhaps with anticipated returns. Its military agreement with Grenada in 1983, co-ordinated with the Soviet Union and Cuba, is one such example.[9] However, in other instances, North Korea appears to have acted relatively independently when initiating military assistance or sales to prospective foreign partners. Its sale of small arms to Peru in 1986, for example, did not seem to have been part of a co-ordinated socialist package.[10]

As a result of these dynamics, the United States' Library of Congress assessed that by the end of the Cold War North Korea had provided

---

[6] *Ibid.*

[7] *Ibid.*, pp. 179–80.

[8] Not all recipients of military support from the communist bloc received assistance from both the Soviet Union and China. The Sino-Soviet split manifested itself in some overseas conflicts. In Angola, for example, the Soviet Union allied itself with a faction opposing the National Front for the Liberation of Angola (FNLA), which China and North Korea supported.

[9] US Department of State and Department of Defense, *Grenada: A Preliminary Report* (Washington, DC: Government Press Office, 1983), pp. 22–24.

[10] Savada (ed.), *North Korea*, chapter on 'Relations with the Third World'.

military assistance to sixty-two state or non-state partners in North America, South America, Africa, Europe, the Middle East and Asia.[11]

The Missile Age

North Korea's defence-industrial complex continued to export its wares after the end of the Cold War, but to a much narrower group of buyers – a decline precipitated by a number of structural factors and international policy developments. In fact, Pyongyang's golden age of foreign military partnerships had started to come to an end already by the late 1980s. Seoul's steadily increasing economic and foreign-policy clout made it harder for Pyongyang to retain its existing clientele or find new markets. The balancing act between Seoul and Pyongyang that many capitals had attempted during the Cold War became less imperative to sustain. Both South Korea and North Korea continued to lean on their foreign partners to scale back ties with the other where they existed, but by the end of the Cold War it had become clear that a positive relationship with South Korea would be more likely to pay dividends.[12]

Moreover, at the end of the Cold War, Pyongyang's ideological and political pull largely withered, spelling the end of many of its military relationships.[13] Defence procurement no longer transpired in the context of superpower rivalry, where countries naturally gravitated to military handouts from, and contracts with, their ideological allies. Whereas North Korean-supplied weapons and training were often previously part of a larger assistance package co-ordinated with other socialist friends, after the end of the Cold War those friends abruptly became competitors in conventional defence exports. Countries seeking to acquire new off-the-shelf systems of the Soviet design heritage with which they were familiar suddenly could compare potential weapons on offer from – amongst others – China, Russia, Ukraine and North Korea.

Adding to North Korea's difficulties in the global arms market, the Soviet Union – under the direction of Mikhail Gorbachev – decided to end the age of handouts. Moscow, facing challenging economic circumstances and increasingly losing interest in its ideological competition with the West, substantially reduced its military aid to foreign partners. One of these partners was North Korea, with Gorbachev ceasing economic and military aid to the country, and instead requesting $5 billion in aid and a

---

[11] *Ibid.*

[12] Armstrong, *Tyranny of the Weak*, pp. 230–33.

[13] An excellent example of the effect of the end of the war of ideas on Pyongyang's military markets is Madagascar. For further details, see Helen Chapin Metz (ed.), *Madagascar: A Country Study* (Washington, DC: GPO for the Library of Congress, 1994).

$2 billion cash loan from South Korea in 1991.[14] As noted by Andrei Lankov:[15]

> [U]ntil the early 1990s Soviet aid was the major reason why North Korea was able to keep its head above water economically ... [T]he newly established Russian Federation halted aid [and] trade declined to one-tenth of its former levels almost overnight. Such changes pushed North Korea into a state of economic collapse.

This intensified economic strains in North Korea – a crisis which became full-blown in the next few years. Moscow also put North Korea on notice that its joint defence-technology programmes and licensing agreements would be suspended until Pyongyang could pay.[16] These dynamics seemed to have changed North Korea's view of the utility of defence exports. In such challenging economic times they were no longer primarily viewed as an instrument of foreign policy. By the 1990s, North Korean arms sales served above all else to generate revenue.

Another effect of the end of Soviet handouts was that many arms recipients had to accept that they would no longer be able to equip their armed forces based on the charity of foreign patrons, but would instead have to pay market or near-market rates. This proved to be a double-edged sword for North Korea, resulting in the end of some of its defence markets but also the opening of new ones. On one hand, after 1990, some countries accepted that they would have to devote unprecedented financial resources to accessing weapons technology, and moved gradually to phase out their Cold War-era Soviet-, Chinese-, or North Korean-designed equipment in favour of newer and more capable weapons from the West. Their withdrawal from active service in many countries therefore diminished Pyongyang's market opportunities.

Yet these dynamics also created opportunities for North Korea in some places. For example, in the late 1980s, shortly before the end of the Cold War, Egypt, Syria and the Palestine Liberation Organization, angered at the fact that their initial requests for additional military assistance had

---

[14] Kathryn Weathersby, 'Dependence and Mistrust: North Korea's Relations with Moscow and the Evolution of Juche', U.S.-Korea Institute, SAIS, Johns Hopkins University, Working Paper 08-08, December 2008, pp. 20–21.

[15] Andrei Lankov, 'N Korea and Russia: A Step towards a Worldwide Anti-Hegemonic Front?', *Al Jazeera*, 22 June 2014.

[16] Sergey Denisentsev and Konstantin Makienko, 'The Arms Trade Treaty and Russian Arms Exports: Expectations and Possible Consequences', United Nations Institute for Disarmament Research, Sources Series, translated by Ivan Khotkhotva, 2013, p. 15, <http://www.unidir.org/files/medias/pdfs/background-paper-the-arms-trade-treat-and-russian-arms-exports-expectations-and-possible-consequences-sergey-denisentsev-and-konstantin-makienko-eng-0-257.pdf>, accessed 20 October 2015.

been rebuffed by Moscow, turned instead to Pyongyang for those items and services.

In addition, many of North Korea's remaining defence-export markets were in countries that dealt poorly with the newfound reality of having to pay market rates for their arsenals. As a result, they opted to maintain and extend the service lives of systems from the Cold War period and of communist-bloc heritage – weaponry that North Korea is familiar with – rather than making substantial new purchases of arms from elsewhere. As Chapters III, IV and V will show, during the 1990s North Korea helped numerous such governments carry out life-extension programmes, particularly as Russia, Ukraine and China had become less able or willing to do so. In other words, Pyongyang began to find success in niche areas: weapons that others were unable or unwilling to export, and maintenance, repairs and upgrades to antique weapons systems that the original designers had moved beyond. In this manner, Pyongyang managed to keep some of its arms-supply partnerships without having to gift or discount goods or services as it did for its friends during the Cold War.

In the late 1980s, North Korea also found a new market niche – ballistic missiles – which helped to counteract its declining opportunities for sales of its conventional-weapons-related services and products. Pyongyang initially developed a ballistic-missile capability by acquiring several Soviet-made 'Scud' missiles from Egypt, sometime in the early 1980s. It reverse engineered them and agreed with Cairo that it would teach it how to produce the system domestically.

This created a substantial opportunity for North Korea. Few countries around the world could make ballistic missiles at the time, even fewer were willing to sell them, and even fewer still were willing to help others learn how to make them themselves. Realising that these systems could be hot-ticket items, Pyongyang added them to its catalogue of available products and marketed them aggressively throughout the Middle East and elsewhere. Over the following fifteen years, Iran, Syria, Libya, Egypt, Pakistan, Yemen, the United Arab Emirates (UAE) and Iraq would all buy or barter for off-the-shelf North Korean short- or medium-range missiles or their production technology.[17]

However, in the late 1980s and early 1990s international policy changes began to undermine the potential attractiveness of North Korean ballistic-missile assistance. In 1987, shortly after the commencement of Pyongyang's missile-exporting campaign, the Missile Technology Control Regime (MTCR) was established. A group of countries, recognising the

---

[17] Joshua Pollack, 'Ballistic Trajectory: The Evolution of North Korea's Ballistic Missile Market', *Nonproliferation Review* (Vol. 18, No. 2, July 2011).

threat posed by the proliferation of WMD-delivery systems, voluntarily sought to establish, co-ordinate and improve export controls on ballistic missiles with a range greater than 300 km. Its existence steadily strengthened a norm that ran counter to Pyongyang's missile exports.[18]

The US, for its part, sought to unilaterally confront demand for North Korean missile products and services, which it had detected in countries like Iran and Egypt during the 1980s. Following the establishment of the MTCR and revelations about ballistic-missile proliferation by North Korea, China and others,[19] the US Congress enhanced restrictions on trade in missile technology and raised penalties under US law for engaging in such activity.[20] It did so through the addition of several sections on missile proliferation to the Arms Export Control Act of 1976, and passed a new Missile Control Act in 1989.[21] Both were used as a basis for the designation of North Korean entities involved in missile proliferation during the 1990s.

Crucially, section 2797 of the Arms Export Control Act determined that, from November 1990, any foreign person who 'engages in the trade of any MTCR equipment or technology that contributes to the acquisition, design, development, or production of missiles in a country that is not an MTCR adherent and would be, if it were United States-origin equipment or technology, subject to the jurisdiction of the United States' shall be denied US government contracts. Those contracts would be denied for no less than two years if the items or technology in question were complete ballistic missiles, major components or production technology. If the items were smaller, dual-use goods, the penalty would be two years. Provisions were included to allow for the waiver of these penalties at presidential discretion.[22]

---

[18]   North Korea allegedly extended the range of the original Scud design it received from Egypt during the reverse-engineering process, making it capable of striking targets 320 km away. As a result, all of North Korea's ballistic-missile exports have been relevant to the Missile Technology Control Regime and the norms it helped steadily to strengthen. Markus Schiller, *Characterizing the North Korean Nuclear Missile Threat* (Santa Monica, CA: RAND Corporation, 2012), p. 24.

[19]   Sharon A Squassoni, Steven R Bowman and Carl E Behrens, *Proliferation Control Regimes: Background and Status* (Hauppauge, NY: Nova Publishers, 2002), p. 52.

[20]   US arms exports to North Korea had already been banned in 1955 with the introduction of the International Traffic in Arms Regulations (ITAR). ITAR is a set of US government regulations designed to control the export and import of US items, technology and services with direct defence applications. It imposes stringent licensing requirements on those dealing with such equipment and services, in order to ensure they are not transferred to foreign persons or entities.

[21]   Squassoni, Bowman and Behrens, *Proliferation Control Regimes*, pp. 52–53.

[22]   22 U.S. Code § 2797b (a)

As will be shown below, between 1990 and 2005 these provisions and threats of penalties were influential in the US securing verbal agreement from numerous North Korean ballistic-missile customers to forswear their missile dealings with Pyongyang. The UAE, which bought a second batch of Scud missiles from North Korea in 1999,[23] was one such example.[24] The US and UK also secured a pledge from Libya in 2004 to renounce military co-operation with North Korea, after Tripoli had been caught red-handed purchasing WMD-relevant technology in breach of the Nuclear Non-Proliferation Treaty (NPT).[25]

Not too long after the establishment of the MTCR and the enactment of US missile-specific restrictions, norms also began to emerge that undermined North Korea's position as a defence supplier more generally, particularly once it was suspected that the country might be violating its commitments under the NPT. North Korea's nuclear-weapons programme was of growing concern in the late 1990s, not least because the 1994 nuclear agreement between the US and DPRK – which imposed restrictions and transparency requirements on North Korea in exchange for certain energy assistance and aid – was crumbling and the US intelligence community correctly believed Pyongyang was pursuing clandestine uranium enrichment.[26] The regime's 1998 rocket launch and active support to regimes like those in Syria, Iran and Burma

---

[23] According to a declassified US National Intelligence Assessment, the UAE bought a first batch of between eighteen and twenty-four Scud missiles from North Korea in 1988. Director of Central Intelligence, National Intelligence Estimate, 'Prospects for Special Weapons Proliferation and Control', NIE 5-91C, Volume II: Annex A (Country Studies), July 1991, p. 6, available at <http://digitalarchive.wilsoncenter.org/document/116907>, accessed 20 October 2015.

[24] 'August 2008 Visit to North Korea by a UAE Delegation for Meetings with KOMID', Cable #08STATE123035, 19 November 2008, accessed via Wikileaks on 27 May 2014.

[25] Admittedly, the promise of rewards for better behaviour on the part of the Qadhafi regime may have been equally significant in his decision to renounce WMD ambitions and ties to North Korea. This will be discussed further below.

See 'Missile Technology Control Regime (MTCR): North Korea's Missile Program', Cable #08STATE105029, 1 October 2008, accessed via Wikileaks on 27 May 2014. There is an active debate over the factors that led Libya to renounce its WMD and missile ambitions. In particular, the degree to which the incident can be portrayed as a success of US non-proliferation policy is contested. For a summary of this debate see John Hart and Shannon N Kile, 'Chapter 14: Libya's Renunciation of Nuclear, Biological and Chemical Weapons and Ballistic Missiles', in *SIPRI Yearbook 2005*, available at <http://www.sipri.org/yearbook/2005/14>, accessed 20 October 2015.

[26] For background on the 1994 Agreed Framework negotiations, see Leon V Sigal, *Disarming Strangers: Nuclear Diplomacy with North Korea* (Princeton, NJ: Princeton University Press, 1998); Scott A Snyder, *Negotiating on the Edge: North*

compounded the effect: even before UN sanctions were imposed, North Korea's legitimacy as an exporter of weapons and related services was threatened.

A final factor hastened the erosion of North Korea's ballistic-missile market: the saturation of the Middle Eastern market for complete missile systems.[27] Most of those who wanted a limited number of off-the-shelf missiles from North Korea had received them. Iraq was a notable exception, though its troubled attempts from 1999 to purchase missiles from North Korea, to which it had paid a $10-million down payment, ended when the US invaded in 2003.[28]

Some clients had also, with North Korea's assistance, learnt to make ballistic missiles themselves. Iran and Pakistan are notable examples, while North Korean assistance with missile production in Egypt had been agreed as part of the original Scud sale in the 1980s. The market opportunities in these and other former missile-buyers – such as Yemen – shifted to spare parts for complete systems purchased earlier, or repair and upgrade services.

New interest in ballistic missiles from other customers also failed to materialise. This was undoubtedly due in part to practical military considerations. As an analysis of the SIPRI Arms Transfer Database highlights, from the late 1990s and early 2000s onwards, many former North Korean customers started to prioritise the procurement of combat aircraft, which Pyongyang does not manufacture.[29] Considering the strategic environment of the majority of these customers, ballistic missiles were less relevant to the type of campaigns that the governments would find themselves most in need of fighting, namely counter-insurgency operations.[30] Sudan and Nigeria both appear to have considered and turned down North Korean offers of ballistic missiles, settling instead for the combat-aircraft purchases that they had been pursuing around the same time.[31]

Korean Negotiating Behaviour (Washington, DC: United States Institute For Peace Press, 1999).

[27] Joshua Pollack, 'Ballistic Trajectory: The Evolution of North Korea's Ballistic Missile Market', *Nonproliferation Review* (Vol. 18, No. 2, July 2011).

[28] *Washington Times*, 'Iraq Paid N. Korea to Deliver Missiles', 4 October 2003.

[29] Analysis by the author of the SIPRI Arms Transfer Database. The author is particularly grateful to Michele Capeleto for his assistance in compiling, reviewing and summarising this information.

[30] Syria's recent use of Scud missiles during its civil war is a notable exception.

[31] US intelligence reports about North Korea's offer to supply Sudan with Scud missile technology can be found in Bill Gertz, 'North Korea Continues to Develop Missiles', *Washington Times*, 28 October 1999. According to Wikileaks, the US believed that Sudan had explored the possibility of purchasing short- and medium-range ballistic missiles and technology from North Korea again in mid-2008.

In short, a variety of structural factors and international policy developments meant that, even before a UN arms embargo was put in place against North Korea in 2006, the country had already been struggling to maintain many of its defence-export relationships.

The Sanctions Regime

UN Security Council Resolution 1718, passed in October 2006, formally identified North Korea's nuclear and missile programmes as threats to international peace and security, and made the obligation to counter them binding and universal under Chapter VII of the UN Charter.[32] The resolution outlined a relatively clear and simple requirement: member states were not to deal with North Korea in major conventional weapons systems, missiles, and nuclear and other WMD-related goods and services. Similarly, they were to ensure that Security Council-designated individuals and entities – a list of which was established under the resolution – did not operate on their territories or with the help of their nationals. Western governments previously active in countering North Korean arms trade thus no longer had to rely exclusively upon complicated domestic legislation to condemn Pyongyang's military customers. The obligation to cease trade with North Korea in these areas was now cemented in international law.

To oversee and review progress in implementing the sanctions regime it had created, the Security Council established a Sanctions Committee (known as the '1718 Committee'). Its formal mandate is to: gather and consider information about measures taken by member states to implement relevant resolutions; examine allegations of violations of the resolutions; update the list of prohibited dual-use goods; designate additional individuals or entities as appropriate; and provide implementation guidelines and assistance to member states.

Resolution 1874 (2009) subsequently broadened the arms embargo to include all conventional weapons and related goods and services, with the exception of small arms and light weapons going to North Korea. Brokering services by North Koreans for non-North Korean-made weapons and related goods were covered by the ban. It also created a UN Panel of Experts (hereafter, the 'Panel' or 'Panel of Experts') to assist

---

'Informing Sudan of U.S. Concerns Regarding Missile Purchases From North Korea', Cable #09STATE10394, 4 March 2009, accessed via Wikileaks on 27 May 2014. For information on Nigeria's discussions regarding North Korea's ballistic missiles, see 'Nigeria and DPRK Missiles', Cable #04ABUJA149, 29 January 2004, accessed via Wikileaks on 27 May 2014.

[32] UN Security Council Resolution 1718 (2006), S/Res/1718 (2006), 14 October 2006, para. 8(a).

the 1718 Committee, originally composed of seven members but expanded to eight in 2013.[33] The Panel is tasked primarily with gathering, examining and analysing information from member states, UN reports, or open sources regarding the implementation of relevant resolutions, particularly incidents of suspected non-compliance. It issues recommendations to the Security Council, 1718 Committee or individual member states, and produces an annual report containing its findings.[34] The Panel can also produce confidential 'Incident Reports' for the 1718 Committee, usually after the inspection and investigation of a major seizure of North Korean weapons-related cargo.

Despite the fact that the UN sanctions regime is universally applicable and has been in existence for nearly a decade, not all countries take it seriously or ascribe it priority. A worryingly small proportion of the international community currently actively engage with the UN sanctions regime against North Korea. Forty-nine per cent of UN member states have never submitted a report detailing their implementation efforts under any of the sanctions resolutions against North Korea, despite their obligation to do so.[35] As observed by the Panel of Experts, non-reporting creates further 'opportunity for the Democratic People's Republic of Korea to continue its prohibited activity'.[36] It is also likely that at least some of the reports that are submitted to the UN include very few details. Only a handful of states actively monitor the activity of North Korean arms dealers, share information with states along likely transit routes, reach out to confirmed or potential clients to express concern, and interdict goods suspected of being illegal.[37] Indeed, the effectiveness of any of the policy tools outlined below would be enhanced by greater participation from across the international community.

In other words, there is substantial variation in international engagement with UN sanctions, with some member states much more active than others. In theory, the UN sanctions regime serves as a

---

[33] The original seven positions on the Panel are filled by representatives of China, France, Japan, Russia, South Korea, the UK and the US. The new eighth position is intended for developing-country nationals. Members can be government officials or non-governmental experts.

[34] These are an important source for this study.

[35] UN Security Council, 'Report of the Panel of Experts Established Pursuant to Resolution 1874 (2009)', 23 February 2015, S/2015/131, p. 12.

[36] *Ibid*. Member states are required to submit a report detailing their efforts to implement a new resolution within a specified timeframe following the resolution's adoption. For instance, Resolution 1874 (2009) specifies a window of forty-five days in which member states must report, while Resolution 2094 (2013) specifies ninety days.

[37] *Ibid*.

minimum obligation, though some states continue to ignore it. In practice, however, numerous states also go above and beyond the minimum requirements by imposing more stringent measures at the national or regional level. The US continues to lead in this respect, as demonstrated by the fact that its list of designated entities and individuals goes some way beyond that managed by the UN. Since 2005, the US Treasury has designated fifty-four North Korean-linked individuals and entities under presidential Executive Order (EO) 13382, issued to counter WMD proliferation.[38] An additional nine designations have been made since 2010 under a separate Executive Order, EO 13551, targeting individuals and entities facilitating North Korean arms sales, procurement of luxury goods and other illicit economic activity.[39] Other individuals and entities have been designated pursuant to Executive Orders concerning certain North Korean customer states. For example, EO 13619 relates specifically to the facilitation of arms trade between North Korea and Burma, and several North Korean military officials and Burma's Directorate of Defense Industries (DDI) have been designated pursuant to it.[40] As will be demonstrated in the remainder of this study, the US is also one of the leading implementers of the array of other policy tools – whether cargo interdictions or normative pressure on North Korea's customer states – outlined below.

The EU, Japan, South Korea, Australia and Canada are also comparatively active implementers of the sanctions regime against the DPRK. They, too, maintain their own list of designated entities and individuals involved in North Korean arms trade. While there is some level of co-ordination between these governments, their lists vary slightly depending upon their respective intelligence streams, as well as the bureaucratic processes and national evidentiary standards involved in making new designations. For example, in June 2015, the EU designated the German office of the Korea National Insurance Company – an entity which does not appear to be designated elsewhere.[41] These governments

---

[38] US Department of the Treasury, 'Testimony of Assistant Secretary Daniel L. Glaser before the House Foreign Affairs Committee Confronting North Korea's Cyber Threat', 13 January 2015, <http://www.treasury.gov/press-center/press-releases/Pages/jl9738.aspx>, accessed 20 October 2015.
[39] *Ibid.*
[40] US Department of the Treasury, 'Treasury Designates Burmese LT. General Thein Htay, Chief of Directorate of Defense Industries', 2 July 2013, <http://www.treasury.gov/press-center/press-releases/Pages/jl1998.aspx>, accessed 20 October 2015.
[41] Official Journal of the European Union, 'EU Council Decision 2015/1066 of 2 July 2015 Amending Decision 2013/183/CFSP Concerning Restrictive Measures against the Democratic People's Republic of Korea', 2 July 2015, <http://eur-lex.europa.eu/legal-content/EN/TXT/?uri=CELEX:32015D1066>, accessed 20 October 2015.

also expend notable diplomatic resources in an effort to curb demand for North Korean military products or services.

Policy Toolbox

In the process of identifying North Korea's military customers in the sanctions era, Chapters III, IV and V will also highlight the range of tools that have been used by national or UN officials in the recent past in support of the sanctions regime. Chapter VI will show that they remain available to those sanctions implementers seeking to reduce demand for North Korean arms, related materiel and services, but should be carefully tailored to take into account the reasons that clients buy from North Korea in the first place.[42] However, as they have formed part of a broader approach by active governments to the implementation of the UN sanctions regime, it is worth considering them briefly here.

Intelligence Sharing

Intelligence sharing in relation to North Korean arms exports is an activity that has merit on its own, but is of greater significance when pursued in relation to the other policy tools outlined below. Independently, it is most useful when pursued *vis-à-vis* a government that may not be aware that either North Korean individuals or entities of concern are active on its territory, or that they are co-operating with nationals of the country in question.

When pursued as part of an effort to implement another policy approach, intelligence sharing can enhance the effect of the other tools in use and improve their chances of success. For example, governments actively monitoring illicit North Korean activity have shared information about suspected movement of North Korean vessels or cargo with states along their likely transit paths in order to interdict the shipment.[43] Selective information sharing has also helped ensure that other governments designate individuals or entities engaged in sanctions-busting activity. In some cases, intelligence has been relayed to suspected customers of North Korean military goods and services in order to exert pressure upon them.[44]

---

[42] Because the focus of this paper is on the customers of North Korean military goods and services, this chapter will not consider in depth the policy tools available for reducing supply.

[43] 'Cancellation of DPRK-Iran Flight: Thanking Central Asian States for their Cooperation', Cable #08STATE91989, 27 August 2008, accessed via Wikileaks on 27 May 2014.

[44] For example, 'Informing Sudan of U.S. Concerns Regarding Missile Purchases From North Korea', Cable #09STATE10394.

Of course, intelligence sharing is an activity that is possible only for those countries with sufficient resources to regularly and actively monitor North Korean arms trade and the entities engaged in it. In the past, countries such as the US, UK, France, Germany and South Korea are known to have shared such information with countries along the suspected transit routes for potentially illicit North Korean cargo, with other countries requiring information to sanction individuals and entities, or with suspected or possible future North Korean customers.[45]

Interdictions and Denial of Access
UN Security Council Resolution 2094 (2013) determined that 'all States shall inspect all cargo within or transiting through their territory that has originated in the DPRK, or that is destined for the DPRK, or has been brokered or facilitated by the DPRK or its nationals, or by individuals or entities acting on their behalf, if the State concerned has credible information that provides reasonable grounds to believe the cargo contains items the supply, sale, transfer, or export of which' is covered by previous resolutions.[46] In other words, UN member states are legally obligated to interdict vessels, aircraft or vehicles they suspect of being relevant to the implementation of the current arms embargo. Should they discover that a cargo contains weapons or related materiel, they are also obligated to detain it, notify the Security Council, and subsequently destroy it.

These provisions do contain some ambiguity. First, the state through which the vessel or aircraft is transiting must have information pointing to an illicit North Korean link to the cargo. This condition highlights the importance not only of attentively monitoring the activities of DPRK arms dealers and facilitators, but also of sharing relevant intelligence between foreign governments. Second, what is 'credible' or offers 'reasonable grounds' are subjective, and countries have previously chosen not to act, or to release cargo later determined to be weapons-related, because they did not feel that there was reasonable grounds to do otherwise.[47]

---

[45] For example, see 'Greece Confirms Missile Parts Included in Suspect Shipment', Cable #07ATHENS2345, 12 December 2007, accessed via Wikileaks on 27 May 2014.
[46] UN Security Council Resolution 2094 (2013), S/RES/2094, 7 March 2013, para. 16.
[47] One example is the government of Singapore, which upon US request detained a cargo of precision lathes destined for the Burma office of the Korea Mining Development Trading Corporation. Singapore subsequently released the items as it determined there was insufficient evidence to conclude they were controlled goods. 'GOS Releases Precision Lathes to Shipper', Cable #07SINGAPORE224, 31 January 2007, accessed via Wikileaks on 27 May 2014. A second example occurred in 2011, when an East African country detained a shipment of milling and slotting

In addition to legal obligations surrounding search and seizure of cargo, the UN Security Council has requested that states 'deny permission to any aircraft to take off from, land, or overfly their territory' if they believe the aircraft to contain goods or personnel contributing to a violation of the same resolutions.[48] Thailand's 2009 seizure of a charter flight laden with North Korean arms bound for non-state actors in the Middle East was an example of the successful use of this particular tool.[49] UN measures focused on preventing the transport of sanctions-busting goods and services via air, sea or land complement the efforts of the seventy-two partner countries in the Proliferation Security Initiative, which seeks to improve countries' capacity to interdict WMD-related goods in transit.[50]

Interdictions and access denial are most immediately useful in preventing supply from reaching the source of the demand. This has short-term benefits in denying the intended recipient its North Korean supply, which can be a particularly high priority when WMD- or missile-related cargo is involved or where non-state actors are the end user, for example. Furthermore, they can give unparalleled insight into the nature of North Korea's relationship with the client in question. Experts can inspect the weapons or related goods, examine documentation on board for information about the contract and other nodes in the proliferation network, and question the crew (where the ship is North Korean-owned and crewed).

---

machines from North Korea bound for Eritrea. Upon inspection it was determined that the contents of the cargo did not meet the criteria in lists of controlled items, and there was no conclusive evidence that they were intended for an arms-related end use. The machines were released, and it was only later that their military application was determined. See UN Security Council, 'Report of the Panel of Experts Established Pursuant to Resolution 1874 (2009)', S/2014/147, 6 March 2014, pp. 33–34.

[48] UN Security Council Resolution 2094 (2013), S/RES/2094, 7 March 2013, para. 18.
[49] UN Security Council, 'Report of the Panel of Experts Established Pursuant to Resolution 1874(2009)', S/2013/337, pp. 33–34.
[50] The Proliferation Security Initiative (PSI) was launched in May 2003 by the US, following its interdiction of North Korean ballistic-missile-related cargo bound for Yemen the previous year. The aim of the initiative is to create a partnership of states and improve their collective ability to pre-emptively interdict cargo suspected of containing WMD- or missile-related goods or materiel. Countries which join the PSI agree to a Statement of Interdiction Principles that commits them to interdict shipments within their jurisdiction, strengthen the processes and legal authority to facilitate interdiction, and develop procedures to exchange information with other partner countries. See US Department of State, 'Proliferation Security Initiative 10th Anniversary High-Level Political Meeting', 28 May 2014, <http://www.state.gov/t/isn/c10390.htm>, accessed 20 October 2015.

Interdictions and denial of access also serve to erode demand by raising the financial and reputational costs of doing business with North Korea. Evading detection is an ever-more difficult affair for North Korean arms dealers, given the increasing (though not universal) awareness of the sanctions regime in place. When overflight is denied, aircraft must be re-routed through countries more friendly to Pyongyang, or at least more willing to overlook suspicions. In early 2008, North Korea scheduled an Air Koryo flight to Tehran, which the US suspected was carrying missile technicians. US démarches to Central Asian governments along the flight path led many of them to deny overflight permission. As a result, the flight had to be re-routed through Mandalay, in Burma, adding over 1,500 km and considerable fuel cost to the flight.[51]

In the event that an illicit cargo is detected and seized, the cost is even greater. At minimum, the cargo must be replaced (by North Korea or a new supplier) under increased international scrutiny, possibly at the client's expense. Depending upon the contract terms and whether a deposit was paid to North Korea, additional costs may be incurred. For example, Pyongyang has refused at least twice to reimburse customer deposits in cases of non-delivery, namely in Iraq and in Yemen.[52] For customers whose decisions to purchase from Pyongyang have been guided primarily by pricing, interdictions could influence future choices of supplier.

As will be argued below, clients that are most sensitive to high-visibility normative pressure may also find the reputational cost of being caught red-handed outweighs the benefits of buying from North Korea. Importantly, reputational damage could also involve loss or denial of aid, and investment and trade opportunities from other countries, which may not wish to incur their own reputational costs for providing assistance to a country in active violation of UN sanctions against Pyongyang.

Sanctions against Individuals and Entities
Economic sanctions have long been a feature of the international community's discussions over how to address North Korea's nuclear

---

[51] 'Cancellation of DPRK-Iran Flight: Thanking Central Asian States for their Cooperation', Cable #08STATE91989, 27 August 2008, accessed via Wikileaks on 27 May 2014. See also 'Air Koryo Flight of Proliferation Concern', Cable #08STATE84151, 5 August 2008, accessed via Wikileaks on 27 May 2014.
[52] See 'Demarche to Yemeni FM Qirbi on DPRK Military Contacts', Cable #03SANAA2769, 23 November 2003, accessed via Wikileaks on 27 May 2014. See also, David E Sanger and Thom Shanker, 'A Region Inflamed: For the Iraqis, A Missile Deal that Went Sour; Files Tell of Talks with North Korea', *New York Times*, 1 December 2003.

pursuits. As part of the UN sanctions regime, member states are obliged to freeze the funds and other financial or economic resources controlled by UN Security Council-listed individuals and entities that are kept on their territory. They also must prevent the travel of designated individuals through their territory.[53] This applies to nationally or regionally imposed lists as well.

Designated individual and entity lists are designed to sever access to the implementing country's financial system, and to restrict interactions between those on the list and the implementing country's nationals. Depending upon the issuing authority in question, other restrictions may also apply. For the most part, the listed individuals and entities are North Korean-controlled, either operating from within North Korea or from offices overseas. The main effect of these lists is to constrain North Korean arms trade from the supply side. At the same time, the elevated costs and hurdles involved in buying from Pyongyang could presumably influence demand-side calculations, though it is difficult to ascertain the extent to which economic restrictions imposed at the UN or national level have raised the cost incurred by the client in previous arms deals with North Korea.

Nevertheless, North Korea has become adept at circumventing restrictions created by designations. Proliferators tend to move much faster than intelligence-gathering and sanctions-listing exercises can. Designated North Korean individuals and entities use aliases and establish shell and front companies, sometimes only for the duration of a single contract. North Korean arms-trading firms also add more links to logistical and finance chains to obscure both the end user of the consignment and their own involvement. In the event that a North Korean entity is formally designated, a simple name change is often sufficient for it to be able to circumvent associated operational constraints in most countries. For this reason, efforts to keep proliferation-focused designations up-to-date are often likened to a game of whack-a-mole.[54]

This is not to say that national or international designations are not worthwhile in the context of demand-focused counter-proliferation strategies. Most of the countries mentioned above that maintain unilateral sanctions lists give a brief explanation of the motivation for new designations when such decisions are taken. Where the entity or individual is North Korean, these explanations frequently hint at where

---

[53] *Ibid.*
[54] Frank Sauer, 'Nuclear Iran? Optimistic Pessimists vs Pessimistic Optimists', International and Security Relations Network, ETH Zurich, 26 February 2014, <http://www.isn.ethz.ch/Digital-Library/Articles/Detail/?id=176995>, accessed 20 October 2015.

they operate overseas, or which foreign countries they have dealt with in the past. They can thus remind a client that their dealings are being watched, draw attention to contemporary North Korean arms-trade activity, and spark further investigations. An example is the US Treasury's recent listing of a representative of the Korea Mining Development Trading Corporation (KOMID) in Namibia, who is alleged to 'represent the southern African interests of KOMID'. The designation highlighted the fact that Washington is aware of KOMID's activity in Namibia and drew attention to North Korean arms traders active in that region.[55]

Designation of Burmese individuals and entities is another example of this dynamic. International attention has been redirected to the continuing illegal military trade taking place between Burmese entities and North Korean ones, despite the former's pledges to abandon them. As suggested above, this could cause not only reputational damage, but also a corresponding loss of business and trade opportunities for Burma generally, and those entities specifically. Risk-conscious companies around the world may in turn remain wary of doing business with military-linked organisations in Burma, out of fear that their reputation may also be damaged. All of these factors can directly and indirectly bring pressure to bear on the consumers of North Korean military products and services, though, as will be argued in Chapter VI, some customers are more immune to it than others.[56]

Threats to Impose Penalties

In select cases, foreign governments with leverage over the customer in question may be able to threaten to impose penalties against them, either publicly or privately, if arms-trade ties with Pyongyang are not severed. Such penalties could take a variety of forms, from trade restrictions to the withholding of benefits and engagement in other areas. Washington has had some success with this strategy, given provisions in the Arms Export Control Act which allow for the denial of US government contracts and co-operation if certain export-control provisions are breached. US

---

[55] US Department of Treasury, 'Treasury Imposes Sanctions against the Government of the Democratic People's Republic of Korea', 2 January 2015, <http://www.treasury.gov/press-center/press-releases/Pages/jl9733.aspx>, accessed 20 October 2015.

[56] Office of Foreign Assets Control, US Department of the Treasury, 'North Korea: An Overview of Sanctions with Respect to North Korea', 6 May 2011, <http://www.treasury.gov/resource-center/sanctions/Programs/Documents/nkorea.pdf>, accessed 20 October 2015. See also US Department of the Treasury, 'Testimony of Assistant Secretary Daniel L. Glaser before the House Foreign Affairs Committee Confronting North Korea's Cyber Threat'.

use of these threats of penalties was mentioned above in relation to the UAE, Libya and Pakistan, all of which probably ceased or reduced their military trade with North Korea over a decade ago partly as a result of this tactic.[57]

Washington pursued the same approach towards Yemen as well. In December 2002, the Spanish navy, acting on US intelligence, seized the North Korean vessel *So San*. Upon boarding, it found the ship laden with North Korean-made Scud-B missiles bound for Yemen. Sana'a protested and the cargo was eventually released – at the time it was not an illegal purchase.[58] However, in August 2002 the US secured a promise from Yemen that it would no longer import missiles or missile-related material from any source, especially North Korea. It allegedly reiterated the commitment in 2003, but informed Washington that North Koreans would be invited back to install replacement parts and repair defective Scuds, and that 'these repairs would mark the end of Yemeni military cooperation with North Korea'.[59] The démarche highlighted Washington's initial threat to impose penalties if Yemen failed to keep its promises: 'Based on [Yemen's] commitment, the United States waived penalties that otherwise would have been required under the U.S. missile sanctions law against Yemeni entities for engaging in missile-related cooperation with North Korea.'[60] Since such a démarche had to be requested again only a few years after Yemen's initial pledge, as will be discussed further in Chapter IV, it appears that this approach, by itself, was not effective.[61] It is, however, one tool that holds promise when a relationship exists that enables the wielder to impose substantial costs upon the target country. These considerations will be explored further in Chapter VI.

---

[57] For further information on negotiations between the UAE and US, see 'August 2008 Visit to North Korea by a UAE Delegation for Meetings with KOMID', Cable #08STATE123035. In Libya, a combination of threats of penalties, normative pressure and conditional incentives was applied by the US and UK. For substantiation of the issuance of threats of penalties, see 'Missile Technology Control Regime (MTCR): North Korea's Missile Program', Cable #08STATE105029. As mentioned above, there remains an active debate about the causes of Libya's disarmament decision. On Pakistan, see Chidanand Rajghatta, 'Pak Cracked under Hard US Proof', *Times of India*, 8 February 2004, <http://timesofindia.indiatimes.com/world/us/Pak-cracked-under-hard-US-proof/articleshow/483777.cms>, accessed 20 October 2015.

[58] *BBC News*, 'Yemen Protests Over Scud Seizure', 11 December 2002.

[59] 'Continuing Cooperation between North Korea's KOMID and Yemen', Cable #09STATE50258, 15 May 2009, accessed via Wikileaks on 27 May 2014.

[60] *Ibid.*

[61] *Ibid.*

Conditional Incentives

'Sticks' are not the only sort of tool available. In some cases, 'carrots' can also be a useful addition to a tailored dissuasion strategy. What would be considered sufficiently enticing for a client to abandon its contracts with North Korea depends on the client's individual circumstances. One approach is the relaxation of existing sanctions or trade restrictions against a country. Such an approach was recently pursued with Burma – a repeated military customer of Pyongyang's – as part of a broader discussion surrounding its transition to democracy.[62] Should the target country demonstrate the desired behaviour (in this case, cessation of sanctions-busting contracts with North Korea), the other party in the arrangement would be expected to fulfil its promise to lift those restrictions.

Another example is Libya. When Western governments became aware of Libya's nuclear weapons programme, its partnership with the A Q Khan network, and the involvement of North Korea in the early 2000s, they set out to negotiate a grand bargain for the Qadhafi regime. This involved both incentives and, presumably, the threat of severe penalties under US non-proliferation legislation if the deal was not upheld. According to the US State Department, Tripoli was 'amply rewarded' for renouncing WMD ambitions and forswearing military co-operation with North Korea.[63] In addition to promised improvements in bilateral relations,[64] the US and UK in effect tacitly sanctioned Qadhafi's purchases of conventional arms from more reputable suppliers than North Korea[65] – something which would have likely been viewed as a highly desirable outcome for Libya.[66]

Such exceptions are likely to be rare: highly visible, substantial benefits that would be easily linkable to the agreement are probably only palatable as

---

[62] Jeffrey Lewis and Catherine Dill, 'Myanmar's Unrepentant Arms Czar', *Foreign Policy*, 9 May 2014.

[63] Arms Control Association, 'Chronology of Libya's Disarmament Relations with the United States', February 2014, <https://www.armscontrol.org/factsheets/LibyaChronology>, accessed 20 October 2015; Paul Kerr, 'Libya Pledges Military Trade Curbs, but Details are Fuzzy', *Arms Control Today*, 1 June 2004.

[64] Arms Control Association, 'Chronology of Libya's Disarmament Relations with the United States'.

[65] The author is grateful to Joshua Pollack for this point.

[66] Qadhafi's son was convinced that 'agreements on military and security cooperation' would follow Libya's disarmament decision. See Norman Cigar, 'Libya's Nuclear Disarmament: Lessons and Implications for Nuclear Proliferation', Marine Corps University, Middle East Studies Monograph No. 2, January 2012, p. 4. In terms of specific arms deals, Libya agreed to inspections of short-range Scud missiles in exchange for permission to purchase Russian SS-26 (Iskander) missiles, for example, though it ultimately chose not to move ahead with the procurement. See Alex Bollfrass, 'Details Bedevil Libyan Grand Bargain', *Arms Control Today*, October 2007.

part of a discussion over how to encourage a country's broader political or security-sector reform, which might include abandoning ties to Pyongyang. This is especially true if the reason that those benefits were not offered earlier is because the behaviour of the government in question was seen as deeply concerning for more reasons than its ties to North Korea. The idea of offering a significant incentive to the Assad regime in exchange for abandoning ties to North Korea would be palatable to few, for example.

Normative Pressure (Public)
Public condemnation of arms-related dealings with North Korea has been important for many reasons. At minimum, it signals the condemning party's determination to improve the implementation of relevant UN Security Council resolutions and to enhance global awareness of the arms embargo. Depending on the type of client being targeted, normative pressure can also be influential in shifting choices of supplier, as will be discussed below in the context of 'reluctant' and 'ad hoc' customers. Like interdictions or sanctions, public pressure can raise the reputational cost of contracting to North Korea. Clients that are relatively integrated into the international community (particularly in terms of economic and trade relations, or dependence upon outside aid) and have much to lose in the event of a backlash to revelations over sanctions breaches, or customers that were not aware that the nature of their contracts with North Korea might constitute violations, may feel compelled to show remorse over their dealings with Pyongyang and pledge to end them.

Public pressure can be applied by national governments, the UN Panel of Experts, 1718 Committee, Security Council, or even members of civil society. Indeed, it is one of the only avenues for civil society to take part in dissuasion strategies. Such pressure can be created through speeches, the calling-in of ambassadors for consultations, or as a corollary of other measures outlined above, such as interdiction or publicised imposition of penalties on individuals and entities linked with the client. The annual, public UN Panel of Experts reports can also have this effect.

Normative Pressure (Private)
Normative pressure has also been exerted upon clients from behind the scenes, particularly through démarches and other forms of outreach by governments. These actions can complement and magnify the effect of public-pressure tactics, and create an avenue for the client to raise any practical issues relating to alternative supply or dependence. Indeed, in some cases it may be wiser to pursue concerns privately rather than publicly, if doing so holds greater promise of breaking the government of concern away from Pyongyang.

Assistance in Finding and Facilitating Alternative Supply

As will be discussed in Chapter IV, some customers turn to North Korea due to a lack of perceived options, either because other suppliers cannot provide the same goods or services or are significantly more costly. In these cases, assistance in securing alternative supply may be effective. Both Yemen and Ethiopia have privately sought help in this regard from the US, and a number of other customers have expressed difficulty in finding viable alternative suppliers.[67] Yemen's plans to have North Korea assist in the construction of a coastal facility for its navy, discussed below, allegedly prompted the US to 'use currently available funding for facilities that serve the Yemen Coast Guard and Navy', and assist with an expert study of possible suppliers other than North Korea.[68] Later, the US asked Romania to make Yemen a competitive offer.[69]

As will be argued in Chapter VI, however, this sort of assistance is not commonly contemplated unless the government making the offer already has a somewhat positive relationship with the other party. Ongoing military conflict involving that country (as is now the case with regard to Yemen, for example) also tends to preclude it from receiving any such assistance.

An Arms Industry Built on Shifting Ground

As this chapter has shown, North Korea's defence-export industry has transitioned through three phases, each bringing increasing difficulties for Pyongyang. The Cold War was undoubtedly its golden era, when interest in North Korean products and services was high. This was partly a result of Pyongyang's aggressive outreach strategies, partly a consequence of the pervasiveness of decolonisation and socialist movements which North Korea's patrons were also eager to see succeed, and partly a result of North Korea's military offerings, which at the time were broadly in line with those of other members of the communist bloc.

The period after 1990 saw the picture change for numerous reasons, some structural and some policy-oriented. The end of the Cold War spelled the widespread disappearance of ideological gravitation towards North Korea as a supplier, and the transformation of its former friends into defence-export competitors. Changing strategic circumstances left many of North Korea's former military partners laden with ageing weaponry that its patrons were becoming uninterested in repairing or servicing. This created

---

[67] *Ibid*. See also 'North Korea: Ethiopia Requests Alternate Supplier Information', Cable #08ADDISABABA952, 7 April 2008, accessed via Wikileaks on 27 May 2014.
[68] 'Yemeni Military Leaders Brief Ambassador on DPRK Contacts', Cable #03SANAA1990, 12 August 2003, accessed via Wikileaks on 27 May 2014.
[69] 'Scenesetter for Under Secretary Bolton's Visit to Yemen', Cable #03SANAA1373, 16 June 2003, accessed via Wikileaks on 15 May 2014.

a market opportunity for North Korea, which was prepared to offer repair services for weapons of that era. At the same time, however, those partners were also unaccustomed to the idea of having to pay market prices for new systems, a fact which clashed with North Korea's intent to turn its military partnerships into revenue streams.

Ballistic-missile sales in the late 1980s and early 1990s helped North Korea overcome some of these issues and generate an important source of income. New markets were opened and, as Chapter III will highlight, existing relationships – like that with Iran – deepened. However, global appetite for North Korean ballistic missiles proved limited. This was aided by gradually progressing domestic production infrastructure, interest in other defence systems, and the strengthening international movement against ballistic-missile proliferation. All the while, North Korea's conventional-weapons catalogue was gradually becoming dated, featuring decades-old Soviet or Chinese designs repeatedly upgraded or modified.

North Korea's 2006 nuclear test internationalised what had previously been a largely Western-held grievance against Pyongyang's military exports. The UN sanctions regime created that year and expanded in 2009 imposed obligations on all UN member states. It spawned new actors tasked with addressing sanctions non-compliance, and it compelled the broader international community to collaborate with a view to monitoring and eroding North Korea's arms trade and the revenue streams it creates.

This study is part of that effort, first considering the effects of the developments mentioned above on North Korea's contemporary defence-export offerings before examining Pyongyang's military customers in the sanctions era, and highlighting the need to tailor the application of policy tools outlined in this chapter to the nature of the North Korean customer in question. In the process, it will become evident that the effect of the aforementioned shifts in the global arms market and North Korea's place within it has been twofold: first, it has made finding new markets for North Korea and its arms traders an increasingly difficult task; and second, it has chipped away most of the clients that were relatively unwedded to Pyongyang, thereby distilling North Korea's sanctions-era customer base down to a group that is mainly defiant of international laws and norms.

II. NORTH KOREA'S CONTEMPORARY DEFENCE-EXPORT INDUSTRY

It may be your grandmother's technology, but grandmother still kicks.

(Indian official, reflecting upon the cargo of the *Ku Wol San*[1])

Numerous state and non-state actors still choose to buy military goods and services from Pyongyang despite the advent of the UN arms embargo described in Chapter I. The reasons they do so remain under-discussed and poorly understood. In order to shed light on this phenomenon, it is first necessary to form a picture of the goods and services North Korea is able to offer prospective clients.

This chapter attempts to reconstruct and detail the country's defence-export catalogue – a product of the national and international developments explored in the previous chapter. It discusses North Korea's pricing decisions, as well as its arms-marketing methods and tools, and as a point of comparison to what Pyongyang has on offer, its competitors. As in the Cold War, North Korea continues to be able to market complete conventional weapons and weapons systems, spare parts and munitions, repair and maintenance services, weapons production technology and assistance, and procurement services. Within these categories, however, its offerings have changed since 1990. In the area of full systems, North Korea has added to its product list with technology such as cruise missiles. At the same time, however, much of its conventional weapons technology has steadily fallen out of date – a trend solidified by the arms embargo in place since 2006. As will be demonstrated below, the age of the majority of technology in North Korea's defence-export catalogue, the price of some of its weapons and services, and Pyongyang's willingness to

---

[1] Jo Warrick, 'On North Korean Freighter, A Hidden Missile Factory', *Washington Post*, 14 August 2003.

provide niche technologies are all likely to influence demand. This analysis lays the ground for the ensuing exploration of which states and non-state actors have bought arms and related materiel and services from North Korea in the sanctions era, what they have bought, and why.

The Catalogue

Former US Representative Heather Wilson, who chaired the Technical and Tactical Intelligence Subcommittee of the House of Representatives' Permanent Select Committee on Intelligence, remarked in 2006 that 'the North Koreans would sell their mother' if a prospective client asked and paid.[2] According to Wilson, anything that North Korea can manufacture, and anything that is in excess of its own requirements, appears to be negotiable for sale.[3]

North Korea's catalogue is indeed vast. It includes: complete off-the-shelf weapons systems and so-called 'knock-down kits';[4] spare parts for those systems and for supporting infrastructure; weapons designs and technology; whole arms manufacturing lines and complexes; repair, maintenance and upgrade services; military training in a wide variety of disciplines; and brokering, procurement and logistical services.

Its catalogue for physical goods depends upon the operation of the country's domestic peacetime defence-industrial complex, which is difficult to assess accurately. Estimates of its size range widely, from fifty to more than 100 sites. According to one interviewee familiar with North Korean arms marketing overseas, the country is home to fifty-four factories that produce conventional arms and related materiel.[5] His contacts in the DPRK asserted that of those fifty-four, eight make infantry weapons, eleven make ammunition and explosive munitions, and thirty-five produce larger weapons systems.[6] US estimates from the 1990s put the number at that time at 134 arms factories,[7] many of which were

---

[2] Katherine Shrader, 'North Korea Arms Trade Seen as Threat', *Washington Post*, 12 October 2006.

[3] *Ibid.*

[4] A 'knock-down kit' is a package containing parts and instructions needed to assemble a final product. In some cases, all parts are produced in one country and are then exported to a second. In other cases, some parts may need to be produced and/or added by the second country.

[5] Author interview with Interviewee C, 6 June 2014.

[6] Author e-mail interview with Interviewee C, 18 September 2014.

[7] Andrea Matles Savada (ed.), *North Korea: A Country Study* (Washington, DC: GPO for Library of Congress, 1994).

believed to be completely or partially underground.[8] At the time, an additional 115 facilities were suspected of having a dedicated wartime materiel-production mission.[9]

Complete Weapons Systems
While the size of the military industrial base is unconfirmed, details about its capabilities are much more readily available. During the early Cold War, both the Soviet Union and China signed licence agreements with North Korea for certain weapons systems, mainly small arms, light weapons and munitions.[10] As mentioned in Chapter I, the design heritage of most of the systems North Korea is able to produce is therefore Soviet or Chinese. Certain designs, such as the AK-47 assault rifle, which North Korea started producing under licence in 1958,[11] or the T-55 tank, date back as far as the late 1940s.

From the 1950s, North Korea sought state-of-the-art technology and the ability to produce larger weapons systems. During this period it agreed a first round of licence agreements with Moscow and Beijing. Thereafter, Pyongyang's quest to produce modern weaponry encountered hurdles. Its conventional military research-and-defence (R&D) capability was, and remains, limited. Largely unable to design and manufacture systems from scratch, it complemented its existing production lines by updating older designs from elsewhere or modifying the designs to suit its preferences. In the late 1960s or early 1970s, Pyongyang began to modify and update the technology it had earlier received from its benefactors and produce indigenously designed variants. Its AK-47 rifles and multiple rocket launchers, for example, feature unique characteristics.[12]

---

[8] Translation of Republic of Korea National Intelligence Service, 'North Korean Military – Munitions Industry', January 1999, available at <http://fas.org/irp/world/rok/nis-docs/defense09.htm>, accessed 20 October 2015.
[9] Savada (ed.), *North Korea*.
[10] There are some exceptions to this. For example, North Korea was permitted to produce a licensed copy of the Chinese Type 63 (YW531) armoured personnel carrier. See US Department of Defense, 'North Korea Country Handbook: Marine Corps Intelligence Activity', May 1997, Appendix A, p. 180.
[11] Shea and Hong, who have examined photographs of North Korean weapons and the weapons themselves, add that, 'in the beginning of manufacturing the Type 58, the rifles appear to have had the receivers made in North Korea, but parts appear to be Soviet. Within a few years all parts appear to be of North Korean origin'. Dan Shea and Heebum Hong, 'North Korean Small Arms', *Small Arms Defense Journal* (Vol. 5, No. 1, March 2013).
[12] North Korea's AK-47s do not have a rate reducer, while its industry produces a unique double-barrelled 107-mm multiple rocket launcher. Roger Davies, 'Sea Tigers, Stealth Technology and the North Korean Connection', *Jane's Intelligence Review*, March 2001, available at <http://www.lankalibrary.com/pol/korea.htm>,

Around this time, Pyongyang also began to augment its technology acquisitions from the Soviet Union and China with an outreach programme aimed at procuring other equipment and dual-use technology. It attempted to purchase US-manufactured helicopters, Japanese trucks and electronics, and Austrian forging equipment that could be used to produce gun barrels.[13] From the early 1970s, the industry began to produce tanks, armoured vehicles, naval craft and other heavy equipment. It later would remind the world of its aptitude in reverse engineering by acquiring Scud-B ballistic missiles from Egypt and quickly rolling out its own production lines for that system, probably between 1984 and 1986. In addition to short-range ballistic missiles, by the 1980s it could also make relatively up-to-date weapons like surface-to-air missiles and anti-tank missiles.

Today, as mentioned above, North Korea has the added challenge of being subject to an arms embargo that forbids all 193 UN member states from selling to Pyongyang anything but small arms and light weapons. For the most part, and particularly in the area of conventional weapons systems, it therefore still relies on modifications to older designs, or reverse engineering weapons it acquires in small numbers, to keep its own arsenal as well as its export catalogue from fading into obsolescence. An example of such modification is presented in the North Korean marketing brochure for its AT-4 Spigot anti-tank missile (also known as the 9K111 Fagot). The system was first spotted in North Korea in a military parade in Pyongyang in 1992, using wire guidance as per the original Soviet design. However, a North Korean marketing brochure confirms that the technology has since been modified so that it uses laser guidance (see Appendix A). More recently, North Korea has similarly displayed a new ship-launched cruise missile that resembles the Russian Kh-35 cruise-missile system. The similarity suggests that the missile was either produced under licence – which is unlikely given that such an agreement would constitute a grave sanctions violation by Moscow – or procured from Russia or another country fielding the system and subsequently reverse engineered.[14] According to Interviewee C, North Korea has also reverse engineered a US-designed and produced minigun.[15]

---

accessed 20 October 2015. It also produced eighteen-tube and twenty-four-tube 107-mm self-propelled multiple rocket launchers, deviating from the standard configuration of twelve tubes. See Federation of American Scientists, 'Type 63 107mm Rocket Launcher', 1999, <http://fas.org/man/dod-101/sys/land/row/type-63-r.htm>, accessed 20 October 2015.

[13] Savada (ed.), *North Korea*.

[14] Joseph S Bermudez, Jr, 'Korean People's Navy Tests New Anti-Ship Cruise Missile', 38 North, 8 February 2015, <http://38north.org/2015/02/jbermudez020815/>, accessed 20 October 2015.

[15] Author interview with Interviewee C, 25 July 2014.

Despite these innovations, the overall quality and sophistication of North Korea's military products continue to lag behind those of other suppliers. Information compiled through open sources and interviews presents a partial but sufficiently detailed picture of the systems North Korea is able to manufacture domestically and market abroad.

Details in public government reports, declassified documents, reports by the UN Panel of Experts, news articles, imagery analysis, and interviews with experts and officials shows that the weapons North Korea produces fall under a broad range of categories.[16] This information is reflected in Table 1, which presents an illustrative list of domestically produced North Korean weaponry. It is not intended to be complete, particularly as it is unclear whether the country mothballs production lines for older technology once it is able to manufacture a newer variant or other system in the same weapons category.

One class of weapons platform which does not appear in Table 1 is jet aircraft, which the country is not yet able to manufacture indigenously. With the possible exception of limited helicopter co-production assistance from China during the Cold War, it does not appear that Pyongyang's benefactors were willing to offer it aircraft designs, technology and production assistance. As a consequence, Pyongyang was forced repeatedly to purchase its jet aircraft from abroad, leaving it at the complete mercy of its patrons.[17] Since the mid-1980s, there has been speculation that this longstanding, glaring gap would drive North Korea to invest heavily in development of an indigenous production capability for jet aircraft at the Panghyon facility in North Pyongan province.[18] Even if attempted, such an achievement has not yet come to pass. These complex and sophisticated systems continue to lie beyond the grasp of North Korea's military R&D complex. In the sanctions era, Pyongyang has grudgingly scrambled to find spare parts abroad to extend the service life of its ageing fleet. In recent years, it has twice been caught attempting to procure jet engines for the MiG-21 aircraft that form the backbone of its interceptor fleet – once from Mongolia and once from Cuba.[19]

Whenever they are sold to foreign customers, the systems and platforms in Table 1 are apparently accompanied by extensive documentation, and can be ordered with supporting equipment (including guidance systems and load and launch vehicles) and munitions.

---

[16] Where applicable, systems usually come complete with guidance systems.

[17] Michael Yahuda, *The International Politics of the Asia-Pacific: 1945–1995* (Abingdon: Routledge, 2005), p. 96.

[18] Savada (ed.), *North Korea*, chapter on 'Military Industry'.

[19] Hugh Griffiths and Roope Siirtola, 'Full Disclosure: Contents of North Korean Smuggling Ship Revealed', 38 North, 27 August 2013, <http://38north.org/2013/08/hgriffiths082713/>, accessed 15 October 2015.

Table 1: North Korean Domestic Manufacturing Capability by Weapons Type.

Weapons Category	Example Types (Closest Foreign Designation Where Applicable)
Small arms and ammunition	Fragmentation hand grenade (F-1, RG-42, RGD-5)
	Anti-tank hand grenade (RPG-43, RKG-3)
	Tokarev pistol (Type 68)
	9x19 mm pistol (close copy of CZ75)
	AK-47 assault rifle (Type 58)
	AKM assault rifle (Type 68)
	SKS assault rifle (Type 63)
	Variants of AK-74, AK-74S assault rifle (Type 88)
	Variant of AK-103 assault rifle (a close derivative of the AK-74M)
	8 mm sniper rifle ('Zastava' M76)
	5.45 mm RPK-74 light machine gun (Type 64)
	7.62×39 mm variant of RPD light machine gun ('Type 62') (at least three versions)
	7.62 mm machine gun (PK series variants)
	7.62 mm Dragunov SVD
	12.7 mm heavy machine gun DShK
	12.7 mm heavy machine gun NSV
Light weapons and munitions	7.62×54 mm minigun (modification of US M134)
	POMZ-2M anti-personnel mine
	40 mm rocket-propelled grenade launcher (RPG-7)
	30 mm automatic grenade launcher (AGS-17)
	93 mm thermobaric rocket launcher
	Man-portable air-defence systems (SA-7, SA-14, SA-16)
	Anti-tank missile (AT-1, AT-3, variant of AT-4)
	82 mm and 107 mm recoilless rifle
Towed and self-propelled artillery and munitions	60 mm, 82 mm, 120 mm and 160 mm mortars
	76 mm field gun
	100 mm self-propelled gun (SU-85)
	120 mm self-propelled combination gun (M-1992)
	122 mm self-propelled howitzer and gun (M-1971, M-1981, M-1991)
	130 mm self-propelled gun (M-1975, M-1992)
	152 mm self-propelled gun-howitzer (M-1974, M-1985)
	170 mm self-propelled gun (M-1978 'Koksan', M-1989)

(Continued)

Table 1: Continued

Weapons Category	Example Types (Closest Foreign Designation Where Applicable)
Multiple rocket launchers and munitions	107 mm multiple rocket launcher (2 tube, 12 tube)
	122 mm multiple rocket launcher (30 tube, 40 tube)
	240 mm multiple rocket launcher (12 tube, 22 tube, possibly 30 tube – range extension available) (BM-24, M-1985, M-1989, M-1991)
	300 mm multiple rocket launcher
Heavy anti-aircraft weapons and munitions	ZPU-1 heavy anti-aircraft machine gun
	ZPU-2 twin heavy anti-aircraft machine gun
	ZPU-4 quad heavy anti-aircraft machine gun
	M-1983 quad 14.55 mm self-propelled heavy machine gun
	M-1990 30 mm Gatling gun
	M-1992 twin 30 mm self-propelled automatic cannon (described by NK as a 'hex gun')*
	37 mm self-propelled anti-aircraft gun (recoil-operated)
	57 mm automatic anti-aircraft gun (single and twin barrel)
Surface-to-air systems	SA-2 Guideline air-defence system
	SA-3 Goa air-defence system
	SA-10 Grumble surface-to-air missile system
Other air defence	Radars
	Radar jammers
	GPS jammers
Tanks and armoured vehicles	M-1992 armoured personnel carrier
	Type 63 armoured personnel carrier (multiple variants, North Korean VTT-323)
	PT-85 light amphibious tank (Type-82)
	M-1985 light tank
	T-55 medium tank
	T-62 medium tank (multiple variants, North Korean 'Chonma-ho') T-628 and T-668, Pokpung-ho
	M-2002 main battle tank** (North Korean 'Pokpung-ho', 'Songun-ho' variants)
Naval craft	Submarines (*Yugo, Yono, Romeo, Sang-O, Sinpo*** class)
	Missile boats (variants of the OSA-1)
	Frigates (*Najin, Nampo* class)
	Corvettes (*Sariwon* class, based on Soviet *Tral* class)
	Torpedo boats
	Hovercraft and specialised infiltration craft (Kong Bang II and III)
	Fire-support patrol craft (*Chaho* class, based on P-6 hull)
	Personnel landing craft (*Nampo* class, based on P-6 hull)
	Mechanized landing craft (*Hante, Hanchon* class)

(Continued)

Table 1:   Continued

Weapons Category	Example Types (Closest Foreign Designation Where Applicable)
Cruise and ballistic missiles	Anti-ship cruise missiles (STYX, Kh-35 variant) Coastal-defence cruise missile (STYX, KN-01) Short-range ballistic missiles (Scud-B/C/D/ER, KN-02 'Toksa') Medium-range ballistic missiles (Nodong, 1,300 km) Intermediate-range ballistic missile (Musudan, 3,500 km) Intercontinental ballistic missiles (TD-2, KN-08, over 10,000 km)
Weapons of mass destruction-related technology	Nuclear reactor design, technology Uranium enrichment and conversion technology Nuclear material (for example, uranium hexafluoride) Plutonium reprocessing technology Nuclear weapons design Chemical munitions production technology Chemical, biological, radiological defence equipment

Source: Interviews and conversations with Interviewee C, conducted throughout 2014; US Army Training and Doctrine Center, 'Worldwide Equipment Guide', September 2001, available at <https://fas.org/man/dod-101/sys/land/row/weg2001.pdf>, accessed 20 October 2015; Federation of American Scientists, 'North Korean Artillery Systems', September 1999, <http://www.fas.org/man/dod-101/sys/land/row/dprk-arty.htm>, accessed 20 October 2015; 'Report of Shwe Mann's Visit to North Korea', Translated by Pascal Khu Thwe for the Democratic Voice of Burma, 2 June 2010, <www.dvb.no/burmas-nuclear-ambitions/burmas-nuclear-ambitions-military-docs/military-docs/9279>, accessed 20 October 2015; US Department of Defense, 'North Korea Country Handbook: Marine Corps Intelligence Activity', May 1997. The author is also grateful to Joseph S Bermudez, Jr for his assistance in refining this catalogue.
Notes:
* Information supplied by Interviewee C.
** North Korean upgrades of the T-62 that also has features of the T-72, T-80, T-90 and the Chinese Type 88. See Military Factory, 'Pokpung-ho', 27 January 2014, <http://www.militaryfactory.com/armor/detail.asp?armor_id=391>, accessed 20 October 2015. See also Kim Eun-jung, 'North Korea Rolls Out 900 Tanks in the Last Seven Years: Source', Yonhap News, 19 June 2013, <http://english.yonhapnews.co.kr/northkorea/2013/06/18/61/0401000000AEN20130618009700315F.HTHT>, accessed 20 October 2015.
*** North Korea's latest submarine has been tentatively given the name 'Sinpo', in the absence of an agreed Western designation.

According to Interviewee C, after-sale services and spare parts can also be negotiated as part of the original contract. An order placed for a full 240-mm multiple-launch rocket system (MLRS) kit would, for example, include technical descriptions of the various types of rocket, the launcher vehicle, loader vehicle and battery fire-control computer. For these components of the system, it would also include operating instructions, parts lists and repair instructions. Supporting documentation for this system totals an estimated 515 pages. At the point of loading and delivery, these items are cross-checked by the North Korean seller with a corresponding list of the agreed items and documents to be supplied.[20]

The quality of North Korea's weapons systems varies. US weapons experts have assessed that its small arms and light weapons are basic in design and their quality is reasonably high.[21] Attesting to this judgement, North Korean small arms bought decades ago by Malta and Peru are still in use by armed forces and police in those countries to this day.[22] Interviewee C added that North Korean multiple rocket launchers were of sound quality, and that they were able to 'do the job'.[23] Some buyers have reported problems with larger systems, indicating that Pyongyang's catalogue is of uneven quality. For example, much to Yemen's chagrin, its US-detected shipment of Scud ballistic missiles from North Korea was defective, necessitating the subsequent return of Korean technicians amidst continued scrutiny by Washington.[24]

Spare Parts and Munitions
Spare parts can be provided by North Korea either as part of a contract for complete systems or separately. In principle, it is able to offer spare parts for any of the systems it manufactures. The same applies to munitions for the types of weapons platforms that North Korean industry is familiar with – whether small arms, light weapons or heavier equipment. As might be expected, there is business to be found for North Korea in selling spare parts and replacement munitions for weapons systems it has previously sold.

North Korea can also provide spare parts or munitions that are compatible with foreign-made weapons of similar, but not necessarily identical, design. This is an important and perhaps growing market opportunity for the country. With one known exception – Guyana – none of North Korea's military clients has ever relied on the country as their only, or even primary, weapons supplier. In fact, the arsenals of most of its Cold War clients were dominated by Soviet or Chinese weaponry. At the time, Moscow and Beijing generously gifted arms or sold them at 'friendship

---

[20] Information and documentation supplied by Interviewee C during interviews with the author in June and July 2014.
[21] Shea and Hong, 'North Korean Small Arms'.
[22] Photographs are available from TheAKForum.net.
[23] Author interview with Interviewee C, 25 July 2014.
[24] 'Yemeni Military Leaders Brief Ambassador on DPRK Contacts', Cable #03SANAA1990, 12 August 2003, accessed via Wikileaks on 15 May 2014.

rates' to allies and partners. Towards the end of the 1980s, that generosity dried up. The Soviet Union under Mikhail Gorbachev dramatically scaled back its military assistance programmes, leaving previous recipients with arsenals they were unprepared to maintain independently. After the Cold War, Russia and China gradually began to build newer variants of the weapons systems they had previously sent abroad, phasing out those based on technology dating from the early-to-mid-Cold War. Earlier beneficiaries thus found it more difficult to locate spare parts and repair services for the weapons systems they became stuck with.

In this void, North Korea has found a market opportunity in continuing to produce variants of systems designed during the golden age of Soviet and Chinese handouts.[25] For example, North Korea has sold spare parts to the RoC and Ethiopia for tanks made in the Soviet Union and Eastern Europe,[26] and supplied ammunition to Cambodia for Soviet-made small arms.[27]

Designs and Production Technology for Weapons and Weapons Systems
In 1996, an unnamed US official remarked upon a more worrying North Korean revenue stream: the sale of weapons manufacturing technology. 'It's one thing to give a man a fish', he said, 'it's another to teach him how to fish.'[28] Pyongyang's offers in this area can be highly attractive: a recipe book for arms manufacturing, all of the needed ingredients and a private instructor. In other words, Pyongyang is open to supplying countries with weapons designs and helping them to establish indigenous defence-industrial capabilities that would in theory later reduce their reliance on external suppliers, North Korea included. China and Russia have in the past occasionally been willing to perform this service as well, though their military and political relationships with the prospective foreign partner are usually already well developed at the time that the sale of production technology is contemplated. Russia's recent deals with India and Venezuela exemplify this.[29]

---

[25] For example, in 2010 North Korea displayed a longer variant of its licensed copy Chinese Type 63 armoured personnel carrier, with new optics. See Military Factory, 'VT-323 (M1973 Sinhung) Armoured Personnel Carrier', 3 May 2015, <http://www.militaryfactory.com/armor/detail.asp?armor_id=394>, accessed 20 October 2015.

[26] 'Ethiopia: Scenesetter for Secretary Rice's December 5 Visit', Cable #07ADDISABABA3430, 30 November 2007, accessed via Wikileaks on 27 May 2014.

[27] 'Blue Lantern Check on Denied License Application 050128842', Cable #09STATE81473_a, 5 August 2009, accessed via Wikileaks on 27 May 2014.

[28] *Risk Report*, 'North Korean Missile Exports', Wisconsin Project on Nuclear Arms Control (Vol. 2, No. 6, November/December 1996), <http://www.wisconsinproject.org/countries/nkorea/north-korea-missile-exports.html>, accessed 20 October 2015.

[29] Gleb Stolyarov, 'Russia's Kalashnikov to Open Weapons Factory in India', *Reuters*, 7 February 2014; *Guardian*, 'Hugo Chavez Announces Kalashnikov and Drone Production', 14 June 2012.

North Korea, by contrast, apparently stands ready to offer such assistance regardless of the depth of the existing relationship.[30] Where it has provided designs and helped to establish weapon production lines overseas, those lines have tended to be for small arms and light weapons and ballistic missiles. For many types of arms, state-of-the-art technology is less likely to be a requirement for prospective clients. An AK-47, though unsophisticated, will perform reliably in a variety of environments and stand the test of time – whether it is of Soviet, Chinese or North Korean manufacture, or of another derivative design. A client wishing to manufacture its own small arms may therefore see little advantage in having Russia or China build the production plant if North Korea has offered to do so cost-effectively and the weapons design is deemed adequate.

A number of countries have granted contracts to North Korea for small-arms and light-weapons plants over the years. Madagascar reportedly contracted for the construction of a North Korean small arms factory in the early 1980s.[31] As will be unearthed throughout Chapters III, IV and V, Yemen, Ethiopia, the Democratic Republic of the Congo (DRC) and possibly Uganda did the same, though some requests were broadened to include light weapons and artillery. In most of these countries, North Korea is not the only arms-factory supplier. For example, China also provided assembly lines for factories in Ethiopia and Uganda. As in other corners of its markets, Pyongyang therefore has competition.

North Korea similarly stands ready to sell ballistic-missile technology regulated by the Missile Technology Control Regime; such transfers, once frowned upon, are now illegal under UN resolutions. Beginning in the late 1980s, North Korea helped to build, supply and operate factories for short-range ballistic missiles in Egypt, Syria, Iran and Libya. In the 1990s, the country helped Iran and Pakistan with medium-range Nodong ballistic-missile production. The extent of North Korea's missile-production assistance to Libya came to light only in June 1999, when Indian customs agents at the port of Kandla requested to board the freighter *Ku Wol San*. The captain, eager to make some extra cash while carrying out his main mission, had decided to detour to pick up sugar in Thailand and attempt to sell it en route to his official destination, Malta. When a deal to sell the sugar to Algerians collapsed, he agreed to sell it to an Indian company and offload the bags in

---

[30] A high-level North Korean delegation surprised its Nigerian counterparts in 2004 by offering to build weapons factories, for instance. North Korea's military and political relationship with Nigeria is not thought to be well developed. *Washington Times*, 'North Korea Offers Nigeria Missile Deal', 28 January 2004.

[31] US Defense Intelligence Agency, 'North Korea: The Foundations for Military Strength', October 1991, available at <https://www.fas.org/irp/dia/product/knfms/knfms_toc.html>, accessed 20 October 2015.

Kandla. There, Indian officials inspected the *Ku Wol San* and after a scuffle with the defensive North Korean crew, discovered what a former White House official described as a 'production kit for missiles'.[32] A committee of Indian missile experts determined that the shipment was 'unimpeachable and irrefutable evidence' of the transfer of a missile production line by North Korea. US intelligence confirmed the end recipient: Libya's Muammar Qadhafi. The fact that the ship's cargo did not include everything needed for missile production suggested that there were earlier shipments, that more were planned, or both.[33]

Of all the forms of North Korean defence exports, the transfer of manufacturing technology is one of the most troubling. As Timothy McCarthy, a former arms inspector in Iraq, pointed out, 'once Libya can make its own missiles, you can't stop them'.[34]

Upgrade, Repair and Maintenance Services
North Korea can also offer upgrade services to previous beneficiaries of its weapon-production technology where it has learnt to make modified or newer variants of the relevant systems. For example, in the late 1980s, Pyongyang assisted Ethiopia in setting up and running two small-arms factories in Ambo and Debre Zeyit. Amongst other things, this included a production line for AK-47 and AK-74 assault rifles at the Debre Zeyit facility.[35] Nearly twenty years later, in 2007, North Koreans were present at the same site, working to retool and upgrade those lines to make a newer variant of the rifles.[36] Similarly, in the last five years North Korean technicians are believed to have assisted Syria in amending its Scud ballistic-missile manufacturing infrastructure to produce variants with an extended range and newer guidance technology.[37]

Repair and maintenance services are also available for some equipment of foreign origin (primarily Soviet or Chinese) in instances where North Korea deploys variants of the same foreign systems or where

---

[32] Warrick, 'On North Korean Freighter, A Hidden Missile Factory'.
[33] *Ibid.*
[34] *Ibid.*
[35] Andrea Berger, 'Is Ethiopia Violating UN Sanctions Against North Korea?', 38 North, 23 December 2014, <http://38north.org/2014/12/aberger122314/>, accessed 20 October 2015.
[36] Tewodros Rufael, 'Design of Enterprise Resource Planning: Framework and its Implementation', supervised by Subhash Chandra at the School of Graduate Studies of Addis Ababa University, November 2007, pp. 8–9.
[37] Robin Hughes, 'SSRC: Spectre at the Table', *Jane's Defence Weekly*, 22 January 2014.

it is able to domestically produce systems of comparable design. As described above, where certain types of equipment are no longer produced by either the Russian or Chinese defence-industrial complexes, those countries are often unable or unwilling to service them, or they do so at a higher price. Vietnamese officials, for example, recently highlighted their consistent frustration that Moscow 'bends [them] over a barrel' for after-sale services for Russian-origin equipment, whether acquired decades ago or more recently.[38] North Korea, by contrast, appears to offer such services relatively inexpensively, as demonstrated by its contracts with the Republic of the Congo (RoC), discussed in Chapter V.

Training Services

Contracting to North Korea for training services is illegal under UN Security Council Resolution 1874 (2009) if that training involves the use of lethal weaponry.[39] This practice has a long history, which has continued into the twenty-first century. Korean People's Army (KPA) officers have instructed counterparts from countries such as Syria, Egypt, Libya, Zimbabwe, Uganda, Benin, Nigeria, the DRC, Mozambique and the Seychelles. Zimbabwe's Robert Mugabe once reminisced that Kim Il-sung 'provide[d] us with training facilities for our cadres ... We thank him today as we did yesterday.'[40] Ugandan President Yoweri Museveni recently recalled with similar fondness North Korea's training of his country's first tank crew.[41] In addition to training provided in the customer's country, training for foreign personnel is also offered in North Korea, particularly at the Kim Il-sung Military Academy.[42] Non-state groups such as Hizbullah

---

[38] Author conversation with Vietnamese officials, 19 November 2014, Hanoi.

[39] The legality of training services was a grey area of the sanctions regime until recently, primarily because the wording of relevant provisions in Resolution 1874 (2009) did not offer a definition of 'related services'. However, as a result of Uganda's repeated military training contracts with North Korea, the UN Panel of Experts on North Korea has clarified that these contracts are in breach of the resolution if they involve the use of lethal weaponry. Chapter III will show that this is indeed the case. UN Security Council, 'Report of the Panel of Experts Established Pursuant to Resolution 1874 (2009)', S/2015/131, 23 February 2015, pp. 38–39.

[40] *Africa Research Bulletin: Political, Social and Cultural Series*, 'Zimbabwe–North Korea: A Controversial Visit' (Vol. 46, No. 5, 2009), pp. 17985B–17986C.

[41] *East African*, 'Museveni Praises North Korea Security Training', 17 April 2014, <http://www.theeastafrican.co.ke/news/Uganda-President-Museveni-praises-North-Korea-security-training/-/2558/2283098/-/f7p3ue/-/index.html>, accessed 20 October 2015.

[42] Other online sources show that North Korea's '711 unit' of the Reconnaissance General Bureau has also hosted foreign students.

and the Palestine Liberation Organization have benefited from these training courses as well.[43]

Information compiled through news reports, academic literature and other publicly available sources highlights the range of disciplines in which KPA officers have trained their foreign counterparts. The most predictable subject covered is the operation of specific weapons systems. North Koreans have helped Libyans and Madagascans to fly MiG aircraft, Ugandans and Congolese to operate tanks, and countless others to use small arms.[44]

Pyongyang has also offered training courses in combat operations, strategy and tactics. Special-forces training seems to have been a particularly attractive offering. In the early 1980s, Robert Mugabe assembled an elite combat unit. The Fifth Brigade, as it became known, was entirely North Korean-trained. Shortly after completing its training, it perpetrated atrocities in Matabeleland, which is still the subject of protests to this date. Mugabe is believed to have repeatedly contracted to North Korea for military training since.[45] Uganda, meanwhile, recently agreed that KPA officers should continue training its marine units, though precisely in what way is unclear.[46]

Leadership-protection courses appear to have been popular, and would be illegal if the use of lethal weaponry were taught during the course. Nigeria is known to have repeatedly sent its army personnel to attend courses on this subject, with the most-recent known contingent placed in North Korea in 2005,[47] perhaps as a direct result of a high-level North Korean visit the year before.

Other known, admittedly legal, training courses include: unarmed combat, in which Zimbabweans and Ugandans have participated in the not-too-distant past; 'homeland security'; intelligence operations and reconnaissance; and (according to a single source) combat engineering.[48]

---

[43] Benjamin R Young, 'How North Korea Has Been Arming Palestinian Militants for Decades', *NK News*, 25 June 2014, <http://www.nknews.org/2014/06/how-north-korea-has-been-arming-palestinian-militants-for-decades/>, accessed 20 October 2015.

[44] Andrea Berger, 'A Legal Precipice: The DPRK-Uganda Security Relationship', 38 North, 13 November 2014, <http://38north.org/2014/11/aberger111314/>, accessed 20 October 2015.

[45] *Africa Research Bulletin: Political, Social and Cultural Series*, 'Zimbabwe–North Korea'.

[46] Savada (ed.), *North Korea*, chapter on 'Relations with the Third World'; Helen Chapin Metz (ed.), *Madagascar: A Country Study* (Washington, DC: GPO for the Library of Congress, 1994).

[47] Information gathered through online sources, obscured to protect the identity of the individuals concerned.

[48] *Ibid.*

In some of the aforementioned areas, such as leadership protection, it is understandable why some foreign governments may believe North Korea has a competitive edge. However, in most others, such as maritime operations, the country's advantage as a provider is unclear, with many other countries providing training in the same subjects. North Korea may be offering more attractive prices. Politics may also be a factor. Training for foreign counterparts is often only palatable to governments other than North Korea when political or military relationships between the two countries concerned are generally positive, or the provider believes that the client is a responsible actor. Training in sensitive disciplines, such as certain types of combat or intelligence operations, may be even more difficult to acquire from reputable suppliers. These dynamics will be explored further in Chapter III in relation to Uganda's recent training contracts with North Korea.

Procurement Services

The UN Security Council recently clarified that buying arms and related materiel from North Korean entities was prohibited, regardless of where they were originally manufactured. Resolution 2094 (2013) notes that previous restrictions, specifically Resolution 1874 (2009), 'apply also to brokering or other intermediary services, including when arranging for the provision, maintenance or use of prohibited items in other States or the supply, sale or transfer to or exports from other States'.[49]

Several North Korean customers are known to have benefited from the country's ability to broker and procure goods from elsewhere. In terms of brokering, Chapter III will explore the Sri Lankan government's allegations that North Korean entities may have facilitated the sale and shipment of Chinese-made arms to the Liberation Tigers of Tamil Eelam. One arms dealer interviewed for this study believes that North Korean brokerage of Chinese-made weapons is facilitated by a standing arrangement between North Korean and Chinese arms firms. This individual asserts that when a North Korean entity negotiates a sale of small arms where the number of units agreed and the timeframe in which delivery is desired exceeds North Korea's manufacturing capacity, Chinese-owned companies based in China will fill the remainder of the contract.[50] North Korea, or brokers working on its behalf, then make the

---

[49] UN Security Council Resolution 2094 (2013), para. 7.
[50] Author interview with Interviewee C, 6 June 2014. The interviewee also claims that in order to facilitate such transactions, North Korean arms dealers price match with their Chinese counterparts.

logistical arrangements for both the Korean- and Chinese-made portions of the consignment. This claim merits further instigation.[51]

Aside from brokering the sale of foreign-made weapons, whenever Pyongyang is involved in establishing a weapons-manufacturing capability in a foreign country, it can also be reasonably assumed that it will take an active role in procuring the machines and components required, often from outside of the Korean Peninsula. North Korea itself uses at least some foreign-sourced components or machines in its weapons production, as demonstrated by UN analysis of the first stage of the country's long-range rocket, launched in December 2012.[52] Undoubtedly, the partial overlap in the North Korean entities – such as the Second Economic Committee – engaged in procurement for North Korea's nuclear and missile programmes and those facilitating arms deals overseas means that the country has had ample opportunity to develop a shrewd and wide-reaching military procurement network. Pyongyang's main arms-dealing entities are thus not only able to obtain products from around the world to support its military development projects in partner countries, but also to largely evade detection in the process of doing so. Both of these capabilities are probable selling features from the perspective of prospective clients, especially those that would prefer a specific weapons-development project to remain clandestine, at least initially.

North Korea's ability to source products from around the globe in support of its foreign military projects is borne out by previous, occasional interdictions of cargo destined for North Korean-assisted production lines in Syria, Libya, Burma and Egypt, amongst others. In 2003, the *Wall Street Journal* reported a raid by Slovakian police on the home of two North Koreans living in Bratislava, where they had been brokering the purchase of supplies from Europe and elsewhere for a North Korean missile project in Egypt. Receipts, invoices and bills of lading left behind in the recently abandoned house showed 'that between 1999 and mid-2001, the pair ordered more than $10 million of products – among them chemicals, trucks, pumps, measuring devices, a high-speed camera and heavy vehicle parts – and billed them to a military factory in Egypt.'[53]

---

[51] Continued investigation would be particularly worthwhile given that it was China that allegedly negotiated the exception in Resolution 1874 (2009) which permits countries to ship small arms and light weapons *to* North Korea.

[52] UN Security Council, 'Report of the Panel of Experts Established Pursuant to Resolution 1874 (2009)', S/2014/147, 6 March 2014, p. 22.

[53] Bertil Lintner and Steve Stecklow, 'Trail of Papers Illuminates North Korea's Arms Trading', *Wall Street Journal*, 6 February 2003.

Pricing

> *North Korea asks only two things of its customers: first, can they pay, and second, can they keep a secret?*

(Michael Hayden, former director, CIA)[54]

North Korean weapons-related goods and services are frequently talked of as being cheaper than others on the market. As outlined in the introduction to this study, commentators that seek to explain a particular country's military relationship with North Korea frequently conclude that cost is a primary factor determining a foreign partner's interest in buying from Pyongyang. Little information is available to substantiate this assertion. Public information about North Korea's pricing – some of which is verified, some unverified – is scattered throughout news reports, testimony by relevant defectors and foreign officials, leaked cables, declassified documents and UN reports. That information is patchy, sometimes dated, lacking the details needed to draw comparisons with other suppliers, and mostly second hand. Nevertheless, the more recent publicly available information broadly supports the hypothesis that North Korea considers the level of competition when pricing its goods and services. As a result, it is plausible that North Korea is comparatively inexpensive in the area of conventional weapons and related goods and services, but may charge steeper prices for ballistic missiles or goods related to weapons of mass destruction (WMD) to those customers that others may not be willing or able to sell to.

Historical information provides the backdrop for this hypothesis. In 1991, the Defense Intelligence Agency assessed that by the end of the Cold War 'North Korea [had] emerged as a significant arms exporter of inexpensive [conventional] weapons'.[55] A 1994 Library of Congress study described North Korea's training services similarly; the country's market edge in the developing world, it said, was 'comparatively inexpensive training programs'.[56] North Korea's Cold War-era costing for these goods and services seemed to be partially politically motivated, and friends such as Cuba and high-priority socialist battleground states like Vietnam often received assistance free of cost.[57] Others seeking weapons on an ad hoc

---

[54] 'Director's Remarks at the Los Angeles World Affairs Council – 16 September 2008', found in *US Central Intelligence Agency Handbook: Strategic Information, Activities, and Regulation* (Washington, DC: International Business Publications Inc., 2013), p. 164.
[55] US Defense Intelligence Agency, 'North Korea', chap. 3 on 'Foreign Policy Goals'.
[56] Savada (ed.), *North Korea*, chapter on 'Relations with the Third World'.
[57] Patrick Oppmann, 'Panama Says Cuban Weapons Shipment Violates U.N. Arms Embargo', *CNN*, 29 August 2013; for further details on North Korea's support to

basis had to pay, but occasionally remarked upon how shockingly inexpensive the final bill was. In April 1986, Peru bought a large number of AK-47s – called 'AK Coreas' in Latin America – from North Korea. The government in Lima defended the purchase, arguing that North Korea's offer was '75 to 80 per cent below world market price'.[58] These weapons are still used by police units, civil guards and the armed forces in Peru today.

It is difficult to extrapolate assessments of North Korean pricing behaviour during the Cold War confidently into the post-Cold War period, particularly given the severity of the country's economic hardships in the 1990s and the priority it consequently assigned to foreign-currency generation. Yet as shown in Chapters IV and V, in recent years, Yemen, Ethiopia and the RoC have still insisted that North Korean goods and services are significantly cheaper than those provided by other suppliers – assessments relating to both the procurement of spare parts and repair services as well as conventional weapons-production technology.

With regards to spare parts and repair services, concrete and reliable details are only available about a 2009 repair and spare-parts contract with the RoC and an attempted 2011 sale of SA-16 man-portable air-defence systems (MANPADS) to Azerbaijan. In the RoC case, the invoice submitted by the General Department of Military Cooperation of the Ministry of People's Armed Forces of the DPRK outlines the cost per unit and in total of repairing various types of equipment. Repairs for B-12 107-mm multiple rocket launchers cost approximately €1,220 per unit,[59] while repairs for

---

North Vietnam, see 'A 7 May 1967 DVO Memo about Intergovernmental Relations between the DPRK and Romania, the DRV, and Cuba', 7 May 1967, History and Public Policy Program Digital Archive, AVPRF f. 0102, op. 23, p. 112, d. 24, pp. 39–42. Obtained for NKIDP by Sergey Radchenko and translated for the North Korea International Documentation Project by Gary Goldberg; available at <http://digitalarchive.wilsoncenter.org/document/116701>, accessed 20 October 2015.

[58] US Defense Intelligence Agency, 'North Korea', chap. 3, 'Foreign Policy Goals'.

[59] In fact, the Congolese contract highlights another important aspect of North Korean pricing: the currency used. According to Interviewee C, in approximately 2008 or 2009, North Korea switched from pricing its military goods and services in US dollars to euros, perhaps as a consequence of the Banco Delta Asia incident and the US Treasury's ability to restrict transactions carried out in dollars. The incident began in September 2005 when the US Treasury designated the Macau-based bank as a 'primary money-laundering concern' under the Patriot Act, because it allegedly facilitated corrupt financial activities by the North Korean government. Some $25 million in North Korean government funds were frozen as a result and numerous financial institutions around the world subsequently began to cut any ties to North Korea out of fear that they might be excluded from the US financial system. Available details of North Korea's arms-related contracts with the Republic of the Congo support the conclusion that North Korea now bills in euros. David Lague and Donald Greenlees, 'Squeeze on Banco Delta Asia Hit North Korea Where It Hurt', *New York Times*, 18 January 2007.

BM-21 122-mm multiple rocket launchers cost €5,520 per unit.[60] For comparison, in 2013 the Ukrainian government contracted one of its own national defence firms to repair four BM-21 multiple rocket launchers, including some repairs to the supporting vehicle chassis. It paid approximately €27,000 per unit. This is approximately five times the price charged to Brazzaville by Pyongyang.[61]

Admittedly, North Korea tends to have few competitors in the market for spare parts and maintenance services for aged, communist-bloc weaponry of the variety it repaired in Congo. Its apparently inexpensive pricing in this category of service may therefore be better explained by the funds customers have available for procurement projects. Indeed, if those clients are opting to extend the life of weapons many decades old rather than purchasing new systems, it is plausible that they have constrained budgets for procurement. North Korea's prices in this category may thus be more reflective of what the market will bear, rather than its level of competition.

In terms of training services – a more competitive market, depending upon the customer state in question – it is reasonable to believe that the Library of Congress study is accurate in its conclusion that North Korea's assistance is comparatively inexpensive. North Korea's inexpensive labour costs (see below) may create a floor for prices for training contracts that Pyongyang is in theory willing to negotiate down in order to remain attractive to potential customers.

In the area of full weapons systems the pricing picture is even more uncertain. It likely varies depending upon the type of system, with a distinction between the competitive conventional defence market and the ballistic-missile and WMD-related market, which is less competitive, particularly in countries of concern. In the conventional-weapons realm, the systems that North Korea produces are generally older variants of the models on offer from competitors. Assuming that the customer is either shopping for a new capability or is looking to replace the weapons fulfilling an existing one, it is possible that North Korea's outdated but cheaper wares are being directly compared to newer and more expensive models. This may make North Korea less attractive to those that have

---

[60] Prices have been adjusted for inflation.

[61] A small portion of the difference may be explained by the extent of work to be done. The Ukraine contract involved minor servicing of the automotive chassis, while this point is unclear in the Congo case. Either way, based on this comparison it seems highly likely that North Korea's services are still substantially cheaper than Ukraine's. See 'Minoborony potratit na remont spetsmashin 5.3 million grn (Hrivnya) [Ministry of Defence Will Spend 5.3 million Hrivnya on the Special Vehicles Overhaul]', facts and comments (with syndicated content from *Ukrainian National News*), 18 October 2013.

specific technological requirements in mind or alternatively pique the interest of customers conscious of their budget and more flexible with their equipment needs.

An example of this pricing dynamic appeared in the case of *Regina v. Michael George Ranger*, the trial of a British arms dealer, Michael Ranger, who was arrested in 2011 and ultimately convicted for failing to secure an export licence when arranging the sale of North Korean-made SA-16 Gimlet (Igla-1) MANPADS to Azerbaijan. Azerbaijan had initially approached Ranger requesting that he find suppliers for 70–100 MANPADS units.[62] Ranger informed Baku that while there was 'no chance' he would be able to source newer-model MANPADS, such as the FIM-92 Stinger, he would be able to procure models based on older Russian technology, namely the SA-16 Gimlet from North Korea.[63] Azerbaijan consented, which highlights its flexibility in terms of military specifications. The initial unit price quoted to Azerbaijan is not referenced in the court transcripts. However, as will be discussed further below, following a dispute over the issue of product testing in the end-user country – something insisted upon by Baku, but resisted by Pyongyang – Ranger sought a new quotation for a reduced number of MANPADS for Azerbaijan. In effect, this small number would serve as a product sample which could be tested before a larger order would be placed. Hesong Trading Corporation, a subsidiary of KOMID, responded that an order of only ten pieces would involve a higher unit price. In manufacturing there is an inverse relationship between the number of units produced and the unit cost. In this instance, according to Hesong, 'The new price of this lot is €28,500 per PCS [€31,000 in 2015 prices]'.[64] It is reasonable to assume that the initial unit price given for the larger quantity would therefore have been much cheaper than this figure.

Assessing North Korea's price competitiveness based on these negotiations is difficult. Individual SA-16 missiles can reportedly be bought on the black market for as little as €4,200,[65] but these figures cannot be taken to indicate the likely costs of a large commercial contract

---

[62] A 'unit' in this case is used to refer to the missile and its launch tube. It does not include the corresponding trigger unit, which is reusable, and whose sale is often negotiated separately.

[63] *Regina v. Michael George Ranger,* Southwark Crown Court, Record of Proceedings for Day Three, 11 July 2012.

[64] *Regina v. Michael George Ranger,* Southwark Crown Court, Record of Proceedings for Day Two, 10 July 2012.

[65] Converted from $5,000 using historical exchange rates at the time of the price's publication in November 2006, and adjusted for inflation. 'Black Market Prices for Man-Portable Air Defense Systems', Federation of American Scientists, June 2010,

between governments. Information about purchases of a comparable number of SA-16 missiles by countries is scarce. This is not only because governments ordinarily contract for a larger number of units than the ten Azerbaijan ultimately was interested in procuring, but also because Russia began producing and (almost exclusively) selling newer and more expensive variants of the 'Igla' system in 2003. The best comparison for the Azerbaijan offer is therefore the 1997 contract between Russia and Ecuador for the sale of 222 SA-16 units (seemingly also excluding trigger components), priced at approximately €80,000 per unit.[66] While there is some margin of error in this comparison, it nevertheless appears that the North Korean SA-16 variants were substantially cheaper than those produced by the original Russian manufacturer. The difference is starker when considering that the unit costs associated with North Korea's initial offer of 100 SA-16s were almost certainly much lower than the €28,500 per piece quoted for ten.

It cannot be ruled out that North Korea may simply be able to manufacture weapons more cost-effectively than others. Experts in communist systems interviewed for this study noted that the cost of labour inputs in the DPRK is either low, poorly calculated or both. The nature of a socialist-planned workforce such as North Korea's makes it extremely challenging to calculate accurately the costs of labour inputs into the defence manufacturing process.[67] It is also possible that North Korean entities with authority to negotiate new deals may have been told by their superiors that generating *revenue* denominated in foreign currencies, rather than profit, is the top priority.[68] If this is the case, this could be another partial explanation for what appears to be North Korea's comparatively low price floor for conventional weapons systems.

In terms of the ballistic-missile or WMD realm, North Korea's competition is much thinner – especially in those markets considering

---

p. 1, <https://fas.org/programs/ssp/asmp/issueareas/manpads/black_market_prices.pdf>, accessed 13 November 2015.

[66] Total contract value was $14 million in January 1998. This has been converted using historical exchange rated from the time, and adjusted for inflation. Paul Holton, 'Small Arms Production in Russia', Saferworld, March 2007, p. 29, <http://www.saferworld.org.uk/resources/view-resource/256-small-arms-production-in-russia>, accessed 13 November 2015.

[67] Author interview with Interviewees A and B, 3 October 2014.

[68] North Korea has sometimes been willing to offer attractive financing arrangements when its customers have shallow pockets, despite the emphasis paid to short-term revenue generation. For one project in Yemen, for example, it agreed to allow Sana'a to pay over a ten-year period. This may be an unusual case, and those terms may have been offered because Sana'a had agreed around the same time to contract to North Korea for other goods and services. 'Yemeni Military Leaders Brief Ambassador on DPRK Contacts', Cable #03SANAA1990.

such programmes. The limited evidence available suggests that Pyongyang recognises it is one of the few countries willing to sell such weapons, facilities, or material to customers under sanctions or pursuing clandestine programmes. As recalled by Thomas Plant and Ben Rhode in *Survival*, North Korea is said to have charged Libya $2 million for three canisters, or 1.7 tonnes, of slightly enriched uranium hexafluoride – about forty times the market rate of $45 per kilogram.[69] If true, this this would again support the hypothesis that North Korea varies its pricing greatly depending upon its competition in the specific market context. It also highlights the possibility that a single big-ticket sale could generate more revenue than all of North Korea's annual conventional-weapons sales and military-services contracts combined. Indeed, during the 1990s, at the zenith of North Korean ballistic-missile exports, the balance of the volume of North Korea's defence contracts may still have been conventional, while the balance of the revenue earned may have been from ballistic missiles.

A further complicating factor in any discussion of pricing is North Korea's penchant for conducting trade through barter arrangements. Cuba, Burma and Iran amongst others have benefited from North Korea's willingness to swap arms and related services for other goods. Representatives of SGS, an independent logistics inspection and certification company active in Burma, suggest that until at least 2009 Burma exchanged rice through military-owned Myanmar Economic Holdings Ltd[70] for 'technical services and equipment' that reportedly included conventional arms.[71] Reports citing other sources speak of a comparable rice-for-arms arrangement.[72] Iran allegedly paid for arms in oil, and the *Chong Chon Gang* shipment from Cuba discussed in Chapter III was part of the country's standing annual barter agreement with Pyongyang.[73] In all of these cases, it is impossible to separate out the discrete price for arms.

---

[69] Thomas Plant and Ben Rhode, 'China, North Korea and the Spread of Nuclear Weapons', *Survival* (Vol. 55, No. 2, April 2013), pp. 65, 67.

[70] Myanmar Economic Holdings Ltd was sanctioned by the US in 2008 for supporting the military junta in Burma. See US Department of the Treasury, 'Recent OFAC Actions', 29 July 2008, <http://www.treasury.gov/resource-center/sanctions/OFAC-Enforcement/pages/20080729.aspx>, accessed 20 October 2015. It remains on the Office of Foreign Asset Control's Specially Designated Nationals and Blocked Persons List as of August 2015. See <https://www.treasury.gov/ofac/downloads/t11sdn.pdf>, accessed 20 October 2015.

[71] 'Burma and North Korea: Rice for Arms', Cable #09RANGOON409, 2 July 2009, accessed via Wikileaks on 27 May 2014.

[72] Bertil Lintner, 'Fog Lifts on Myanmar-North Korea Barter', *Asia Times Online*, 4 March 2011.

[73] Author interview with Interviewee J, 29 April 2014. Corroborated by Interviewee E, in conversation with the author on 8 May 2014.

While a clear picture of North Korea's cost modelling is nigh-impossible to reconstruct from open sources, there is some reason to believe that portions of its catalogue – namely conventional weapons, parts maintenance and repair services, and training services – are competitively priced. As a result, the remainder of this Whitehall Paper operates under the assumption that in terms of these categories, North Korea is often less expensive than other suppliers, and that clients that have claimed this factor to have influenced their defence procurement decisions are being at least somewhat truthful. However, as subsequent chapters will show, the narrative that price provides the best explanation for why countries buy military goods and services from Pyongyang is an oversimplification that applies better to some categories of customers than others.

Marketing Methods and Tools

North Korea has unique challenges in attracting custom as a result of the national and UN sanctions against it, its international reputation, and the international political influence of its adversaries, including the US and South Korea. As highlighted in Chapter I, these difficulties emerged prior to the introduction of UN sanctions against North Korea, but have expanded and solidified as a result of them. In order to overcome them and find markets for its military products and services, Pyongyang applies a variety of methods and tools. Currently available information is insufficient to determine whether or not a clear, centrally co-ordinated strategy underpins these marketing efforts.

Various actors are involved in Pyongyang's quest to open new markets or strike fresh deals with existing clients: senior officials; the overseas offices of North Korean firms; diplomatic staff at North Korea's embassies; and even brokers of foreign nationality.

North Korea sometimes uses high-level political meetings to initiate discussions over new arms sales. In August 2003, a senior North Korean delegation led by then-Deputy Defence Minister Jong Chon-dok visited Nigeria – a country with which North Korea was not known to have significant (or perhaps even any) military ties. According to Nigerian officials, during his visit Jong met with the Nigerian Chief of Defence Staff 'to discuss the possible sale of a wide variety of weapons systems to Nigeria. According to … Abuja sources … the North Korean delegation confessed it badly needed hard currency and was willing to sell "anything in their inventory" to Nigeria.' Offers were made for conventional arms, submarines, a radar system and possible assistance in defence manufacturing.[74] The two countries also signed a memorandum of understanding during the visit. A few months later, in

---

[74] 'Nigeria and DPRK Missiles', Cable #04ABUJA149, 29 January 2004, accessed via Wikileaks on 27 May 2014.

January 2004, the vice president of the Presidium of the Supreme People's Assembly of the DPRK visited Nigeria. Afterward, the Nigerian vice president's spokesperson shocked the world by announcing that North Korea had proposed sharing ballistic-missile technology – and by implying that the offer was being considered.[75] This disclosure sparked a strong reaction from the US and France, amongst others.[76] Nigeria's national security advisor subsequently backtracked, saying that 'North Korea had offered to sell missiles and/or missile technology, but the [Government of Nigeria] had turned the offer down'. It is not clear whether other forms of proposed assistance were accepted. However, the incident highlights North Korea's penchant for beginning discussions over new arms sales at the very top. Pyongyang has continued to periodically apply this approach to opening new markets for its goods and services in the sanctions era. In 2009, during a visit to Brazil, North Korea's foreign minister extended similarly unprompted offers to his Brazilian interlocutors. These included numerous proposals for co-operation, including one of an unspecified 'maritime nature' that may have included deep-water oil technology. This mimics the blunt tactics used by the North Korean delegation in Nigeria to expand discussions over bilateral co-operation.[77]

At the same time, some contacts also appear to be initiated through a 'bottom-up' approach, namely by North Korean companies involved in arms trading and their representatives, as well as brokers of foreign nationality, rather than senior political figures. Responsibility for facilitating arms exports is spread between a number of North Korean organisations, many of which use front or brass-plate companies to facilitate their dealings. Figure 1 shows the three main defence-export entities active overseas – the Korea Mining Development Trading Corporation (KOMID), the Korea Ryonbong General Corporation and the Green Pine Associated Corporation – as well as their main associated financial entities, their subsidiary organisations and aliases. It excludes entities affiliated with the Second Academy of Natural Sciences. While subsidiary organisations of the Second Academy have on occasion helped procure goods for North Korean defence projects overseas, the Academy engages primarily in procurement for North Korea's domestic defence programmes, rather than in the export of goods and services.

The first defence-export entity depicted, KOMID, is a 'primary arms dealer and main exporter of goods and equipment related to ballistic missiles and conventional weapons' under the direction of the Second

---

[75] *BBC News*, 'Nigeria Seeking N Korea Missiles', 29 January 2004.
[76] 'Demarche Delivered to French Government on North Korean Arms Trade', Cable #05PARIS6530, 23 September 2005, accessed via Wikileaks on 27 May 2014.
[77] See 'North Korean Foreign Minister Makes "Generic" Visit to Brazil, May 9–13', Cable #09BRASILIA694, 4 June 2009, accessed via Wikileaks on 27 May 2014.

Figure 1: A Basic Outline of North Korea's Defence-Export Bureaucracy.

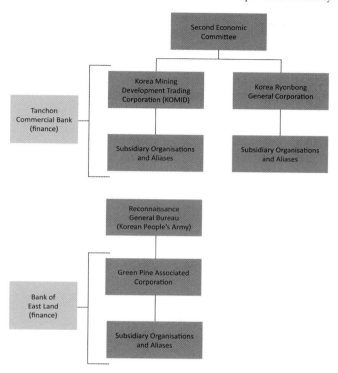

Economic Committee.[78] Also under the direction of this entity is the Korea Ryonbong General Corporation, which, as will be shown in Chapter IV, has been active in countries such as Ethiopia. According to the UN, it is a 'defense conglomerate specializing in acquisition for DPRK defense industries and support to that country's military-related sales'.[79]

The Green Pine Associated Corporation (hereafter, 'Green Pine') operates under the direction of the KPA's Reconnaissance General Bureau and 'specializes in the production of maritime military craft and

---

[78] UN Security Council, 'Narrative Summaries of Reasons for Listing: Korea Mining Development Trading Corporation', 29 October 2014, <www.un.org/sc/suborg/en/sanctions/1718/materials/summaries/entity/korea-mining-development-trading-corporation>, accessed 13 November 2015.

[79] UN Security Council, 'Narrative Summaries of Reasons for Listing: Korea Ryongbong General Corporation', 29 October 2014, <https://www.un.org/sc/suborg/en/sanctions/1718/materials/summaries/entity/korea-ryonbong-general-corporation>, accessed 13 November 2015.

armaments, such as submarines, military boats and missile systems, and has exported torpedoes and technical assistance to Iranian defence-related firms.[80] Due to their involvement in prohibited proliferation activity, all three have been designated by the UN and numerous countries worldwide.

KOMID is believed to have offices in various countries, including China, Russia, Iran, Syria, Uganda and Namibia, the latter of which is responsible for marketing North Korean arms and related services in southern Africa. Interviewee C claims that when arranging transactions in which North Korea was involved, he was often asked to contact his North Korean business partners (employees of a KOMID subsidiary) at their offices in Peru.[81] Like KOMID, Green Pine is currently believed to have representatives in Iran, perhaps indicating that North Korea–Iran co-operation continues to have a maritime dimension. Some of the KOMID or Green Pine offices may be regarded as permanent arrangements, while others are likely more temporary, designed to tap into growth markets or facilitate a given transaction.[82]

In either case, they often receive support from local North Korean diplomatic staff. North Korean embassy representatives have on many occasions been caught facilitating arms deals. Green Pine was paid for a military contract in Iran through a bank in Germany; the account paid into belonged to the North Korean embassy in Tehran.[83] Similarly, North Korean embassy staff signed off on a 2008 invoice to the government of the RoC for weapons-related repair services by North Korean contractors.[84] Given these cases, it is reasonable to assume that embassy staff members may be involved at both the marketing and post-contract logistics phase.

Interviews and recent court cases illuminate a final method by which North Korea identifies new arms markets: employing non-Korean brokers. It is not known how commonly this practice is used, but its origins pre-date the implementation of UN sanctions against North Korea. Interviewee C claims he was encouraged by his North Korean interlocutors to take progressively greater initiative to probe discreetly for new market

---

[80] UN Security Council, 'Narrative Summaries of Reasons for Listing: Green Pine Associated Corporation', 29 October 2014, <https://www.un.org/sc/suborg/en/sanctions/1718/materials/summaries/entity/green-pine-associated-corporation>, accessed 13 November 2015.

[81] Author interview with Interviewee C, 6 June 2014.

[82] North Korean-controlled logistics and shipping firms also have offices overseas in countries such as Russia, China and Brazil, which help delivery on an agreed contract.

[83] 'Message on Ongoing Proliferation Finance Activities by Iran and North Korea Passed to Germany', Cable #07BERLIN1571, 17 August 2007, accessed via Wikileaks on 27 May 2014.

[84] UN Security Council, 'Report of the Panel of Experts Established Pursuant to Resolution 1874(2009)', S/2013/337, pp. 112–15.

opportunities. In approximately 2009, for instance, he claims to have been asked by his counterparts to find buyers for a new radar jamming system that North Korea had developed.

He was assisted in this task by hard-copy marketing material, which North Korean entities seem to use to support face-to-face outreach. As shown in Appendix A, North Korean companies have produced English-language product brochures, and it is likely that versions are available in other languages as well given North Korea's marketing activities in Africa. The example presented is for an AT-4 anti-tank missile, originally wire-guided, which the North Koreans have adapted to use laser guidance. The anti-tank missile brochure uses the NATO designation for the product closest in design – a seemingly common practice, in light of the fact that North Korean blueprints for short-range missiles were found aboard the *Ku Wol San* labelled 'Scud-B' or 'Scud-C', the better-known foreign designator.[85] Brochures comparable to that in Appendix A are allegedly available for the full catalogue of complete weapons systems that Pyongyang manufactures.

Complicating North Korea's ability to secure contracts in new markets for the sale of complete weapons and systems is the issue of product demonstrations. While North Korea is happy to send personnel for in-country contract negotiations, they are allegedly reluctant to entertain requests to demonstrate products in the customer country before agreeing a sale. Doing so would not only add cost for North Korea, which it may not wish to bear if contracts have yet to be signed, but would also add risk for both sides. To demonstrate a product, North Korean technicians would have to clandestinely transfer a single unit to the prospective client. While this would have to be done for a larger volume in the event of a sale, product testing abroad would create another opportunity to get caught, especially if the unit also had to be returned. These challenges were highlighted during the trial of Michael Ranger,[86] when it came to light that North Korea had refused to allow Azerbaijan to test the system in-country before buying, prompting Azerbaijan to reduce the number of units it was willing to procure from 100 to ten. Neither party was willing to compromise on this issue of quantity, making it possible that the contract would have organically fallen through had Michael Ranger not been arrested first.

Given Pyongyang's reluctance to allow in-country demonstrations, customers may be invited to view tests in North Korea, as was offered to

---

[85] Warrick, 'On North Korean Freighter, A Hidden Missile Factory'.

[86] *Regina v. Michael George Ranger*, Southwark Crown Court, Record of Proceedings for Day One, 9 July 2012; Crown Prosecution Service, 'Michael Ranger Sentenced For Organising Arms Deals between North Korea and Azerbaijan', 20 July 2012, <http://www.cps.gov.uk/news/latest_news/michael_ranger_sentenced_for_organising_arms_deals/>, accessed 20 October 2015.

Azerbaijan in its contract negotiations. Interviewee C supplied photographs allegedly showing the demonstration of a minigun in North Korea to 'buyers from Sri Lanka'.[87] He claimed that in 'all' of his dealings, demonstrations were undertaken 'strictly in North Korea'.[88] This constraint creates difficulties for North Korean arms exporters looking to sell complete weapons systems to new markets, especially as North Korean products have a reputation for being of comparatively low or uncertain quality. Product testing, a regular practice in the global defence industry, would therefore be helpful in increasing the prospective customer's confidence in North Korea's wares. However, Pyongyang does not appear to have this luxury.

In short, North Korea is an adaptable marketer, but within the constraints imposed by international sanctions. It uses a mixture of high-level political visits and company-level outreach to probe opportunities for new arms contracts, has over the past decade seemingly begun to incorporate non-Korean nationals into its marketing activity, and has developed marketing material to support its aims. As outlined in the section on pricing, North Korean entities seem to show flexibility in their pricing structure and may actively assess what the market will bear. At the practical level, however, their efforts to open new markets have been impeded by their lack of willingness to risk conducting product demonstrations in-country.

A Niche Supplier

Though the history of its defence-export industry has been fraught with challenges, North Korea has maintained the ability to offer a wide range of weaponry, spare parts and munitions, repair and upgrade services, military training, production technology and assistance, and procurement services. Its limited ability to innovate and keep its catalogue current has been a double-edged sword. On the one hand, it has meant that customers looking for newer wares take little interest in what Pyongyang has to offer. On the other, North Korea remains one of the few available suppliers for those laden with antique weaponry.

In fact, in the sanctions era, Pyongyang has aptly identified and exploited its competitive advantages, continuing to serve a market niche in repairing and upgrading antique systems. North Korea is able to provide weapons or related materiel and services that others will not or cannot, such as ballistic-missile modifications and spare parts. In addition, it markets some of the above cheaply and aggressively, attracting numerous foreign clients with its offerings.

---

[87] It is unclear whether the prospective buyers in question were members of the Sri Lankan military or Liberation Tigers of Tamil Eelam. The latter group was known to be a regular customer.

[88] Author e-mail conversation with Interviewee C, 26 January 2015.

III. RESILIENT CUSTOMERS

Not all North Korean clients are alike in their reasons for choosing the country as a supplier. Their considerations in doing so range from: longstanding bilateral political and military relations, often with attendant appreciation of Pyongyang's dependability as a supplier; the North Korean leadership's personal relationships with particular leaders or ruling families, such as the House of Assad in Syria; North Korea's willingness to assist with the establishment of new indigenous capabilities; reliance upon North Korean spare parts, or production or repair equipment; a lack of alternative suppliers; and, of course, cost. Decisions are sometimes taken in ignorance of the boundaries of the sanctions regime against North Korea and sometimes in defiance of them.

These differences in motivation are essential to bear in mind when examining Pyongyang's arms-trade activity. It is crucial to appreciate not only who buys from North Korea and what is on their shopping lists, but also why they choose this particular supplier. Efforts to improve implementation of the sanctions regime and peel customers away from North Korea must be tailored to reflect the drivers behind the demand.

This chapter focuses on the category of recent customers that are most difficult to convince to discontinue their custom: those whose ties to North Korea have weathered decades, including the nearly ten years in which sanctions have been in place. As mentioned in Chapter I, the number of state and non-state actors purchasing arms and related services has continually dwindled since the end of the Cold War. However, Syria, Iran, Uganda, the Democratic Republic of the Congo (DRC), Burma and Cuba have been steadfast, continuing to contract out to Pyongyang for arms and related materiel and services in spite of taboos and legal restrictions against doing so. Some non-state groups appear to have been 'resilient customers' during the sanctions era as well, including Palestinian militant groups, Hizbullah and the now-degraded Liberation Tigers of Tamil Eelam (LTTE). A number of other likely customers may also be in this category, but are not included here because of a dearth in publicly available evidence through which to characterise their respective relationships with North Korea.

Unlike some of North Korea's other clients, this 'resilient' group is fully aware of the illicit nature of continuing to buy arms and related materiel and services from the country. Because their business probably accounts for most of North Korea's recent revenue through arms sales, and because they appear to operate in disregard of international regimes, they represent the most significant problem for those working to improve sanctions implementation.

This chapter outlines each of the main resilient customers during the period since 2006 and analyses their common traits. As with the rest of this study, it relies entirely on open-source information and expert interviews in order to reach an assessment of the probable 'resilient' nature of the client in question. That information is more abundant for some customers than others. Should additional information on their ties to North Korea come to light in the future, it may become evident that they in fact belong in another camp. Similarly, though all of the state and non-state groups in this chapter have been categorised as 'resilient' because they demonstrate certain characteristics, there is still variation in the degree of their closeness to North Korea.

Syria

Of all of North Korea's defence-export markets, Syria is one of the oldest, most stable and most lucrative. Visible signs of the military relationship date back to the Arab–Israeli War of 1967, when Pyongyang sent dozens of pilots to fly Syrian jets.[1] From 1970, North Korean pilots, tank operators, missile technicians and instructors were regularly stationed in-country. They assisted Syrian forces in their campaigns against Israel in 1973 and participated in significant air battles. Throughout the 1970s and 1980s, North Korean officers trained Syrian forces both in Syria and in the DPRK.[2]

The relationship grounded in military services and training was consummated with weapons sales. From the late 1970s, North Korea sold Syria a myriad of systems. This included small arms and ammunition, armoured vehicles and anti-tank missiles. In addition, 122-mm multiple rocket launchers, which the DPRK sold to a number of other clients in the Middle East and elsewhere, also appeared in the Syrian arsenal during the 1982 Lebanon War. Israel is said to have captured one of these rocket launchers, killing the Korean People's Army (KPA) personnel operating

---

[1] Alexandre Mansourov, 'North Korea: Entering Syria's Civil War', 38 North, 25 November 2013, <http://38north.org/2013/11/amansourov112513/>, accessed 20 October 2015.
[2] *Ibid.*

it.[3] North Korea proved itself to be a friend loyal enough to put itself on the front lines of Syria's defence and to shed Korean blood in the process if necessary.

Syria eventually put North Korea at the centre of its most important defence procurement and development programmes. Foremost amongst these is the country's ballistic-missile programme. By the late 1980s, Damascus possessed approximately 300 Soviet-made Scud missiles with a range of 300 km.[4] Seeking ballistic missiles of a longer range, it requested to buy the SS-23 missile from the Soviet Union. With its request rebuffed,[5] as Mikhail Gorbachev sought to rein in Soviet military assistance worldwide, Damascus instead turned to Pyongyang for Scud-C missiles and launchers, and deliveries from North Korea began in 1991 and continued throughout the decade.[6] Production technology for ballistic missiles was provided at this time as well, as Syria, like numerous others that have sought Pyongyang's help with their military programmes, wished to develop a level of indigenous manufacturing capability. This specific form of assistance would become a major feature of North Korea's relationship with Syria. In addition to providing North Korean-made missiles, components and technology, Pyongyang also put its proliferation network on offer. Its traders helped the Syrian government to procure goods from around the world for North Korean-assisted missile manufacturing projects at two new factories near Aleppo and Hama.[7] Equipment destined for those factories was believed to be on board the *Dae Hung Ho* when it evaded a US naval task force and docked in Syria in March 1992.[8]

Syria's eagerness to procure unconventional deterrent capabilities did not end with ballistic missiles, and the fruitful military relations between

---

[3] Joseph S Bermudez, Jr, 'North Korea's Chemical Warfare Capabilities', 38 North, 10 October 2013, <http://38north.org/2013/10/jbermudez101013/>, accessed 20 October 2015.

[4] Director of Central Intelligence, National Intelligence Estimate, 'Prospects for Special Weapons Proliferation and Control', NIE 5-91C, Volume II: Annex A (Country Studies), July 1991, p. 6.

[5] *Risk Report*, 'Syria Missile Milestones: 1972–2005' (Vol. 11, No. 5, September/October 2005), <http://www.wisconsinproject.org/countries/syria/syria-missile-miles.html>, accessed 27 November 2015.

[6] *Risk Report*, 'Syria Missile Development – 1997', Wisconsin Project on Nuclear Arms Control (Vol. 3, No. 2, March-April 1997), <http://www.wisconsinproject.org/countries/syria/missiles.html>, accessed 20 October 2015.

[7] Joseph S Bermudez, Jr, 'A History of Ballistic Missile Development in the DPRK', Center for Nonproliferation Studies Occasional Paper No. 2, 1999, p. 18.

[8] George Lardner, Jr, 'Probe Ordered in Failure to Track N. Korean Ship', *Washington Post*, 14 March 1992. See also Douglas Waller, 'Sneaking in the Scuds', *Newsweek*, 22 June 1992, pp. 42–46.

Damascus and Pyongyang spread into other areas. Syria also sought WMD-related capabilities from North Korea in the form of a nuclear reactor and possibly chemical-weapons-relevant technology. According to the US Central Intelligence Agency, 'as early as 1997', Syria and North Korea began a project to construct a gas-cooled, graphite-moderated nuclear reactor along the lines of North Korea's plutonium-production reactor at Yongbyon.[9] The installation, located in the desert at Al-Kibar, was destroyed by Israeli air strikes as it was nearing operational status in September 2007.

It is also widely suspected but unconfirmed that Syria received assistance in producing chemical warheads for its newly acquired North Korean ballistic missiles. According to the former director of the US Defense Intelligence Agency, Lieutenant General Michael Maples, 'North Korea's chemical warfare capabilities probably includes [sic] the ability to produce bulk quantities of nerve, blister, choking and blood agents.'[10] The country is believed by many to have at minimum shared its expertise in producing and weaponising such agents with Syria, though this has not been confirmed.[11] Multiple chemical-related shipments from North Korea have been detected in the sanctions era, adding credence to the idea that Pyongyang may have been involved in Syria's chemical-weapons programme in some way. South Korea detained four containers of OZK chemical protection suits, bound for the Environmental Study Centre in Syria via Saudi Arabia.[12] UN experts determined that the suits had a primarily military application in the protection against certain chemical agents.[13] Another shipment of 13,000 OZK suits identical to those seized by South Korea, as well as gas-indicator ampoules for chemical detection, was impounded by Greece in November 2009.[14] These two shipments were likely part of the same contract.[15]

---

[9] The Central Intelligence Agency provided a video briefing to Congress in 2008, reproduced by the BBC. *BBC News*, 'Syria Had Covert Nuclear Scheme', 25 April 2008. See also Peter Crail, 'U.S. Shares Information on NK-Syrian Nuclear Ties', *Arms Control Today* (Vol. 38, No. 4, May 2008).

[10] Paul Eckert, 'Specter of North Korea Lurks in U.S. Debate on Syria's Chemical Weapons', *Reuters*, 15 September 2013.

[11] Bermudez, Jr, 'North Korea's Chemical Warfare Capabilities'.

[12] UN Security Council, 'Report of the Panel of Experts Submitted Pursuant to Resolution 1874 (2009)', S/2010/571, 5 November 2010, pp. 25–26. See also 'DPRK: Sanctions Committee Presses on 1874 Implementation', Cable #10USUNNEWYORK36, 22 January 2010, accessed via Wikileaks on 12 May 2014.

[13] UN Security Council, 'Report of the Panel of Experts Submitted Pursuant to Resolution 1874 (2009)', S/2010/571.

[14] UN Security Council, 'Report of the Panel of Experts Submitted Pursuant to Resolution 1874 (2009)', S/2012/422, 14 June 2012, pp. 27–28.

[15] *Ibid.*

Following the confirmation of the Syrian government's use of chemical weapons against its civilians in August 2013, and the subsequent threat of a military response by Western forces, President Bashar Al-Assad pledged to dismantle the country's chemical arsenal with international assistance and verification. Though not problem-free, that unexpected dismantlement campaign likely dried up the demand for North Korean chemical-weapons-related assistance, barring any decision by Damascus to reconstitute this capability. The lack of interdictions of chemical-related goods from North Korea to Syria after August 2013 does not prove the absence of any such interactions. Yet equally, despite intense international scrutiny, there is also no evidence that sanctions-busting co-operation between the two continues to take place in this field.

Missile and conventional-weapons co-operation has also been detected in the sanctions period and, in contrast to possible chemical-weapons collaboration, can be reasonably assumed to be ongoing. Multiple instances of missile-related proliferation incidents involving the two countries have been recorded between 2006 and the time of writing. In 2007, acting on a tip-off from French intelligence, Greek authorities detained the *MV Anemone,* which was transiting the Mediterranean en route to Syria. On board, they discovered 'missile parts originating in North Korea'.[16] Another consignment seized in 2007 included double-base propellant for Scud missiles.[17] The following year was a particularly active one for North Korean entities procuring foreign goods on behalf of the Syrian missile programme. Efforts were made to acquire missile-related steel, electrical relays which arm a missile's warhead,[18] and a variety of electronics useful for Scud guidance and navigation.[19] Trade in missile-related goods persisted after the outbreak of the Syrian civil war in 2011, during the course of which the Syrian government has been using Scud missiles and thereby depleting its arsenal. In 2012, the vessel *Xin Yan Tai* was stopped in the port of Busan, where South Korean authorities discovered 445 graphite cylinders en route to the Electric Parts Company in Syria, a front for the Syrian Scientific Studies and Research Centre (SSRC). The cylinders were consistent with material used in Syria's

---

[16] 'Greece Confirms Missile Parts Included in Suspect Shipment', Cable #07ATHENS2345, 12 December 2012, accessed via Wikileaks on 27 May 2014.
[17] UN Security Council, 'Report of the Panel of Experts Submitted Pursuant to Resolution 1874 (2009)', S/2012/422, pp. 24–25.
[18] 'Shipment of North Korean Parts with Missile Applications from China to Syria', Cable #08STATE44906, 29 April 2008, accessed via Wikileaks on 27 May 2014.
[19] 'Missile Technology Control Regime (MTCR): North Korea's Missile Program', Cable #09STATE103755, accessed via Wikileaks on 27 May 2014.

ballistic-missile programme, and were thus determined by the UN to be a violation of Security Council Resolution 1718 (2006).[20]

Some of these shipments may have been related to North Korean efforts to further develop Syria's ballistic-missile capability. The US report to a 2009 Missile Technology Control Regime (MTCR) experts meeting concluded that 'North Korea probably provided assistance to Syria's development of a maneuvering reentry vehicle (MaRV) for its Scud ballistic missiles.'[21] Other sources reference evidence of an ongoing bilateral project with a similar focus. A 2014 IHS Jane's report, citing 'Syrian and EU Foreign and Security Policy sources', says that a MaRV programme is indeed taking place in Syria with North Korean assistance:[22]

> Engineers from North Korea's Tangun Trading Corporation are supplying technology and expertise to ... Project 99 at Jabal Taqsis to upgrade Syrian 'Scud D' variants with a MaRV and global navigation satellite system ... The upgrade, which incorporates a bespoke canard system, will enable the MaRV of the Scud to alter its original planned trajectory when it re-enters the atmosphere, significantly improving its accuracy and increasing warhead survivability by making its flight path problematical to assess for missile-defence interceptors.

The same report alleges that a North Korean entity operating out of China, Rayn Hap-2 (believed by this author to be referring to 'Ryonhap', a common alias for the Ryonha Machinery Joint Venture Corporation), regularly ships not only metal for Scud engines, but also missile guidance-and-control equipment and computer numerically controlled (CNC) machines to the SSRC – the organisation which oversees Syria's missile and WMD programmes.

Conventional weapons trade has featured in the sanctions era as well, although it is unclear whether a portion of these consignments was destined to be passed on to Hizbullah.[23] France inspected the *MV San Francisco*

---

[20] UN Security Council, 'Report of the Panel of Experts Submitted Pursuant to Resolution 2050 (2012)', S/2013/337, 11 June 2013.
[21] 'Missile Technology Control Regime (MTCR): North Korea's Missile Program', Cable #09STATE103755.
[22] Robin Hughes, 'SSRC: Spectre at the Table', *Jane's Defence Weekly*, 22 January 2014. Tangun Trading Corporation is an entity subordinate to the Second Academy of National Sciences, which is primarily responsible for procuring commodities for North Korea's own defence development programmes. This demonstrates the involvement of select procurement-focused entities in the country's defence-export activity.
[23] As will be shown later in the chapter, some North Korean material seems to have found its way into Hizbullah's hands, and Syrian complicity in its procurement is plausible.

Bridge in November 2010 and discovered brass discs and copper rods used to manufacture artillery shells, as well as rocket-usable aluminium alloy tubes, originating in North Korea and destined for Syria. In 2012, Iraq denied overflight permission to an Air Koryo flight bound for Syria, which it was 'convinced' was carrying weapons.[24] In a further incident in April 2013 that received little media attention, Turkey is said to have seized 1,400 North Korean rifles, 30,000 ammunition cartridges and gas masks believed to have been intended for overland shipment to the Syrian regime.[25]

Additional, unconfirmed reports point to potential North Korean command-and-control and logistical assistance to Syrian forces fighting in the civil war. Citing pro-Assad militia sources, the director of the Syrian Observatory for Human Rights claimed that 'between 11 and 15 North Korean officers' are 'taking part alongside the regular forces in the fighting in Aleppo'. They are 'deployed at several fronts such as the defense factories southeast of Aleppo and at the regular forces' bases inside the city itself' and are 'offering logistical support in addition to drawing up the military operations maps. They are also supervising the regular army's artillery shelling.' The same organisation later claimed that North Korean helicopter pilots were also assisting the Assad government.[26] This author has not been able to verify any of these assertions, though they merit continued investigation.

The above evidence makes clear that Damascus has previously and continues to actively circumvent sanctions against the DPRK. The ongoing Syrian civil war seems to have strengthened their partnership. The two countries have been eager to advertise their commitment to one another by publicising their regular high-level visits. Comprehensive analysis of reports by the official Korean Central News Agency (KCNA) on bilateral political and military exchanges between North Korea and the countries outlined in this chapter show that the volume of interaction is highest in the Syrian case. Senior North Korean officials met with President Assad at least twice in 2014, for instance.[27]

---

[24] Suadad Al-Salhy, 'Iraq Blocks Syria-Bound North Korean Plane, Suspects Weapons Cargo', *Reuters*, 21 September 2012.
[25] Barbara Demick, 'North Korea Tried to Ship Gas Masks to Syria, Report Says', *LA Times*, 27 August 2013.
[26] *Jerusalem Post*, 'Behind the Lines: Assad's North Korean Connection', 11 February 2013.
[27] The author is particularly grateful to Caroline Cottet for her assistance in completing this data. NK Leadership Watch, 'DPRK Foreign Minister Meets with Bashar Al-Assad', 19 June 2014, <https://nkleadershipwatch.wordpress.com/2014/06/19/dprk-foreign-minister-meets-with-bashar-al-assad/>, accessed 20 October 2015. See also *Syrian Arab News Agency*, 'President Al-Assad Receives a

This pattern is by no means surprising. By the time sanctions against North Korea were enacted in 2006, the North Korean–Syrian military relationship was nearly forty years old, having grown consistently stronger during that time. Yet their deep history of military co-operation is not the only factor explaining the contemporary bilateral relationship. Syria seems to tick almost every box on the above list of major considerations for countries that buy weapons and military-related services from Pyongyang. It has a longstanding bilateral and military relationship with North Korea, and judging by the regularity of public interaction between officials of the two countries, it probably also appreciates North Korea's dependability. Personal relationships may be influential as well. The Kim and Assad families are firmly established partners, with the former's assistance to the latter having covered nearly every category of weapons and related services: small arms; light weapons; heavy systems; ballistic missiles; and WMD-relevant technology. North Korea's willingness to offer Damascus the goods and services it needs during its civil war, often in violation of many national and EU-level arms embargoes against Syria, may also be a factor in play. Finally, Syria appears to remain partially dependent upon Pyongyang to facilitate modifications, upgrades and range extensions to its ballistic-missile designs.

Iran

Tehran demonstrates many of the same general characteristics as Damascus when it comes to its military relationship with Pyongyang. Iran's ties to North Korea are longstanding. Archival documents show that prior to the 1979 Iranian revolution, North Korea's outreach efforts to Tehran had yielded little success.[28] Two factors seem to have shifted the winds in Pyongyang's favour. The first was the overthrow of the Western-oriented shah of Iran and his replacement with the theocratic Supreme Leader Ayatollah Khomeini. The new Islamic Republic pledged to counter US influence in the Middle East, a tune that played well with Kim Il-sung. Second, Tehran's strategic reorientation soon collided with urgent operational requirements. The overthrow of the shah led to the termination of Iran's military supply links with its traditional suppliers,

---

Delegation from the Democratic People's Republic of Korea (DPRK) Headed by DPRK Foreign Trade Minister Ri Ryong Nam', 29 May 2014, <http://www.sana.sy/en/?p=18497>, accessed 20 October 2015.

[28] 'TELEGRAM 075.345 from the Romanian Embassy in Tehran to the Romanian Ministry of Foreign Affairs', 24 May 1978, History and Public Policy Program Digital Archive, AMAE, Folder 784/1978, 7 January 1978 – 23 September 1978. Obtained and translated for NKIDP by Eliza Gheorghe; available at <http://digitalarchive.wilsoncenter.org/document/116429>, accessed 20 October 2015.

including the US and the UK. Then, shortly thereafter, Saddam Hussein's Iraq, seeing an opportunity for military victory in chaotic post-revolutionary Iran, invaded the country in September 1980. To defend itself during the ensuing eight years of war, Iran turned to willing and able suppliers whose interests now broadly aligned with its own. In the early years of the war, it awarded an estimated $15 billion in arms contracts to foreign partners,[29] and received corresponding deliveries throughout the remainder of the decade. North Korea, eager to seize the substantial business opportunity presented by the Iran–Iraq War, was among them. It sacrificed much of its more modest military co-operation with Baghdad and turned towards Tehran, signing its first arms agreement with the latter in 1980.[30] Military sales between the two countries expanded greatly during the 1980s, with Iran becoming North Korea's most lucrative buyer. The former US Arms Control and Disarmament Agency estimated that Iran ordered $1.8 billion of arms from North Korea in the first three years of the Iran–Iraq War,[31] and Iran may have accounted for as much as 78 per cent of North Korea's arms exports between 1980 and 1987.[32]

Iran procured a variety of weapons from Pyongyang during the conflict, including 122-mm rockets and launchers.[33] Ballistic missiles were, however, the more coveted item for Tehran. After quickly depleting its small stock of existing Scuds during the early years of the war against Iraq, Iran turned to North Korea. It received its first consignment of North Korean Scud-Bs in 1987 and subsequent deliveries under the same contract into the early 1990s.

---

[29] US Arms Control and Disarmament Agency, 'World Military Expenditures and Arms Transfers', 1989.

[30] Charles K Armstrong, *Tyranny of the Weak: North Korea and the World, 1950–1992* (Ithaca, NY: Cornell University Press, 2013), pp. 185–86.

[31] Original figure provided was $1 billion. Adjusted for inflation from the publication date of the World Military Expenditures and Arms Transfers report in June 1989. See US Arms Control and Disarmament Agency, 'World Military Expenditures and Arms Transfers 1988', ACDA Publication 131, June 1989, <http://www.state.gov/documents/organization/185653.pdf>, accessed 20 October 2015.

[32] Andrea Matles Savada (ed.), *North Korea: A Country Study* (Washington, DC: GPO for Library of Congress, 1994), chapter on 'Relations with the Third World'. Data in the study are drawn from the annual 'World Military Expenditures and Arms Transfers' reports that were produced by the Arms Control and Disarmament Agency during the 1980s. The agency was merged into the Department of State in 1999. US Defense Intelligence Agency, 'North Korea: The Foundations for Military Strength', October 1991, available at <https://www.fas.org/irp/dia/product/knfms/knfms_toc.html>, accessed 20 October 2015.

[33] Andrea Berger, 'North Korea, Hamas, and Hezbollah: Arm in Arm?', 38 North, 5 August 2014, <http://38north.org/2014/08/aberger080514/>, accessed 20 October 2015.

North Korea also offered training to the Iranian military, in part to help it overcome problems of interoperability experienced as a result of having sourced weapons from around the world. North Korea trained Iranian gunners to operate Chinese mobile surface-to-air systems, and taught the Iran Revolutionary Guard Corps (IRGC) unconventional warfare techniques.[34]

After the war, Iran attempted to achieve a greater degree of strike capability by pursuing aircraft-, ballistic-missile-, and submarine-related co-operation with its reliable supplier, North Korea. According to defector testimony, in 1994 the Korean People's Air Force commander travelled to Iran to sign a new arms agreement. Under the terms of the deal, North Korea allegedly agreed to supply MiG aircraft parts[35] in exchange for Iranian-supplied fuel for its own MiG fleet.[36]

Missile-related co-operation with North Korea continued its upward trajectory after the end of the Iran–Iraq War in 1988. Iran received North Korean assistance in converting a maintenance facility into one able to assemble and manufacture Scud missiles, allowing Iran gradually to learn to produce the system independent of its original supplier.

Iran soon set its sights on longer-range systems as well. The DPRK is believed to have allowed Iranian observers to monitor a test flight of its 1,300-km-range Nodong missile, and subsequently provided a small number of complete missiles or kits, and possibly also the associated launchers, to Tehran.[37] The Nodong would eventually serve as the basis for Iran's Shehab-3 missile.[38] Leaked US State Department cables from

---

[34] Savada (ed.), *North Korea*, chapter on 'Relations with the Third World'.

[35] Iran purchased MiG-29s from the Soviet Union shortly after the Iran–Iraq War ended, and kept in service a number of captured Iraqi MiG aircraft that had flown into Iranian airspace during the Gulf War of 1991. Much later, in 2000, Tehran contracted to Moscow to undertake a comprehensive programme of repairs of the aircraft it had previously sold. See Alla Kassianova, 'Russian Weapon Sales to Iran', PONARS Policy Memo No. 427, pp. 2–3, available at <http://csis.org/files/media/csis/pubs/pm_0427.pdf>, accessed 20 October 2015.

[36] Statement of Choi Ju-hwal, 'North Korean Missile Proliferation: Hearing Before the Subcommittee on International Security, Proliferation, and Federal Services of the Committee on Governmental Affairs', US Senate, First Session, 105th Congress, 21 October 1997.

[37] Bermudez, Jr, 'A History of Ballistic Missile Development in the DPRK', pp. 21–25.

[38] North Korean defectors with knowledge of the two countries' joint missile-development efforts noted that US surveillance and interdiction activity began to pose difficulties for facilitating technology transfer. In order to evade detection when delivering contracted missile-related goods to Iran and Syria, the DPRK began to send components rather than complete systems, and often split cargo between maritime and air transport. In addition, it routed shipments through off-track destinations such as Pointe-Noire in the Republic of the Congo. See 'North Korean Missile Proliferation: Hearing Before the Subcommittee on International

2008 highlight a belief that North Korea provided Iran with the technology for its even longer-range Musudan (or BM-25) liquid-propellant ballistic missile around 2005.[39] The system has a range of 3,500 km and the transfer therefore represented a significant advancement in the range of Iran's ballistic-missile capability.

In addition to assisting with aircraft and ballistic missiles, North Korea provided Iran with midget submarines, likely in the early 2000s. A 2009 report by the US Office of Naval Intelligence (ONI) stated that by 2007 Iran had seven 'Yono-class midget submarines', referring to the North Korean designation. While only four had been launched, ONI expected there to be additional *Yono*-class launches.[40] These claims added credence to other official reports of midget-submarine transfers from North Korea. For example, a member of the South Korean team investigating the 2010 sinking of the ROKS *Cheonan* outlined North Korea's submarine-warfare capabilities and said it was confirmed that North Korea had exported 130-ton submarines (a description which aligns with the *Yono*-class) to Iran in 2003.[41]

Tehran's pattern of military co-operation with Pyongyang is thus well established. Rooted in the substantial assistance during the Iran–Iraq War, and cemented through decades of close political and military co-operation since, the relationship has long been viewed by Western analysts as deeply troubling. Both countries see the US and its allies in their respective regions as strategic adversaries. It is not surprising, therefore, that North Korea has provided arms and related services to Iran's non-state allies taking on Israel, possibly at Tehran's behest. In addition, both regimes have missile ambitions, which they have previously worked together to realise.

Yet despite the volume of information on Iran–North Korea co-operation prior to 2006, and in comparison to the amount of available information on sanctions-era arms-related sales to Syria, surprisingly little conclusive, detailed evidence of an active military partnership between Pyongyang and Tehran exists for the sanctions era. This may be partly a product of their prowess in evading international detection. In larger part, it may be a result of the evolution of the defence ties between the two countries, or a shift in the focus of their collaboration. As with Syria and

---

Security, Proliferation, and Federal Services of the Committee on Governmental Affairs', US Senate, First Session, 105th Congress, 21 October 1997.
[39] 'Missile Technology Control Regime (MTCR): Iran's Ballistic Missile Program', cable #08STATE105103, 1 October 2008, accessed via Wikileaks on 27 May 2014.
[40] Office of Naval Intelligence, 'Iran's Naval Forces: From Guerrilla Warfare to a Modern Naval Strategy', 2009, p. 20.
[41] *Chosun Ilbo*, 'Seoul Rebuts NK Denials in Cheonan Sinking', 31 May 2010, <http://english.chosun.com/site/data/html_dir/2010/05/31/2010053101481.html>, accessed 20 October 2015.

other partners, North Korea helped Iran to develop its ability to manufacture missiles indigenously. In contrast with Syria, however, the Iranian scientific complex seems to have been more successful in reducing its dependence on North Korean supply of ballistic-missile-related goods. Iran's graduation to this rank of relative independence is indicated by its ability to export its own ballistic-missile systems.[42] This is not to say that Iran no longer necessarily has a need or an interest in North Korean ballistic-missile assistance. Instead, their bilateral co-operation may merely have shifted to less tangible forms. An anonymous US official described this process of evolution as long ago as 1996: 'North Korea's missile trade is like a localized cancer that starts to spread. First you see the missile sales, but then it spreads to services and production technology and becomes harder and harder to track'.[43]

The most concrete indicator that Iran and North Korea have conducted weapons-related trade since the enactment of Resolution 1718 in 2006, and indeed may still have such trade today, is the continued presence in Iran of the Korea Mining Development Trading Corporation (KOMID), which has both an office and representatives there.[44] As outlined in the introduction to this study, KOMID's primary function is to 'facilitate weapons sales for the North Korean government'.[45] In January 2015, the US Treasury designated two new KOMID representatives working at the company's Iran office. It can safely be assumed that their presence would not be necessary if there were no market for KOMID's products and services.

One possible explanation is that KOMID representatives are still involved in missile-related activity in Iran, which appears to have continued into the early sanctions era at least. A supporting indicator for this possibility was the scheduling of a suspicious passenger flight in 2008. That year, Air Koryo scheduled a round-trip charter flight to Iran. When Central Asian states suspected it of carrying ballistic-missile technicians

---

[42] Joshua Pollack, 'Ballistic Trajectory: The Evolution of North Korea's Ballistic Missile Market', *Nonproliferation Review* (Vol. 18, No. 2, July 2011), p. 415. See also Office of the Director of National Intelligence, 'Unclassified Report to Congress on the Acquisition of Technology Relating to Weapons of Mass Destruction and Advanced Conventional Munitions, Covering 1 January to 31 December 2009', 2010, p. 7.

[43] *Risk Report*, 'North Korean Missile Exports', Wisconsin Project on Nuclear Arms Control (Vol. 2, No. 6, November/December 1996), <http://www.wisconsinproject. org/countries/nkorea/north-korea-missile-exports.html>, accessed 20 October 2015.

[44] US Department of Treasury, 'Treasury Imposes Sanctions against the Government of the Democratic People's Republic of Korea', 2 January 2015, <http://www. treasury.gov/press-center/press-releases/Pages/jl9733.aspx>, accessed 20 October 2015.

[45] *Ibid.*

and denied it overflight permission, the flight was re-routed through Mandalay, in Burma. The change added considerable distance and cost to the flight, reinforcing the assumptions about its passengers and the financial revenue they may have represented.[46]

A record of cargo shipments of concern similarly suggests that Iran has not entirely lost its need for North Korean ballistic-missile-related parts. In November 2007, staff from the US embassy in Beijing démarched the Arms Control and Disarmament Department at the Chinese Ministry of Foreign Affairs because it had information about an 'ongoing transshipment via Beijing of ballistic missile parts from North Korea to Iran'. Specifically, the shipment contained jet vanes, controlled under the MTCR and firmly proscribed under UN Security Council Resolution 1718.[47] The consignee was Shahid Bagheri Industrial Group (SBIG), which is subordinate to the state-owned Aviation Industries Organization, and is responsible for Iran's solid-propellant ballistic-missile programme. While North Korea is best-known for assisting Iran's liquid-fuelled missile development efforts, at the time Iran was in the process of testing systems for its new solid-propellant Sejjil missiles.[48] In 2010, Singapore also seized aluminium powder from North Korea headed for Iran aboard the *STX Patraikos* that would have been usable in solid propellant for missiles or artillery rockets.[49]

In fact, the two aforementioned incidents suggest that as Tehran's missile ambitions have evolved and expanded, it has sought to maintain its partnership with North Korea. This conclusion is further borne out by

---

[46] 'PRC Informed of DPRK-To-Iran Flight of Proliferation Concern', Cable #08BEIJING3047, 7 August 2008, accessed via Wikileaks on 27 May 2014. Note that in May 2012, the Security Council also designated the Amroggang Development Banking Corporation for its assistance to Iran's ballistic-missile programme. Though the timeframe for this assistance is not clear, this formal designation means that the members of the Sanctions Committee felt there was compelling evidence of Amroggang's involvement in proscribed activities after the introduction of Resolution 1718 (2006). See UN, 'Security Council Committee Determines Entities, Goods Subject to Measures Imposed on Democratic People's Republic of Korea by Resolution 1718 (2006)', SC/10633, press release, 2 May 2012, <http://www.un.org/press/en/2012/sc10633.doc.htm>, accessed 20 October 2015.

[47] 'Post Raises Ongoing Missile Proliferation Matter with MFA', Cable #07BEIJING7063, 9 November 2007, accessed via Wikileaks on 27 May 2014.

[48] Peter Crail, 'Iran Lauds Development of Solid Fuel Missile', *Arms Control Today* (Vol. 38, No. 1, January/February 2008).

[49] Iran Watch, 'Iran-Bound Rocket Fuel Component Seized in Singapore', 1 September 2010, <http://www.iranwatch.org/our-publications/enforcement-news-summary/iran-bound-rocket-fuel-component-seized-singapore>, accessed 20 October 2015.

leaked US State Department cables from 2008, which highlight a belief that North Korea provided Iran with its Musudan liquid-propellant, intermediate-range ballistic-missile technology.[50]

This same trend may apply to cruise-missile co-operation as well. In 1994, 1997, 2003 and 2007,[51] North Korea tested an indigenous, upgraded variant of the Chinese-designed Seersucker (CSS-C-3) coastal-defence cruise missile. Unconfirmed reports emerged that suggested that Iranian representatives, contemplating buying the system, were present for the first two tests.[52] A similarly unverified 2003 report alleged that Iranian IL-76 cargo planes had transported at least six cargoes of cruise missiles from Sunan airport in Pyongyang back to Iran.[53] Diplomatic cables add credence to the notion that Iran and North Korea were actively co-operating in this space. In November 2008, the US stated its belief that KOMID intended to send 'cruise-missile related items' to Iran.[54] The consignment was reportedly expected to be loaded aboard the *MV So Hung 1*, bound for Iran via Singapore.

Unconfirmed allegations have swirled about the possibility of collaboration between Tehran and Pyongyang in nuclear technology. Specifically, it has been alleged that Iranians were present for North Korean nuclear tests and may even be benefiting from North Korean test data, negating their need to publicly explode a weapon themselves to assess its functionality.[55] Some cite the suspicious nature of a scientific co-operation agreement signed by the two countries in Tehran in September 2012.[56] The text of the accompanying statement, which unsurprisingly does not mention military or nuclear co-operation, bears a striking resemblance to a similar agreement signed between North Korea and Syria ten years earlier, when the two were probably formulating contractual arrangements for the ill-fated Al-Kibar nuclear reactor.[57] The

---

[50] 'Missile Technology Control Regime (MTCR): Iran's Ballistic Missile Program', Cable #08STATE105103.

[51] *Jane's Defence Weekly*, 'North Korea Tests Short-Range Missile', 30 May 2007.

[52] *Jane's Defence Weekly*, 'North Korea tests Anti-Ship Cruise Missiles', 28 February 2003.

[53] *Time*, 'Is North Korea Peddling Nuclear Weapons?', 7 July 2003.

[54] 'PSI: North Korean Vessel of Possible Proliferation Concerns', Cable #08STATE12403222, November 2008, accessed via Wikileaks on 27 May 2014.

[55] Siegfried S Hecker and William Liou, 'Dangerous Dealings: North Korea's Nuclear Capabilities and the Threat of Export to Iran', *Arms Control Today*, March 2007. See also *Kyodo News*, 'N. Korea Conducts Nuke Test in Presence of Iranian Scientists: Source', 15 February 2013.

[56] Yeganeh Torbati, 'Iran, North Korea Agree to Cooperate in Science, Technology', *Reuters*, 1 September 2012.

[57] Jay Solomon, 'Iran, North Korea Pact Draws Concern', *Wall Street Journal*, 8 March 2013.

similarities between the agreements sparked fears that Iran too would become a beneficiary of North Korean nuclear technology. Adding to the concern was the presence of the head of the Atomic Energy Organization of Iran, Fereydoun Abbasi-Davani, and the minister of defence of armed forces logistics, Ahmad Vahidi, at the signing ceremony and subsequent banquet in Tehran.[58]

While these allegations and suspicions cannot be proven, at least at present, two other facets of Iran–North Korea co-operation can: conventional-weapons trade and, relatedly, the sharing of proliferation networks. In the past few years, multiple cargoes of conventional weapons from the DPRK have been seized en route to Iran. In 2008, two containers of Iran-bound, DPRK-produced fuses for 122-mm rockets were discovered by an unspecified UN member state.[59] The consignee was Arshia Trading Company, affiliated with Iran's SBIG. Shortly thereafter, in 2009, in containers aboard the *ANL Australia*, UAE authorities found 'military equipment including detonators, rocket launchers, munitions, and explosives including ammunition for rocket-propelled grenade weapons'.[60] Later that year, Thailand grounded a charter flight from Pyongyang laden with 35 tons of conventional arms – including 240-mm rockets, man-portable air-defence systems (MANPADS) and RPG-7s. That shipment also contained fuses identical to those found in 2008, indicating that they were also for 122-mm rockets.[61]

It should be noted that, though all of the aforementioned cargoes were bound for Iran, it may not have been the intended end user. In fact, Iran is now able to produce some of these same weapons systems domestically. Additionally, it was not at the time itself embroiled in conflicts where such weapons would have been expended, and which would have necessitated the acquisition of new stock. Instead, it is widely believed that the arms seized between 2008 and 2009 were bound for non-state groups in the Middle East that Iran supports. For example, the shipment seized by Thailand was alleged by Israel to have been bound for Hamas and

---

[58] *Ibid*.

[59] It was only under UN Security Council Resolution 1874 (2009) that states became obliged to report any searches and seizures pertaining to the UN sanctions regime against the DPRK. As a result, this particular incident was not reported until sometime after its occurrence. For further information on the cargo discovered in this incident, see UN Security Council, 'Report of the Panel of Experts Submitted Pursuant to Resolution 1874 (2009)', S/2013/337, p. 31.

[60] 'DPRK: UAE Reports Sanctions Violation to 1718 Committee', Cable #09USUNNEWYORK775, 17 August 2009, accessed via Wikileaks on 24 May 2014.

[61] UN Security Council, 'Report of the Panel of Experts Submitted Pursuant to Resolution 1874 (2009)', S/2013/337, pp. 31–34.

Hizbullah,[62] although a White House official's statement on the seizure only mentioned Hamas.[63]

These incidents highlight the sharing of arms-supply networks between North Korea and Iran. The involvement of state-affiliated SBIG in facilitating what appears to have been onward shipment of 122-mm rocket fuses to Iranian proxies in the region is telling. Similarly, diplomatic sources linked to the UN Sanctions Committee on North Korea told the *Financial Times* that the consignee of the cargo aboard the *ANL Australia* was Three Star Services Co, an entity linked to the IRGC.[64] Three Star Services has been listed as an entity of proliferation concern by numerous countries, which believe it to be involved in Iran's WMD-relevant procurement.[65] In other words, SBIG and Three Star Services are companies with official links, that appear not only to have been involved intimately with Iran's own missile and WMD programmes, but also with the procurement of conventional armaments from North Korea, presumably for onward transfer to armed non-state groups in the Middle East.

North Korean weapons assistance to Palestinian and Lebanese non-state actors connected to Iran may be provided as part of the wider North Korea–Iran relationship (and, in the case of Hizbullah, possibly also as part of the relationship with Syria).[66] This observation could offer another explanation for the continued presence of a KOMID office in Iran. While Iran is also able to produce many of the same weapons that North Korea has apparently shipped to Hamas and Hizbullah, it may prefer to facilitate North Korean supply for a number of reasons. Perhaps it cannot always fill orders independently. Perhaps it is more cost-effective to buy from the DPRK rather than to start domestic production lines when Iranian forces are not in need of these goods themselves. Or perhaps North Korean stocks are preferable because they offer a greater degree of plausible deniability – a burden that Pyongyang seems happy to bear.

---

[62] Yoko Kubota, 'Israel Says Seized North Korean Arms Were for Hamas, Hezbollah', *Reuters*, 12 May 2010.

[63] White House Office of the Press Secretary, 'Press Gaggle by Press Secretary Jay Carney and Deputy National Security Advisor for Strategic Communications Ben Rhodes', 17 November 2012, <http://www.whitehouse.gov/the-press-office/2012/11/17/press-gaggle-press-secretary-jay-carney-and-deputy-national-security-adv>, accessed 20 October 2015.

[64] Simon Kerr, 'N Korea Arms for Tehran Seized, Says UAE', *Financial Times*, 29 August 2009.

[65] Germany listed the entity as a proliferation concern before the incident with the *ANL Australia*, while Canada, Japan and the UK did so after the event. Iran Watch, 'Iranian Entities: T.S.S Co', 13 July 2011, <http://www.iranwatch.org/iranian-entities/tss-co>, accessed 20 October 2015.

[66] Author conversation with Balázs Szalontai, April 2014.

While the Iran–North Korea arms-supply bond has changed with time, it remains resilient. Like other clients discussed in this chapter, Tehran has numerous reasons to continue to seek weapons-related assistance from Pyongyang, for itself or for its regional proxies: its interest in indigenously developing major new weapons systems, including ballistic and cruise missiles; its isolation and lack of ability to access such technology or weapons-related supplies and assistance from other foreign countries; the long history of their military partnership; Pyongyang's track record of being a dependable supplier over a period of more than three decades, especially in times of acute need; the likely existence of strong personal connections between the Iranian and North Korean regimes as a result of these longstanding ties; and the two countries' significantly overlapping geopolitical outlook and shared distaste for the US and Israel. As a consequence of some of these dynamics, it is perhaps to be expected that there is less evidence of the exact nature of their interactions in the sanctions era. Iran has, over time and with North Korean help, become relatively technologically adept. Even in areas where it has become capable, such as in ballistic and cruise missiles, Tehran has been prepared to involve North Korea in the expansion of that capability.

The recently concluded nuclear deal between the P5+1 and Iran, if it reaches the implementation stage, is unlikely to dissuade Iran from doing business with North Korea entirely, especially as Iran's missile development was not comprehensively addressed in the deal. Under the terms of UN Security Council Resolution 2231 (2015), which brings the existing UN sanctions framework in line with the deal, Iran is only 'called upon' to refrain from developing missiles capable of delivering nuclear weapons for the first eight years of the agreement.[67] It may purchase missiles and missile-related goods with prior approval from the Security Council,[68] though it seems unlikely that Tehran will seek permission for such programmes given the slim chances that the US and European members of the Security Council would grant it. As the evidence presented in this chapter has demonstrated, Iran has shown little regard for the sanctions in place against it, and has pursued its missile programmes with North Korean assistance for many years in defiance of UN resolutions. This pattern of behaviour could well continue under the first eight years of the deal, after which Iran's missile programmes are formally unrestricted. Similarly, there is no reason to believe that Iran will cease its practice of arming its non-state-actor allies in the Middle East as a result of the newly concluded nuclear agreement.

---

[67] UN Security Council Resolution 2231 (2015), S/RES/2231, p. 99.
[68] *Ibid.*, p. 100.

Uganda

After watching the graduation ceremony of 700 North Korean-trained Ugandan police officers in 2014, the country's president, Yoweri Museveni, thanked 'the government of the Democratic People's Republic of Korea'. 'They always give us technical support', he said.[69] Museveni is not the first Ugandan president to welcome KPA officers to the country, and he is unlikely to be the last.

Unlike in Syria and Iran, North Korea has never been a primary supplier of a particular weapons system or class of system for Uganda. Instead, Pyongyang seems to have been called upon periodically to provide support services, such as training and arms maintenance, and help fill in smaller equipment gaps where the Ugandan leader of the day was not able to acquire the required arms or services from his most generous patrons – whether the Soviet Union, Tanzania or Libya.

During the Cold War, Uganda passed through four power transitions. Each new government, having come to power as a result of violence and internal divisions, remained painfully aware of the fact that it, too, may one day have to defend its position with force. In 1971, the commander of the armed forces in Uganda, Idi Amin, seized power in a military coup. He arranged for Ugandan forces to receive training and weapons from North Korea over the course of his rule.[70] That relationship survived Amin's overthrow in 1979 at the end of the Uganda–Tanzania War. On a visit to Pyongyang in 1981, the new president, Milton Obote, signed a co-operation agreement covering a variety of technical, economic and cultural areas. Pyongyang subsequently deployed a military team of thirty officers to Uganda, reportedly to manage equipment repair and infantry training in Gulu in the north of the country. A Library of Congress study asserts that, under Obote, North Korean officers even led combat units in operations against anti-government guerrillas.[71]

In a six-month period in 1985–86, two further coups took place in Uganda. Yoweri Museveni, the current president, took office in January 1986. Not long thereafter, he asked the KPA to return to Uganda to train police forces and National Resistance Army fighters to use the weapons that preceding governments had acquired from Pyongyang. Having recently engaged in a 'bush war', and conscious of the possibility of

---

[69] *East African*, 'Museveni Praises North Korea Security Training', 17 April 2014, <http://www.theeastafrican.co.ke/news/Uganda-President-Museveni-praises-North-Korea-security-training/-/2558/2283098/-/f7p3ue/-/index.html>, accessed 20 October 2015.

[70] US Defense Intelligence Agency, 'North Korea'.

[71] Rita M Byrnes (ed.), *Uganda: A Country Study* (Washington, DC: GPO for Library of Congress, 1992).

continuing armed conflict, Museveni ordered new arms stocks as well. A consignment of North Korean weapons arrived at Dar es Salaam in Tanzania in 1987, destined for onward shipment to Uganda. It contained a mixture of Soviet- and indigenously built weapons, namely SA-7 Grail MANPADS, anti-aircraft guns, truck-mounted multiple rocket launchers, armoured personnel carriers and ammunition.[72] Additional multiple rocket launchers were reportedly delivered the following year.[73]

After the Cold War, Uganda continued to receive North Korean training delegations, including for marine units and local law-enforcement personnel.[74] In addition, Kampala began to prioritise the creation of a domestic arms-manufacturing capability, reducing dependence upon outside supply. In 1996, the Nakasongola factory came online, manufacturing products such as ammunition, firearms and landmines.[75] Activities at Nakasongola have also included repair services for a variety of small and large weapons systems. Numerous reports in the years after its opening indicated that Nakasongola was operated with the assistance of both China and North Korea,[76] though other reports indicate it may have only been China.[77] The specific nature of that assistance was never reported. Given North Korea's history of facilitating weapons repairs in Uganda since the 1970s, it is plausible that North Koreans continued to be involved in Ugandan defence affairs in this way.

The factory at Nakasongola is managed by Luwero Industries Limited – a subsidiary of the National Enterprise Corporation, originally set up as the commercial arm of the National Resistance Army. In 2004, residents near the Nakasongola complex complained about the presence of North Koreans. Their main grievance was that North Koreans living on Luwero Industries land[78] had been given unlimited permission to fish in nearby

---

[72] *Ibid.*

[73] Christopher W Hughes, *Japan's Economic Power and Security: Japan and North Korea* (London: Routledge, 1999), p. 144.

[74] Steven Candia, 'North Korea to Solve Police Housing Crisis', New Vision, 12 June 2013, <http://www.newvision.co.ug/news/643881-north-korea-to-solve-police-housing-crisis.html>, accessed 20 October 2015.

[75] *IRIN News*, 'Uganda: Kampala Reportedly Increasing Arms Manufacturing Capability', 30 March 1999, <http://www.irinnews.org/report/5863/uganda-kampala-reportedly-increasing-arms-manufacturing-capacity>, accessed 20 October 2015.

[76] *Ibid.*

[77] 'Audition de M. Georges Berghezan, chargé de recherche au Grip pour l'Afrique et les transports d'armes', Sénat de Belgique, Session ordinaire 2001-2002, Commission d'enquête parlementaire «Grands Lacs», 5 July 2002, <http://www.senate.be/crv/GR/gr-35.html>, accessed 20 October 2015.

[78] North Koreans were apparently permitted to settle between Nakasongola Barracks and Lwampanga.

lakes and had depleted fish stocks in the process.[79] If these reports are accurate, they would suggest that North Korean personnel remained involved in the day-to-day operations of Luwero Industries' business in the area until at least 2004.

North Korean military assistance has thus been a fairly consistent feature of Uganda's foreign relations for decades. This fact does not appear to have changed since the passage of sanctions. Of particular concern is that the bilateral co-operation that has been disclosed by Kampala in many respects sits in the areas of the sanctions regime where the legality of the activity has yet to be clarified by the Sanctions Committee or Panel of Experts, and in other respects clearly breaches the Security Council resolutions.

Until at least 2007, the US continually requested access to the government of Uganda's classified budget, out of suspicion that it would contain information on the transfer of man-portable air-defence systems between North Korea and Uganda. It was rebuffed. According to leaked State Department cables, 'The [government of Uganda's] military sales relationship with North Korea might hinder engagement [with the US]'. In 2009, US embassy cables from Kampala revealed that KOMID had an office in the city. 'The KOMID office,' it said, 'has been primarily facilitating arms sales with the Ugandan People's Defence Force'.[80] In 2010, another cable stated that 'while preferring Western partners for military training and doctrine, Uganda relies on China and other old eastern bloc countries like North Korea and Russia for arms and hardware'.[81] While the US conviction that arms sales were taking place at least until 2010 is clear, it has not been separately confirmed in other open sources. North Korea has also had a role in providing training in Uganda, despite the contrary US assessment in 2010.

Developments in the years since confirm that North Korea continues to be involved in the Ugandan defence market, sometimes in violation of UN sanctions. In October 2014, Kim Yong-nam, chairman of the Presidium of the DPRK's Supreme People's Assembly, was welcomed in Kampala with much ceremony. Over four days, Kim met with the Ugandan president, prime minister and foreign minister amongst others, and attended a state banquet in his honour. The reported purpose of his visit was to enhance bilateral security co-

---

[79] Records obtained by the author, the details of which have been withheld to ensure anonymity.
[80] '2008 Security Environment Profile Questionnaire (SEPQ), Kampala', Cable #09KAMPALA272_a, 12 March 2009, accessed via Wikileaks on 27 December 2014.
[81] 'Chinese Engagement in Uganda', Cable #10KAMPALA77, 17 February 2010, accessed via Wikileaks on 14 May 2014.

operation.[82] His Ugandan counterparts – some of whom, like the current deputy chief of the defence staff,[83] trained in North Korea – seemed highly receptive to this initiative.

At the time, Uganda explained that North Korea provides it with 'non-lethal' arms and training in marine operations and rescue, martial arts, and 'security and technical training courses for the Ugandan Police Special Force, Police Construction Unit, Criminal and Forensic Investigation.'[84] As it was not immediately evident that these courses used lethal weaponry, which would have been unequivocally 'arms-related' and therefore in breach of the resolutions, the UN Panel of Experts sought further detail.

The 2015 report of the UN Panel of Experts on North Korea reproduces the Panel's communication with Uganda, which clarifies the matter:[85]

> On 19 December 2014, Uganda replied to the Panel's follow-up inquiry with details of the cooperation, stating that the 'Field Force Unit Training' carried out by Democratic People's Republic of Korea instructors at the police training schools at Kabalye, Masindi and Butiaba, Wantembo … included training on the use of AK-47s and pistols. The training for the Marine Police Unit included sharp shooting.

The Panel concluded that 'this type of training is a violation of paragraph 9 of resolution 1874 (2009)'.[86] Uganda's reply to the Panel also indicates that North Korea's maritime training courses, held for six months in both 2010 and 2013, were probably motivated in part by the flare-up with Kenya over territorial claims to the Migingo Island in Lake Victoria in 2009 and 2013.[87]

Despite this censure, Uganda is unlikely to eschew the assistance of the KPA any time soon. In fact, in May 2015, *Africa Intelligence* reported that

---

[82] *Times Live*, 'Top North Korean Leader in Uganda to Boost Security Ties', 29 October 2014, <http://www.timeslive.co.za/africa/2014/10/29/top-north-korean-leader-in-uganda-to-boost-security-ties>, accessed 22 October 2015.

[83] Sulaiman Kakaire, 'New Army Big Wigs: Who Are They?', *Observer,* 29 May 2013, <http://observer.ug/index.php?option=com_content&view=article&id=25566:-new-army-big-wigs-who-are-they>, accessed 22 October 2015.

[84] UN Security Council, 'Report of the Panel of Experts Established Pursuant to Resolution 1874 (2009)', S/2014/147, 6 March 2014, p. 37.

[85] UN Security Council, 'Report of the Panel of Experts Established Pursuant to Resolution 1874 (2009)', S/2015/131, 23 February 2015, p. 38. Full details of the training are available on pp. 100–01.

[86] *Ibid.,* p. 39.

[87] Jeffrey Gettleman, 'Ripples of Dispute Surround Tiny Island in East Africa', *New York Times*, 16 August 2009.

North Korea had been training a new cadre of 400 Ugandan police officers since 18 April.[88]

As demonstrated by the type of goods and services Kampala has previously sought from Pyongyang, it is clear that their co-operation is not a product of unfortunate historical dependence, but a conscious choice from a range of viable suppliers. The armed forces of numerous other nations operate AK-47s and are experienced in sharp-shooting, and could offer training services to this effect. So, why North Korea? Price may be an important factor. Alongside the training services and non-lethal arms mentioned above, Uganda also contracted with North Korea to build housing units for the police, allegedly because it could do so more inexpensively than even domestic contractors.[89]

It also appears that Uganda's long history of military-to-military ties with North Korea and its desire to maintain a generally positive relationship with Pyongyang are influential considerations. The bilateral security relationship has outlasted numerous changes of power in Uganda, as well as the growth of the taboo around security co-operation with North Korea that has accompanied the strengthening of UN sanctions. Successive Ugandan leaders seem to have come to view North Korea as a 'no-strings-attached' supplier, and Uganda does not appear poised to change tack now. Kampala's defiant response to recent questions and criticisms surrounding DPRK–Uganda co-operation is indicative of its determination to maintain strong political and probably military ties. It has explicitly said that it will not abandon its ties to North Korea as a result of sanctions or pressure from the UN. According to Foreign Affairs Permanent Secretary James Mugume, 'countries are not like people. The fact that you have an enemy does not mean he is our enemy'.[90] Other officials have flatly stated that Uganda has a right to engage with whomever it chooses, even if the country is subject to a UN arms embargo. Such statements may also indicate that the continuing

---

[88] UN Security Council, 'Report of the Panel of Experts Established Pursuant to Resolution 1874 (2009)', S/2015/131, pp. 100–01. See also Barbara Among, 'Uganda, Tanzania in Trouble with UN over "Arms Deals"' with North Korea', *East African*, 12 April 2014, <http://www.theeastafrican.co.ke/news/Uganda–Tanzania-on-UN-radar-over-North-Korea-links-/-/2558/2277334/-/w54donz/-/index.html>, accessed 22 October 2015; Barbara Among, 'North Korea Training 400 Police Officers', *Africa Intelligence* (No. 1402, 1 May 2015), <http://www.africaintelligence.com/ION/politics-power/2015/05/01/north-korea-training-400%C2%A0police-officers,108071813-BRE>, accessed 22 October 2015.
[89] Candia, 'North Korea to Solve Police Housing Crisis'.
[90] Among, 'Uganda, Tanzania in Trouble with UN over "Arms Deals"' with North Korea'.

relationship with North Korea even offers Ugandan officials a positive symbol of the country's foreign-policy independence.

The history of the Uganda–DPRK relationship, the nature of their military contracts, and Kampala's recent rhetoric therefore make Uganda unsuitable for the 'reluctant' and 'ad hoc' categories of customer outlined in this Whitehall Paper. They have earned Uganda a place among North Korea's most resilient buyers of arms-related goods and services.

Democratic Republic of the Congo

North Korea has found a solid foothold elsewhere on the African continent. Mobutu Sese Seko, president of Zaire (now the DRC) from 1965–97, was particularly fond of Pyongyang. After Mobutu's 1974 visit to Pyongyang, his rhetoric against the US became notably similar to that of North Korea.[91] He also contracted with the North Koreans to help him establish and train an elite brigade consisting of a number of tribes or segments of Zairian society. The fully North Korean-trained (and, possibly, equipped) 11th Brigade of the Kaymanyola Division was called into battle only six months after its establishment, although the effectiveness of this training was questionable, given that the Brigade fell apart after its first armed exchange and had to spend two days reorganising.[92] After a brief dispute over North Korea's policy towards the civil war in Angola – in which North Korea backed the National Front for the Liberation of Angola (FNLA) alongside China and Romania[93] – further training assistance was provided in the early and mid-1980s.

Kinshasa continued to seek North Korean assistance, probably in three forms, between 1990 and 2006. The first was an extension of earlier co-operation, namely training assistance to the Congolese armed forces. In 1998, shortly after the overthrow of Mobutu by Laurent Kabila, the new government's Presidential Guard Brigade – which now included the earlier Kaymanyola elite division – was reported to be receiving training by the KPA.[94] It is possible that part of this training included the operation of main battle tanks. The same year the country's 10th Brigade rebelled

---

[91] Some scholars and researchers also believe that Korean People's Army (KPA) soldiers visiting Zaire as part of a North Korean delegation in 1967 clashed with mercenaries who were attempting to overthrow Mobutu. See David Axe, *Shadow Wars: Chasing Conflict in an Era of Peace* (Dulles, VA: Potomac Books, 2013), p. 7.

[92] Thomas P Odom, 'Shaba II: The French and Belgian Intervention in Zaire in 1978', Combat Studies Institute, April 1993.

[93] Sandra W Meditz and Tim Merrill (eds), *Zaire: A Country Study* (Washington, DC: GPO for Library of Congress, 1994). See in particular the section on 'Relations with the Communist World'.

[94] Tom Cooper, *Great Lakes Conflagration: Second Congo War, 1998–2003* (London: Helion and Company, 2013) p. 7.

against the central government.[95] That rebellion was swiftly crushed and the reconstituted brigade was subjected to nine months of North Korean re-training.[96] In 1999, the DRC government announced that a new tranche of Korean soldiers had arrived in Kinshasa to provide further training services.[97]

The second form of co-operation may have included the North Korean-assisted construction and operation of an ammunition-production facility at Likasi. The plant was set up by a parastatal company called Société Africaine D'explosifs (AFRIDEX) to produce ammunition and explosives, initially with a military application. At the turn of the century, several reports emerged pointing to the conclusion that North Korea had assisted AFRIDEX in setting up and operating certain production lines. Interviews conducted with diplomatic staff in Kinshasa around the time likewise suggested that North Korea was helping to 'produce' and 'assemble' 250-kg and 500-kg bombs. Allegedly, the poor quality of the weapons contributed to the deadly explosion at Kinshasa airport on 14 April 2000. Bombs from the North Korean production line had been stored in a building near the airport, which caught fire and caused the cache to explode.[98] A report in 2001 also confidently linked North Korea to explosives production in the DRC, and accused the UN Group of Experts on the DRC of 'fail[ing] to mention North Korean involvement in Afridex'.[99] In fact, the existence of an ammunition and explosives factory at Likasi only came to the attention of the Group in 2011, when a regional body informed it that the DRC was able to produce ammunition. The group visited the plant in April 2012 and found that it had not been producing explosives for military purposes 'for seven years' – since 2005. Now owned by Société Commerciale et Industrielle D'explosifs (SOCIDEX), the site is instead periodically used to produce explosives for use in the mining sector.[100]

---

[95] 'Case Concerning Armed Activities on the Territory of the Congo', *Democratic Republic of the Congo v. Uganda*, International Court of Justice, Judgment of 19 December 2005, p. 192.

[96] Cooper, *Great Lakes Conflagration*, p. 54.

[97] Ghislaine Dupon, 'Combats signalés au sud. On annonce l'arrivée de troupes nord-coréennes', *Radio France Internationale*, Paris, radio broadcast in French at 1230 GMT, 29 June 1999.

[98] ICG Rapport Afrique No. 26, 'Le partage du Congo : Anatomie d'une sale guerre', 20 December 2000, p. 52.

[99] *Africa Confidential*, 'War Economy' (Vol. 42, No. 9, 4 May 2001).

[100] Letter dated 21 June 2012 from the chair of the Security Council Committee established pursuant to resolution 1533 (2004) concerning the Democratic Republic of the Congo (DRC) addressed to the President of the UN Security Council, S/2012/348, p. 34.

Finally, it is suspected that North Korea also transferred weapons to the DRC. Members of the UN Group of Experts[101] on the DRC interviewed senior officers of the Democratic Forces for the Liberation of Rwanda (FDLR), a Rwandan Hutu rebel group active in North Kivu province of the DRC, along the border with Rwanda and Uganda. The group had served as a proxy for Congolese President Joseph Kabila's government in the early 2000s. The Experts heard accounts that 'until at least October 2003', FDLR units in North Kivu were given weapons by the DRC government in exchange for access to 'natural resources', presumably in the territory the FDLR controlled. This was said to be part of a deal between Kinshasa and Pyongyang, where the weapons would be flown into the DRC by aircraft manned with Russian-speaking crew before being trucked overland from Shabunda airport in South Kivu province.[102]

Suspicion persists that some, possibly even all, of the deals mentioned above were conducted as barter deals, with payment to the North Koreans in the form of access to mines. In particular, it is thought that North Koreans may have had access to uranium mines at Shinkolobwe – an idea that is difficult to comprehend in light of the DPRK's significant domestic uranium resources.[103] US diplomatic cables from 2004–07 reveal conversations with foreign government officials, UN representatives and miners who all claimed to have witnessed the presence of 'unidentified' Korean businessmen and workers at uranium mines.[104] Other US cables probing the DPRK–DRC relationship and its possible connections to the mining sector show that embassy staff believed these individuals to be North Korean. These suspicions remain unsubstantiated. Should new information come to light to confirm them, it would suggest that affordability was a factor affecting the DRC's decision to buy from Pyongyang.

---

[101] 'Groups of Experts' perform the same function within the UN system as 'Panels of Experts' and 'Monitoring Groups'.

[102] UN Security Council, 'Report of the Group of Experts Submitted Pursuant to Resolution 1533 (2004)', S/2004/551, 15 July 2004, p. 87.

[103] Andrea Berger, 'What Lies Beneath: North Korea's Uranium Deposits', *NK News*, 28 August 2014, <http://www.nknews.org/2014/08/what-lies-beneath-north-koreas-uranium-deposits/>, accessed 22 October 2015.

[104] 'Recent Allegations of Uranium Trafficking in the Democratic Republic of Congo', Cable #07KINSHASA797, 11 July 2007, accessed via Wikileaks on 14 May 2014. See also 'MONUC Fears Uranium Smuggling in Congo', Cable #04KINSHASA1492, 8 September 2004, accessed via Wikileaks on 19 August 2014; 'DRC Visit to China, N. Korea – Hydroelectricity and Roof Tiles Major Prospects', Cable #04KINSHASA2122, 19 November 2004, accessed via Wikileaks on 27 May 2014.

While details of the DRC–North Korea relationship in the years immediately prior to the introduction of UN sanctions against Pyongyang are hazy, information in the sanctions era clearly points to the relationship's extension in defiance of UN resolutions. The UN Group of Experts on the DRC registered its concern over a North Korean consignment of arms aboard the *Bi Ro Bong,* which docked at Boma port on 21 January 2009. Interviews conducted by the Group confirmed that the ship contained full weapons systems and ammunition, though specific types of equipment could not be verified.[105] A DRC government document indicated that the ship offloaded 3,434 tons of military equipment. However, Congolese port authorities were forbidden by the DRC army from approaching the ship, and official importation procedures and logistical channels were completely bypassed. The army transported the equipment to the military camp at Kibomango in Kinshasa, rather than through its standard equipment-distribution site.[106] US diplomatic cables suggest that a KOMID delegation had also travelled to sub-Saharan Africa to be present for the arrival of the cargo and any subsequent related activity.[107] The volume of military equipment in the *Bi Ro Bong* shipment is also noteworthy. Exporting large volumes of equipment to a country could create long-term demand for corresponding spare parts and ammunition, contracts which would be in violation of UN sanctions against North Korea.

Continuing their long history of providing training services to the DRC, instructors from the KPA arrived in Kinshasa in May 2009. It is unclear whether this training contract was related to the weapons delivered by the *Bi Ro Bong* a few months earlier. The regularity with which North Koreans have been involved in military activity in the DRC, especially in military training and arms and related supplies, is noteworthy. Successive governments in Kinshasa have sought and received Pyongyang's help. It is difficult to assess the precise considerations behind these decisions, especially in recent years. Analysis of the age and type of equipment deployed by the DRC government forces, as well as numerous non-state groups they have supported, suggests that North Korea would also be a suitable source of replacement stock for many of the existing weapons systems deployed in the DRC.[108]

---

[105] 'Final Report of the Group of Experts on the Democratic Republic of the Congo', S/2009/603, 23 November 2009, pp. 61–62.

[106] *Ibid.*

[107] 'Possible North Korean Shipment of Proliferation Concern', Cable #09STATE4103_a, 15 January 2009, accessed via Wikileaks on 14 May 2014.

[108] Institute for International Strategic Studies, *The Military Balance 2009* (Routledge: London, 2009), pp. 297–98.

The nature and persistence of the conflict in the DRC probably also means that price and the availability of supply are important, intertwined considerations. In terms of the availability of supply, this may be particularly important in light of the arms embargo covering the DRC. Since July 2003, the UN has prohibited sales or diversion of arms and other military assistance to any non-state groups operating in North Kivu, South Kivu or the Ituri district. This includes assistance by foreign governments as well as the government of the DRC. Restrictions were also in place from 2003–08 on the sale of arms to DRC government units outside of specific command structures or operating in certain territories.[109] If North Korea had provided arms to the FDLR at the behest of the DRC government, the consignments would have been in violation of these provisions. It is therefore likely that, at least for some time, North Korea was a preferred supplier for the DRC because it was willing to circumvent UN restrictions and adopt a 'no-strings-attached' approach.

Pyongyang is in this sense a dependable supplier for the DRC. Indeed, it has proven its dependability over decades. Both current President Joseph Kabila, his predecessor and father Laurent Kabila, and Mobutu Sese Seko before him repeatedly turned to North Korea for military assistance – and Pyongyang delivered. That said, while it is clear that the DRC has been a fairly recent customer of North Korea's, since 2009 no evidence has come to light to demonstrate that it continues to purchase arms and related goods and services.

Burma

A newly elected government came to power in Burma in November 2010 and was immediately asked by the US to 'quit North Korea'.[110] The country's generals, however, have not listened. Compared to many of the other North Korean customers discussed in this chapter, Burma's military trade with Pyongyang has a brief history. In October 1983, three North Korean operatives bombed a mausoleum in Rangoon, where South Korean President Chun Doo-hwan and other members of the Cabinet were due to lay wreaths. South Korea's foreign minister, minister of commerce and deputy prime minister were amongst those killed in the blast. In reaction to the North Korean bombing, Burma severed all diplomatic relations with Pyongyang.

---

[109] For more information, see Stockholm International Peace Research Institute (SIPRI), 'UN Arms Embargo against the DRC (Non-Governmental Forces)', 12 June 2015, <http://www.sipri.org/databases/embargoes/un_arms_embargoes/drc>, accessed 22 October 2015.
[110] Jeffrey Lewis and Catherine Dill, 'Myanmar's Unrepentant Arms Czar', *Foreign Policy*, 9 May 2014.

Relations were not formally restored until 2007. However, Burma had quietly begun to procure military goods and services from North Korea in the 1990s, following the August 1988 crackdown by the ruling Burmese junta on pro-democracy protesters, which left thousands dead. Thereafter, the army launched a programme to significantly expand and modernise the country's military capacity.[111] New procurement, within resource constraints, would have been a natural part of this effort – a balancing act that a number of countries had also previously grappled with before choosing to turn to North Korea for a portion of their military goods and services.

Burma's resource constraints were worsened by the sanctions imposed by the US and others on the Burmese government for its brutality in 1988. According to the former Americas Division director of the Burmese Ministry of Foreign Affairs, 'given sanctions, Burma really [had] no other options but to develop the relationship with North Korea', which was outside of Western control regimes.[112] Until 2005, dealings between the two countries are believed to have included conventional arms and missiles or associated technology.

In the area of conventional arms, Burma's military expansion project led to new contracts with China, Pakistan and Ukraine amongst others.[113] North Korea appears to have been part of this list as well, though initially in terms much smaller than the volume or value of Chinese contracts, for example. North Korean conventional arms were regarded as similar to the Chinese designs that Burma was already familiar with, but even cheaper.[114] Pyongyang's willingness to accept barter deals may have been attractive as well.[115]

---

[111] Andrew Selth, 'Burma's Armed Forces: Looking Down the Barrel', Griffith Asia Institute, Regional Outlook Paper No. 21, 2009, <http://www.griffith.edu.au/__ data/assets/pdf_file/0003/148350/Selth-Regional-Outlook-Paper-21.pdf>, accessed 22 October 2015. See p. 11 for an overview of the various expansion estimates, most of which arrive at the conclusion that the Burmese armed forces doubled in size after 1988.

[112] 'Burma Official Confirms Burma-DPRK "Peaceful" Nuclear Cooperation', Cable #09RANGOON502, 7 August 2009, accessed via Wikileaks on 14 May 2014.

[113] Andrew T H Tan (ed.), *The Global Arms Trade: A Handbook* (Abingdon: Routledge, 2014), pp. 23–24. Supplemented by information from the SIPRI Arms Transfer Database.

[114] Bertil Lintner, 'Burma's WMD Programme and Military Cooperation between Burma and the Democratic People's Republic of Korea', March 2012, <http://issuu. com/asia_pacific_media_services/docs/burma-dark-post>, accessed 22 October 2015.

[115] Bruce Hawke, 'Rice Buys Artillery for Myanmar', *Jane's Defence Weekly*, 5 August 1998, p. 8.

Jane's Defence Weekly offers two suggestions for the types of conventional arms or related materiel that may have been purchased during the 1990s. In 1991, it reported that Rangoon had placed an order for 20 million rounds of 7.62-mm ammunition for AK-47 rifles.[116] In 1998, the same publication alleged that North Korea had delivered its first shipment of artillery pieces to Burma.[117] While these reports are the principal evidence cited for conventional trade between the two countries,[118] US Deputy Assistant Secretary of State for East Asian and Pacific Affairs Matthew Daley concurred in 2004 that 'Burma and North Korea do have a military trade relationship'.[119]

In the same State Department transcript, Daley acknowledged Washington's concern over expansion of the Burma–DPRK relationship into the sphere of ballistic missiles.[120] Months earlier, in November 2003, an article published by the *Far Eastern Economic Review* cited US and Asian officials in alleging that Burma had embarked on negotiations for the purchase of surface-to-surface missiles from North Korea.[121] Daley subsequently confirmed that an offer had been made by the North Koreans but nothing had been agreed and the deal had not come to fruition. More concrete missile-related co-operation between the two did eventually materialise, as noted by the US Department of Defense in 2012, though it is unclear whether this was for off-the-shelf missiles or production technology.[122]

---

[116] 'Burma Buys AK-47 Rounds', *Jane's Defence Weekly*, 2 February 1991, p. 139.

[117] Hawke, 'Rice Buys Artillery for Myanmar'.

[118] The Burmese military may have also explored the possibility of purchasing one or two small submarines from North Korea in 2002, but there are no grounds to conclude that the sale took place. See Andrew Selth, 'Burma's North Korean Gambit: A Challenge to Regional Security?', Strategic and Defence Studies Paper, Canberra Papers on Strategy and Defence No. 154, Australian National University, 2004, p. 4.

[119] 'Developments in Burma', testimony by Matthew P Daley before the House International Relations Committee, Washington, DC, 25 March 2004, available from <http://2001-2009.state.gov/p/eap/rls/rm/2004/30789.htm>, accessed 22 October 2015.

[120] *Ibid.*

[121] Bertil Lintner and Shawn W Crispin, 'Dangerous Bedfellows', *Far Eastern Economic Review*, 20 November 2003.

[122] A 2012 report by the US Department of Defense cites Burma as one 'client for North Korea's ballistic missiles', amongst others. See Department of Defense, 'Military and Security Developments Involving the Democratic People's Republic of Korea: A Report to Congress Pursuant to the National Defence Authorization Act for Fiscal Year 2012', 5 February 2013, p. 16. See Robert E Kelley and Ali Fowle, 'Nuclear Related Activities in Burma', published for the *Democratic Voice of Burma*, 25 May 2010, available at <http://www.washingtonpost.com/wp-srv/world/documents/060410.pdf>, accessed 22 October 2015. See also Geoffrey

It is possible that the ruling military junta in Burma also began attempts to develop an indigenous nuclear programme with North Korean assistance in the early 2000s. However, while Burma did attempt to establish a nuclear programme with Russian help,[123] lengthy speculation over the possibility of concerted North Korean involvement in those plans is based on weaker, hotly contested evidence. It will thus not be treated in detail here.[124]

Relatively robust information is available to suggest that North Korean military sales to Burma continued after sanctions were imposed in 2006, and even after the latter's general elections in 2010. In 2007, Singapore held a shipment of precision lathes with a variety of potential military applications en route from Taiwan to the Burmese office of KOMID. It ultimately released the shipment, convinced that it lacked the legal grounds to continue its detention.[125] In early 2008, Japanese media reported North Korean sales of multiple rocket launcher systems to Burma,[126] and shortly thereafter, staff at the South Korean embassy in Rangoon confirmed that North Korea was still transferring artillery, and that North Korean technicians were present at various sites in the country.[127]

Forden's analysis of photographs released by the *Democratic Voice of Burma*, showing facilities and materials belonging to the Burmese military's indigenous ballistic-missile programme. Geoffrey Forden, 'Now It Can Be Told: Inside BOB', Arms Control Wonk, 3 June 2010.

[123] The Burmese government publicly announced its plans to acquire a research reactor in 2002. In 2007, it signed an agreement with Russia for the supply of a 10-MWe light-water research reactor. That project was suspended in 2010 'due to inadequacy of resources and the government's concern for misunderstanding it may cause' in the international community. For more information see US Department of State, 'Adherence to and Compliance with Arms Control, Non-Proliferation and Disarmament Agreements and Commitments', July 2014, pp. 21–23, <http://www.state.gov/documents/organization/230108.pdf>, accessed 22 October 2015.

[124] See, for example, Robert Kelley, 'Expert Says Burma Planning Nuclear Bomb', *Democratic Voice of Burma*, 3 June 2010, <https://www.dvb.no/news/expert-says-burma-%E2%80%98planning-nuclear-bomb%E2%80%99/9527>, accessed 22 October 2015. For a more comprehensive collection of sources alleging a North Korea–Burma nuclear link, see 'A Sourcebook on Allegations of Cooperation between Myanmar (Burma) and North Korea on Nuclear Projects', reproduced by the Federation of American Scientists, 22 September 2014, <http://www.fas.org/man/eprint/burma.pdf>, accessed 22 October 2015.

[125] 'GOS Releases Precision Lathes to Shipper', Cable #07SINGAPORE224, 31 January 2007, accessed via Wikileaks on 27 May 2014.

[126] *CNBC*, 'N Korea Exporting Multiple-Launch Rockets to Myanmar – Report', 2 April 2008.

[127] 'Burma: Visit of DPRK Vice Foreign Minister', Cable #08RANGOON90, 19 November 2008, accessed via Wikileaks on 27 May 2014.

In November 2008, US officials reported that they had evidence indicating 'ongoing and potentially increasing conventional arms sales'.[128] That same month, Burma sent a large military delegation to North Korea, led by General Shwe Mann, then chief of coordination for the Burmese armed forces and the current speaker of Burma's lower house of parliament. The leaked trip report indicates that the delegation visited a Scud missile factory as well as underground facilities producing: ammunition; 'anti-tank laser beam missile guidance' (perhaps in reference to the AT-4 mentioned in Chapter II); radars and radar jammers; and SA-16 MANPADS. They also visited and expressed special interest in an underground radar site and an underground aircraft hangar. The report concludes that 'the military of the two countries will have to conduct joint military training and practice. The Burmese military proposes to have priority in training for special unit, military security, for tunnel inspections, air defense, and language learning of the two countries.' Furthermore, 'the military of the two countries will provide aid and have joint efforts in building tunnels to keep air planes and ships and other military buildings and underground buildings ... [They] will have joint efforts in modernizing weapons and military equipment and exchange experiences.'[129]

It is unclear which aspects of the co-operation the Burmese were already undertaking in partnership with North Korea, and which of those described by the delegation as desirable actually came to fruition. However, available evidence suggests that, at minimum, the construction of underground facilities and conventional-arms sales continued. Indeed, analysis undertaken in 2009 of the construction of a military complex in the Setkhaya Mountains in Burma indicates possible North Korean assistance with tunnelling and underground facilities[130] – co-operation which may have pre-dated the 2008 delegation visit.[131] A Burmese defector with alleged access to documentation on North Korean tunnelling operations in the country spoke out in support of this conclusion, though his claims cannot be substantiated.[132]

---

[128] *Ibid.*

[129] 'Report of Shwe Mann's Visit to North Korea', translated by Pascal Khu Thwe for the Democratic Voice of Burma, 2 June 2010, <www.dvb.no/burmas-nuclear-ambitions/burmas-nuclear-ambitions-military-docs/military-docs/9279>, accessed 20 October 2015.

[130] See, for example, 'O'Connor on the BOB', Arms Control Wonk, 5 August 2009, <http://lewis.armscontrolwonk.com/archive/2412/oconnor-on-the-bob>, accessed 22 October 2015.

[131] Bertil Lintner, 'Myanmar and North Korea Share a Tunnel Vision', *Asia Times*, 19 July 2006, <http://www.atimes.com/atimes/Southeast_Asia/HG19Ae01.html>, accessed 22 October 2015.

[132] Andreas Persbo, 'The Box in Burma: Preliminary Analysis', Arms Control Verification Blog, 13 August 2009, <http://www.armscontrolverification.org/2009/08/box-in-burma-preliminary-analysis.html>, accessed 22 October 2015.

With regards to weapons sales, a few months after the visit, the US Treasury designated a handful of North Korean entities involved in transactions with Burma. Washington alleged that since 2008, the Tanchon Commercial Bank[133] had been using an entity called the Korea Kwangson Banking Corporation to facilitate payments from North Korean arms dealers in Burma to China. Kwangson was therefore designated by the US Treasury for arranging payments for what appeared to have been weapons contracts with Burma.[134]

That year, US and Japanese export-control authorities also began working together to prevent North Korea from procuring machines and components with missile-related applications for an end user in Burma. On the shopping list in July 2008 were three Japanese cylindrical grinding machines, which KOMID was collaborating with a Chinese company to purchase and ship to Southeast Asia.[135] In addition to the cylindrical grinding machines, they also allegedly shipped magnetometers, which could be used to produce magnets for missile-guidance systems. Some analysts believed that these goods may have been intended for a different end user or perhaps even North Korea itself.[136] Leaked diplomatic cables, however, show that Washington did not doubt that the end user was in Burma. Japanese authorities eventually arrested two Japanese nationals and one North Korean in 2009 for these offences.[137]

Also in 2009, the USS *John S McCain* pursued the North Korean-owned and flagged *Kang Nam I,* believing it to be carrying proscribed weapons bound for Burma. When countries in the region refused the ship access to their ports, the *Kang Nam I* changed course and returned to the DPRK.[138]

Finally, between 2008 and 2011, construction was ongoing for Burma's F11 *Aung Zeya* frigate. When it entered into service in 2011, it became clear

---

[133] The Tanchon Commercial Bank is a subordinate of Korea Ryonbong General Corporation, which is suspected of having been involved in Ethiopian arms factories, as discussed in Chapter IV.

[134] 'E.O. 13382 Designation of Kwangson Banking Corporation', Cable #09STATE84276, 13 August 2009, accessed via Wikileaks on 27 May 2014.

[135] 'Follow-Up on Attempts by North Korea's KOMID to Evade Japanese Export Controls', Cable #08STATE126248, 1 December 2008, accessed via Wikileaks on 27 May 2014.

[136] Catherine Boye, Melissa Hanham and Robert Shaw, 'North Korea and Myanmar: A Match for Nuclear Proliferation?', Bulletin of the Atomic Scientists, 27 September 2010, <http://thebulletin.org/north-korea-and-myanmar-match-nuclear-proliferation>, accessed 22 October 2015.

[137] *Z News India,* 'Tokyo Trader Charged with Selling Sensitive Machine to Myanmar', 24 July 2009.

[138] 'Final Report of the Panel of Experts Submitted Pursuant to Resolution 1874 (2009)', S/2010/571, 5 November 2010, p. 24.

that the frigate was carrying variants of the Russian Kh-35 anti-ship cruise missile. Subsequently, it became apparent that the supporting racks and canisters resembled those installed on North Korean vessels deploying the system, not the racks and canisters used by Russia. Presumably, these missiles were acquired from North Korea, or produced in Burma with Pyongyang's help, during the ship's construction period.[139]

More transactions between North Korea and Burma have taken place since the latter's 2010 general election and the country's subsequent pronouncement that it had not had military transactions with North Korea since early 2011. In May 2011, a US Navy vessel hailed the *MV Light* (now renamed *Victory 3*), suspecting it of carrying arms from North Korea to Burma. The ship's captain refused to let the ship be inspected and instead sailed back to North Korea.[140] Following the event, General Shwe Mann, by this time speaker of Burma's lower house, amended the country's earlier statements about arms trade with Pyongyang. He insisted that while Burma would pursue no new weapons purchases, it was still receiving weapons deliveries under older contracts.[141]

Continuing evidence of Burmese military interaction with North Korea, and the US reaction to that evidence, suggests that there may be more than old contracts at play, however. In July 2012, the US Treasury designated Burma's Directorate of Defense Industries (DDI) – the military-controlled entity which has traditionally been at the heart of the bilateral relationship with North Korea – for continuing its illegal pursuits.[142] Weeks later, Japan seized the *Wan Hai 313* carrying weapons-usable metal pipes and high-specification aluminium alloy bars from North Korea to Burma.[143] More designations followed. First was Lieutenant General Thein Htay, the head of the previously sanctioned DDI, who had 'disregarded international requirements to stop purchasing military goods from North Korea, the revenues from which directly support North Korea's illicit activities', said US Under Secretary for Terrorism and

---

[139] Stijn Mitzer and Joost Oliemans, 'North Korea Kh-35 Anti-Ship Missiles Shed Light on a Modernizing Navy', Oryx Blog, 12 June 2014, <http://spioenkop.blogspot.co.uk/2014/06/north-korean-kh-35-anti-ship-missiles.html>, accessed 22 October 2015.
[140] 'Report of the Panel of Experts Submitted Pursuant to Resolution 1874 (2009)', S/2012/422, p. 23.
[141] Yoshiro Makino, 'Japan Intercepts N. Korea Weapons-Grade Material Bound for Myanmar', *Asahi Shimbun*, 24 November 2012.
[142] *Federal Register*, 'Designation of Two Entities Pursuant to Executive Orders', (Vol. 77, No. 196, October 2012), <http://www.gpo.gov/fdsys/pkg/FR-2012-10-10/html/2012-24181.htm>, accessed 22 October 2015.
[143] Makino, 'Japan Intercepts N. Korea Weapons-Grade Material Bound for Myanmar'.

Financial Intelligence David Cohen.[144] Thereafter, the US designated three companies and one individual: Asia Metal Company Ltd, Soe Min Htike Co Ltd, Excellence Mineral Manufacturing Co Ltd, and Lieutenant Colonel Kyaw Nyunt Oo.[145] Of the companies, the US Treasury added:[146]

> As recently as June 2013, Soe Min Htike Co. Ltd. and Excellence Mineral were companies working with North Korean officials to import materiel for military weapons programs. As of December 2012, Asia Metal constructed buildings and supplied construction materials on a DDI factory compound where approximately 30 North Koreans were still working.

As for Lieutenant Colonel Oo, a senior member of DDI, he too was alleged to be continually assisting the sale of North Korean arms to Burma.

Further demonstrating continuing illicit military ties between the two countries, in November 2015 the US designated several KOMID representatives stationed in Burma. In an unprecedented move, it also designated the North Korean ambassador to Burma for facilitating KOMID's activities and negotiations with defence officials in the country.[147]

Mindful of the delicate diplomatic situation and the fragility and reversibility of Burma's recent reforms, the US Treasury clarified that these were not sanctions against the country's government, but against specific individuals and entities. This disclaimer highlights a number of possibilities regarding the nature of the contemporary North Korea–Burma relationship. On the one hand, it is possible that information about arms and related materiel procurement from North Korea is knowledge to which the civilian government in Burma is privy and tacitly condones – a fact which the US may merely prefer to address behind the scenes. On the other, it is also possible, and perhaps more likely, that the civilian government is not aware of this activity as it occurs. Arms procurement from North Korea may be propelled at the sub-state level by DDI, and it may therefore not form part of any central government strategy for the

---

[144] US Department of the Treasury, 'Treasury Designates Burmese LT. General Thein Htay, Chief of Directorate of Defense Industries', 2 July 2013, <http://www.treasury.gov/press-center/press-releases/Pages/jl1998.aspx>, accessed 20 October 2015.

[145] US Department of the Treasury, 'Treasury Designates Burmese Companies and an Individual with Ties to the Directorate of Defense Industries', 17 December 2013, <http://www.treasury.gov/press-center/press-releases/Pages/jl2247.aspx>, accessed 20 October 2015.

[146] *Ibid.*

[147] US Department of the Treasury, 'Treasury Sanctions Supporters of North Korea's Weapons of Mass Destruction and Illicit Finance Networks', 13 November 2015, <http://www.treasury.gov/press-center/press-releases/Pages/jl0269.aspx>, accessed 13 November 2015.

bilateral relationship with North Korea. This would not be the first time that North Korean arms dealers have profited from stove piping or personal relationships with key military decision-makers in customer states.

At best, the international community has made progress in eroding political support in Burma for continued military procurement from North Korea, enough to mean that this type of activity is now driven primarily by a single entity. Should this be the case, it could be argued that Burma in fact belongs in the 'reluctant' category of clients outlined in Chapter IV. Yet the evidence presented above indicates that such a reclassification would be premature.

At worst, Burma has found a way to maintain its ties to North Korea as well as to the international community. It may continue to be attracted by Pyongyang's ability to sell missile technology and conventional arms unavailable elsewhere. Perhaps it is swayed by the rather unique ability to barter dry goods such as rice for North Korea's products and services, as outlined in Chapter II.

Either way, it appears that sanctions violations continue, despite Burma's prospects of being reintegrated into the international community, with all of the benefits that that would entail. As will be discussed further in Chapter VI, even the application of carefully selected carrots and sticks has not yet been enough to convince Burma's generals to quit their North Korean habit entirely.

Cuba

It is no surprise that North Korea and Cuba, two isolated communist states, have consistently maintained a military relationship. During the Cold War, the two were important partners. As then-Deputy Premier Raul Castro said in 1968: 'If someone is interested in what the Cubans' opinion is on certain questions, he should ask the Koreans. And if someone asks what Korea's standpoint may be in certain cases, he can safely ask the Cubans about that. Our views are completely identical in everything.'[148] Pyongyang offered Havana political and military support in its overseas endeavours, including in Vietnam and Yemen. Cuba may also have benefited from North Korean military services. In 1960, Zhou Enlai, then-premier of the People's Republic of China, encouraged Ernesto 'Che' Guevara to ask North Korea for military advice. 'Talk to them, to see what

---

[148] 'Report, Hungarian Embassy in Cuba to the Hungarian Foreign Ministry, 25 January 1968', 25 January 1968, History and Public Policy Program Digital Archive, MOL, XIX-J-1-j Cuba, 1968, 59. doboz, 1, 001121/1968. Translated by Balázs Szalontai; available at <http://digitalarchive.wilsoncenter.org/document/116665>, accessed 22 October 2015.

secret defensive works could be constructed in mountainous areas', he said.[149] A former Cuban intelligence officer has suggested that while the Cubans did indeed study North Korean operations during the Korean War, they did not receive military hardware.[150] This claim may have been true of the first few years of Cuba's post-revolutionary history, as no concrete evidence of North Korean weapons shipments exists in open sources for this period. However, archival documents reveal that in 1967, 'at the request of the Cuban government [North Korea] agreed to send a group of up to 700 volunteers with weapons and equipment to Cuba'.[151]

Aidan Foster-Carter, a Korea expert at Leeds University, describes historical relations between Havana and Pyongyang as periodically lukewarm.[152] This is a plausible conclusion in the context of North Korea's provision of military assistance to Cuba. Archival documents show that the Soviet Union was keen to be the primary supplier of arms to Cuba, though it would sometimes endorse supplementary shipments from Czechoslovakia and Bulgaria, for example. Large orders were filled with little question and on generous credit (although this often did not cover the total value of the order), and reserve supplies were even offered as gifts.[153] Despite its ideological commonalities with North Korea, Cuba would have had little reason to look beyond the aforementioned countries unless they could not supply specific equipment or the quantity required. The 1967 request may have been such an example.

---

[149] 'Memorandum of Conversation between Vice-Chairman Zhou Enlai, Party Secretary of the Cuban Popular Socialist Party Manuel Luzardo, and Member of National Directory Ernesto Che Guevara', 21 November 1960, History and Public Policy Program Digital Archive, Chinese Foreign Ministry Archive, No.204-00098-03, pp. 1–19. Translated for CWIHP by Zhang Qian; available at <http://digitalarchive.wilsoncenter.org/document/115154>, accessed 22 October 2015.

[150] *Cuba News*, 'Cuba-N. Korea Relationship More Complex than it Seems', 1 March 2005.

[151] 'From a 2 June 1967 Memo of the Soviet Embassy in the DPRK (1st Secretary V. Nemchinov) about Some New Factors in Korean-Cuban Relations', 2 June 1967, History and Public Policy Program Digital Archive, AVPRF f. 0102, op. 23, p. 112, d. 24, pp. 53–57. Obtained by Sergey Radchenko and translated by Gary Goldberg; available at <http://digitalarchive.wilsoncenter.org/document/116706>, accessed 22 October 2015.

[152] Aidan Foster-Carter, 'Cuba and North Korea: A Difficult Relationship', *Wall Street Journal*, 17 July 2013.

[153] See, for example, 'Ivan Budinov, Minister of Foreign Trade, Report to Todor Zhivkov, Chairman of the Council of Ministers, Report on Granting a Credit to Cuba', December 1962, History and Public Policy Program Digital Archive, Bulgarian Central State Archive, Fond 1-B, Opis 64, a.e. 303, pp. 2–3. Translated by Greta Keremidchieva and edited by Jordan Baev. Obtained by the Bulgarian Cold War Research Group; available at <http://digitalarchive.wilsoncenter.org/document/116255>, accessed 22 October 2015.

In the 1980s, however, the Soviet Union's generosity receded. Fidel Castro wrote in 2013 that when Moscow refused to fill an order for 100,000 AK-47s in the 1980s, Havana turned to another communist friend: Pyongyang. North Korea delivered the hardware requested, along with tens of millions of rounds of ammunition,[154] and as Castro fondly reminisced, 'they did not charge us a cent'.[155]

Cuba became North Korea's primary, and perhaps even sole, remaining customer in Latin America after the end of the Cold War. The two countries signed a twenty-year co-operation agreement with a military component in 1986,[156] and it is reasonable to conclude that co-operation continued throughout the duration of that agreement, although precise details cannot be confirmed. It is possible that North Korea provided spare parts and services for some of its Soviet-made aircraft, as will be outlined below.

More recently, there have been unusually frequent and high-ranking exchanges of Cuban and North Korean military delegations. In November 2010, then-chief of the KPA General Staff, Ri Yong-ho, visited Cuba for meetings with senior Cuban military representatives. He also toured Cuban defence-industry sites, with one photograph showing him inspecting a GAZ-51 engine, used in light armoured vehicles.[157] In September 2012, the vice minister of the Cuban Revolutionary Armed Forces travelled to Pyongyang with an accompanying military delegation. He was separately taken to an exhibition of North Korean military equipment.[158] Then in June 2013, Kim Kyok-sik, Ri's successor as chief of the KPA General Staff, led an army delegation to Cuba consisting of over a dozen officers.[159] During his stay, he met the Cuban president, minister and vice minister of the Revolutionary Armed Forces – the latter of whom had been in Pyongyang a year earlier. Kim discussed 'boosting the friendly

---

[154] Foreign Broadcast Information Service Daily Report (Asia), 12 March 1986, p. D10.
[155] Patrick Oppmann, 'Panama Says Cuban Weapons Shipment Violates U.N. Arms Embargo', *CNN*, 29 August 2013.
[156] United States Information Agency, Office of Research and Policy, *Cuba Annual Report: 1986* (New Brunswick, NJ: Transaction, 1988), p. 81.
[157] Michael Madden, 'Gen. Kim Kyok Sik Visits Cuba', NK Leadership Watch Blog, 30 June 2013, <https://nkleadershipwatch.wordpress.com/2013/06/30/gen-kim-kyok-sik-visits-cuba/>, accessed 22 October 2015.
[158] Michael Madden, 'Kim Jong Gak Meets with Cuban Military Delegation', NK Leadership Watch Blog, 9 September 2012, <https://nkleadershipwatch.wordpress.com/2012/09/09/kim-jong-gak-meets-with-cuban-military-delegation/>, accessed 22 October 2015.
[159] CCTV, 'Raul Castro Meets with Kim Kyok-Sik in Havana', 2 July 2013, <http://english.cntv.cn/program/newshour/20130702/104201.shtml>, accessed 22 October 2015.

relations between the two armies', and visited numerous Cuban military units, including the Grand Rescue Tank Unit.[160]

It now appears that another, more specific purpose of Kim's visit to Cuba in 2013 was to check that military equipment from Cuba had been successfully loaded onto a North Korean vessel, the *Chong Chon Gang,* before being concealed with bags of sugar. Just over a week after the delegation departed Cuba, the vessel was subject to an anti-drug inspection while passing through the Panama Canal. The ship was found to contain twenty-five containers with Cuban military equipment, including but not limited to:

- Two anti-aircraft missile complexes
- Nine missiles in spares and parts
- Two MiG-21 jet aircraft
- Fifteen MiG-21 jet engines
- Machines for loading and aligning 5.56-mm cartridges
- Ammunition for both small arms and light weapons
- Artillery ammunition
- 57-mm anti-tank guns
- Miscellaneous items, such as a tank-track section, parts for a Soviet rotary cannon, one pair of night-vision binoculars and an assortment of gauges.[161]

Upon announcement by Panamanian authorities that the illicit cargo had been discovered, the Cuban authorities reacted within hours, articulating a detailed but ultimately unconvincing legal explanation for the cargo on the ship. In fact, the swiftness and detail of the statement raises suspicions that not only was the Cuban bureaucracy aware of the transaction, but also that the statement may in fact have been partially prepared in advance.[162] In its response, the Cuban Ministry of Foreign Affairs acknowledged ownership of the arms and related materiel. However, it insisted that the items were being shipped to be repaired and returned. It also argued that 'maintenance', as forbidden by paragraph 8 (c) of UN Security Council Resolution 1718, was distinct from 'repair', which Cuba claimed was the basis of its contract with Pyongyang.[163]

The UN Panel of Experts on North Korea subsequently determined that the Cuban explanation was unsatisfactory, and that the incident was an unequivocal violation of Resolutions 1718 and 1874.[164] Some of the

---

[160] Madden, 'Gen. Kim Kyok Sik Visits Cuba'.
[161] 'Report of the Panel of Experts Established Pursuant to Resolution 1874 (2009)', S/2014/147, Annex VII, p. 70.
[162] Author interview with Interviewee E, 8 May 2014.
[163] 'Report of the Panel of Experts Established Pursuant to Resolution 1874 (2009)', S/2014/147, p. 29.
[164] *Ibid*.

cargo onboard was new and in its original packaging, and some had calibration certificates dated just prior to packing,[165] clearly indicating it was not meant to be repaired and returned, as the Cubans alleged.[166]

As is the case in the Burma–North Korea relationship, the *Chong Chon Gang* shipment was allegedly facilitated through a standing barter agreement between the two countries, which includes non-military goods. The sugar loaded aboard the vessel was payment for the inbound cargo delivered by the *Chong Chon Gang* (rolled steel plates and locomotive wheels). North Korea would therefore have been expected to pay for the military equipment sent by Cuba with a subsequent shipment.[167]

In terms of the military trade component of this broader relationship, most analysis of the *Chong Chon Gang* incident suggests that this was evidence only of a one-way arms relationship between Cuba and North Korea, where Cuba was the supplier and North Korea the customer.[168] In other words, the generally held view is that Cuba was selling arms-related goods intended to stay in North Korea, not the other way around. However, a closer look at the ship's cargo provides hints that Cuba had previously been, and may have wished to continue to be, a client for North Korean military goods as well.

Two observations contribute to this assessment. First, examination of the tail fins of the complete MiG-21 fuselages aboard the *Chong Chon Gang* show they have been marked 'left' and 'right' in Korean. Given that these tail fins were already attached to the connecting section of the fuselage when they were loaded onto the ship, there is no reason for them to have been marked in this way. Instead, this strongly suggests that the tail fins may originally have been North Korean spare parts supplied to Cuba's air force, and installed by Korean technicians in the country. The UN Panel of Experts on North Korea hinted at the same, and quietly warned in its report that if these markings were made because of prior North Korean

---

[165] These certificates provide essential information about an instrument's condition, and specifically any out-of-tolerance or special measurement conditions. They are often required by end users in a sale to ensure that the product has been tested prior to shipment.

[166] Hugh Griffiths and Roope Siirtola, 'Full Disclosure: Contents of North Korean Smuggling Ship Revealed', 38 North, 27 August 2013, <http://38north.org/2013/08/hgriffiths082713/>, accessed 22 October 2015.

[167] Author interview with Interviewee J, 29 April 2014. Corroborated by Interviewee E, in conversation with the author on 8 May 2014.

[168] Melissa Hanham, 'North Korea's Cuban Missile Crisis', 38 North, 1 August 2013, <http://38north.org/2013/08/mhanham080113/>, accessed 22 October 2015; see also Griffiths and Siirtola, 'Full Disclosure'.

involvement with the Cuban air force, that it would have been another violation of the resolution.[169]

Second, the collection of miscellaneous items in the shipment points to the conclusion that these were a sample that Cuba wished North Korea to match and supply. North Korea has no conceivable need for a single pair of night-vision binoculars nor for part of a tank track, given its well-known ability to produce and export tanks and other armoured vehicles. The same can be postulated for the assorted parts of the Soviet 30-mm rotary cannon, variants of which can be used on MiG-27 aircraft or on naval platforms.[170]

The information presented above shows that Cuba exhibits many of the same characteristics as North Korea's other resilient customers. The historical importance of the country's military ties to North Korea, and the longstanding nature of their partnership, likely have some influence on Havana's supplier choice. Similarly, personal relationships may play a role, as highlighted by the glowing praise of the country's military relationship with North Korea recently uttered by the Castro family.[171]

However, limitations on Cuba's supplier options, weaponry requirements and budget are also explanatory factors. Cuba presently has few potential sources for military hardware. The CIA notes that 'the collapse of the Soviet Union deprived the Cuban military of its major economic and logistic support and had a significant impact on the state of Cuban [military] equipment'.[172] Data from the World Military Expenditures and Arms Transfers (WMEAT) database indicates that Russia did in fact provide some limited, undefined support during the 2000–10 period,[173] and several arms shipments from China to Cuba have been revealed by the press as well.[174] Few others appear to have any interest in arming

---

[169] 'Report of the Panel of Experts Established Pursuant to Resolution 1874 (2009)', S/2014/147, p. 79.

[170] Interviewee E agreed that this was likely the intention behind the shipment of miscellaneous items, during an interview with the author on 8 May 2014.

[171] Oppmann, 'Panama Says Cuban Weapons Shipment Violates U.N. Arms Embargo'.

[172] CIA, 'World Factbook: Cuba', military section last updated 2013, <https://www.cia.gov/library/publications/resources/the-world-factbook/geos/cu.html>, accessed 22 October 2015.

[173] Data sourced from the 2013 World Military Expenditures and Arms Transfer (WMEAT) Database, Table III.

[174] A string of Chinese shipments of arms-related parts were reported in 2001. They were said to be part of a contract for maintenance and upgrade of Cuban weapons. See *Washington Times*, 'China Secretly Shipping Cuba Arms', 12 June 2001. A Chinese vessel laden with similar parts, as well as ninety-nine 'rockets', all produced by China's largest state-owned defence firm and bound for Cuba, was seized in Colombia in May 2015. See Miles Yu, 'Colombians Catch Illegal Arms on Chinese Ship Bound for Cuba', *Washington Times*, 5 March 2015.

Cuba, and the US and EU members, amongst others, have unilaterally imposed restrictions on arms-related trade with the country. US law allows for the imposition of national penalties on any country which supplies arms to designated State Sponsors of Terrorism, which Cuba was until 29 May 2015.[175] This may have been a deterrent for many countries, even if defence-related trade with Cuba was not prohibited under their own national legislation.

Lack of interest on the part of most major defence suppliers in selling Cuba new weaponry makes it necessary for Havana to continue to extend the service lives of its Cold War-era systems. As Cuba's and North Korea's Cold War-era arsenals – heavily populated by systems of Soviet design heritage – have aged together, the two countries have co-operated to ensure that they remain militarily capable. As discussed in Chapter II, antique weapons systems are a notable market niche for North Korea, and it has managed to generate numerous contracts because of this specialisation. Cuba appears to be one of them.

The preference for life extension is probably compounded by budgetary constraints as well. Though concrete and reliable statistics on Cuba's defence budget are not available,[176] its standing barter arrangement with Pyongyang may be taken as an indicator of financial resource considerations when conducting its defence trade.

It remains to be seen what effect fledgling rapprochement between Washington and Havana will have on this partnership. It is possible that, like with some of Pyongyang's other previous clients – including Libya and Burma – Washington will eventually demand that ties with North Korea be severed. However, Cuba has an ageing arsenal, with the service lives of many of its systems coming to an end. Havana may not be able to wait for its economic and foreign-relations climate to warm to the point that it has a wider range of willing military suppliers, with a procurement budget that allows it to replace its Soviet-era weapons and turn away from Pyongyang. There is a risk, therefore, that in the coming years, it will continue to be tempted by what Pyongyang has to offer. Alternatively, it is also possible that China will seek to gain a greater foothold in what it may view as a growth market, undercutting some of North Korea's comparative advantages in Cuba.

---

[175] Felicia Schwartz, 'Cuba Officially Removed from U.S. State Sponsors of Terrorism List', *Washington Post*, 29 May 2015.
[176] WMEAT's statistical notes for 2013 indicate the problems with the sources and veracity of data for Cuba. The CIA World Factbook's collection of defence budget data does not contain information for Cuba; and the Stockholm International Peace Research Institute's Arms Transfer Database shows no transfers to Cuba after 1991.

Non-State Groups

During the 1970s and 1980s, Pyongyang offered modest amounts of military training and armaments to a host of revolutionary groups. Aid often came in co-ordination with, or in parallel to, assistance from other friends such as Cuba, China, Iran or Syria. Africa and Latin America were particularly important regions for North Korea's broader efforts to enable anti-government forces. In the latter case, assistance was given to groups operating in Argentina, Bolivia, Brazil, Chile, Guatemala, Mexico, Nicaragua, Paraguay, Peru and Venezuela amongst others.[177] North Korea's relationships with Palestinian groups and with Hizbullah, which received training and weapons from the DPRK, also took off in earnest during this period.

Lack of funds or expertise was undoubtedly a consideration for these groups when accepting handouts from North Korea. Another important binding agent was the moral and political support that North Korea lent to their anti-imperialist objectives. Some non-state groups drew parallels with North Korea's efforts to cast off US and South Korean oppression. One such figure, Yasser Arafat, famously awarded Kim Il-sung the 'Star of Palestine' for the support he had lent to the Palestinian cause.[178] For many non-state recipients, Pyongyang was not merely a supplier of convenience, but an ideological supporter.

In the sanctions era, a handful of non-state groups have continued to receive military assistance from North Korea. They need both stock and training, depending on the regularity and intensity of their campaigns. Some may still appreciate North Korea's solidarity with their political objectives. Like a number of Pyongyang's more committed and internationally isolated state customers, these clients do not feel normatively constrained by externally imposed sanctions regimes or arms embargoes. They also share – to an even greater extent – the isolation that these states experience.

Armed Palestinian Organisations and Hizbullah

North Korea's initial military involvement with Hizbullah and Palestinian organisations during the 1970s and 1980s was mainly to provide training for their fighters and commanders. More information has recently come to light to suggest that co-operation in the post-Cold War period had additional dimensions. In June 2014, a US district court ruled in *Chaim*

---

[177] Savada (ed.), *North Korea*, chapter on 'Relations with the Third World'.

[178] Benjamin R Young, 'How North Korea Has Been Arming Palestinian Militants for Decades', *NK News*, 25 June 2014, <http://www.nknews.org/2014/06/how-north-korea-has-been-arming-palestinian-militants-for-decades/>, accessed 20 October 2015.

Kaplan et al. vs. Hezbollah et al., that 'North Korea and Iran are liable for damages because they provided material support and assistance' to the defendant, enabling its rocket attacks during the 2006 war with Israel. The memorandum opinion states that:[179]

> North Korea provided Hezbollah with a wide variety of material support and resources ... This material support included professional military and intelligence training and assistance in building a massive network of underground military installations, tunnels, bunkers, depots and storage facilities in southern Lebanon. Moreover, North Korea worked in concert with Iran and Syria to provide rocket and missile components to Hezbollah. North Korea sent these rocket and missile components to Iran where they were assembled and shipped to Hezbollah in Lebanon via Syria.

Much of the court's conviction regarding the North Korea connection stemmed from testimony given by Bruce Bechtol Jr, an associate professor at Angelo State University.[180] While some of the claims offered in his testimony require further substantiation, there is evidence supporting the link. For example, a 2010 Congressional Research Service report provides an overview of the available allegations of North Korean assistance in tunnel construction,[181] including the reported dispatch of North Korean trainers to southern Lebanon to assist with the design and construction of underground military facilities. A Japanese daily, the *Sankei Shimbun*, later cited a 'document of an international organ' in describing a meeting between Syrian President Bashar Al-Assad and North Korean officials in which the former apparently requested help in designing and building such structures. It suggests that these tunnel networks enabled Hizbullah to conceal its rocket launchers during the 2006 war, thereby reducing their vulnerability to Israeli strike. None of these reports has been confirmed, but due to the weight of the evidence and North Korea's known involvement in tunnel-construction projects in countries such as Burma, it is reasonable to suggest that it may have successfully marketed its extensive experience in this area in Lebanon.

On weapons sales, the 2007 UN secretary-general's report pursuant to Resolution 1559, which would have been based largely on information from

---

[179] Memorandum Opinion, *Chaim Kaplan et al. v. Hezbollah et al.*, United Services District Court for the District of Columbia, 23 July 2014.
[180] 'Declaration of Professor Bruce Bechtol', *Chaim Kaplan et al. vs. Hezbollah et al.*, United Services District Court for the District of Columbia, 8 September 2011.
[181] Mark E Manyin, 'North Korea: Back on the Terrorism List?', Congressional Research Service, Report 7-5700, 29 June 2010, <http://fas.org/sgp/crs/row/RL30613.pdf>, accessed 22 October 2015.

the preceding year, states that Hizbullah regularly receives 'weapons *produced outside the region* [which] arrive via third countries and are brought clandestinely into Lebanon through the Syrian-Lebanese border'.[182] Israeli analysis of the nearly 4,000 rockets fired by Hizbullah during the conflict concludes that over 75 per cent were 122-mm rockets. While many of these were confirmed to be Chinese-made weapons with cluster warheads, there is reason to believe that at least some of Hizbullah's stock of 122-mm rockets came from North Korea, though precisely when – and how – is unclear.[183]

It is nevertheless difficult to show conclusively that any North Korean-made weapons in Hizbullah's arsenal were transferred as the result of a contract between the two parties. Numerous analyses of the weapons used by Hizbullah in the 2006 conflict conclude that much of the stockpile was instead originally Iranian army stock, and none of the statements referenced above actually confirms that North Korea sold these weapons directly. In fact, because Iran and Syria are known to have previously and consistently acquired some of these same systems from North Korea, it is possible that one of these regional states – and not Pyongyang – offered Hizbullah access to weapons produced in North Korea. The case of the *MV Francop* illustrates just such a pattern of behaviour. The vessel was stopped and searched by Israel in November 2009 on its way from Iran to Syria, carrying cargo allegedly intended for Hizbullah. This included North Korean-made 122-mm rockets manufactured at the time of the Iran–Iraq War, and therefore likely from Iranian surplus stock.[184]

Either way, North Korea–Hizbullah ties appear to have been active at the time of the 2006 conflict between Hizbullah and Israel, shortly before UN Security Council Resolution 1718 was passed that October. It is reasonable to assume that they continued thereafter as well. Indeed, Israel has stated its belief that Hizbullah was one of the intended recipients of the North Korean cargo aboard the charter flight detained in Thailand in 2009.[185]

Palestinian organisations are confirmed to have attempted to import, and are believed to have received, North Korean arms as well. In late 2008, Hamas became embroiled in a short but damaging war with Israel. The group expended significant quantities of munitions in the battle, making it

---

[182] Emphasis added. 'Fifth Semi-annual Report of the Secretary-General to the UN Security Council on the Implementation of Security Council Resolution 1559 (2004)', S/2007/262, 7 May 2007, para. 28.

[183] Human Rights Watch, 'Civilians Under Assault: Hezbollah's Rocket Attacks on Israel in the 2006 War', Vol. 19, No. 3, August 2007, pp. 29, 43, <http://www.hrw.org/reports/2007/iopt0807/iopt0807web.pdf>, accessed 22 October 2015.

[184] Berger, 'North Korea, Hamas, and Hezbollah'.

[185] Kubota, 'Israel Says Seized North Korean Arms Were for Hamas, Hezbollah'.

plausible that the North Korean light-weapons shipments destined for Hamas (and possibly Hizbullah) and seized by Thailand in 2009 were part of a restocking campaign. In July 2014, the *Daily Telegraph* claimed that another such campaign was underway, following the Israel–Hamas conflict that took place during that month. Hamas, it said, is 'looking for ways to replenish its stocks ... because of [the] large numbers it has fired at Israel in recent weeks' and is therefore negotiating a new arms deal with North Korea. Probably the result of leaked information from foreign officials, the story is unverifiable using open sources.[186]

Suggestions that Hamas may need to restock its arms caches seem plausible in light of its summer 2014 confrontation with Israel. Small arms, mortar bombs, anti-tank and anti-personnel light weapons, and surface-to-surface rockets and launchers may be particularly desirable,[187] as a large number of these types of munitions were expended in the latest exchanges. Hamas apparently fired over 3,200 rockets during the 2014 conflict, for instance.[188]

A closer look at promotional material and parades by Hamas forces seems to confirm that supply has recently met demand in one of these weapons categories: anti-tank weapons. Analysts at IHS Jane's and elsewhere have spotted what appear to be North Korean variants of 9K111 anti-tank missiles (of Russian-origin design) being used by the group.[189] Similar weapons have materialised in videos of the Al-Nasser Salah Al-Deen Brigades – a wing of the Popular Resistance Committees in the Gaza Strip.[190] The North Korean heritage of those weapons is apparent when still frames from the footage are compared with a North Korean marketing brochure (see Appendix A), which uses the NATO designation 'AT-4' rather than the Soviet '9K111'. This is one example of North Korea's ability and willingness to produce and supply the types of weapons that the armed Palestinian organisations and Hizbullah have repeatedly used in their battles.[191]

The non-state groups mentioned above have had long histories with North Korea, which has consistently supported their political and military

---

[186] Con Coughlin, 'Hamas and North Korea in Secret Arms Deal', *Daily Telegraph*, 26 July 2014.

[187] Berger, 'North Korea, Hamas, and Hezbollah'.

[188] Colleen Curry and Seni Tienabeso, 'Israel Says Public Bus Was Target of Terror Attack', *ABC News*, 4 August 2014.

[189] Jeremy Binnie, 'Analysis: Hamas Displays Long-Range Rockets', *IHS Jane's Defence Weekly*, 17 December 2014. See also Arms Control Wonk, 'Oryx Blog on DPRK Arms Exports', 25 June 2014, <http://lewis.armscontrolwonk.com/archive/7370/oryx-blog-on-dprk-arms-exports>, accessed 22 October 2015.

[190] *Ibid.*

[191] Binnie, 'Analysis: Hamas Displays Long-Range Rockets',

objectives, and it is clear that Iran and Syria condone Pyongyang's involvement as well. Looking ahead, these armed groups will almost certainly have cause to fight in coming years – and when they do, they will wield arms that North Korea is able to manufacture cheaply and easily. Given their decades-long military co-operation with North Korea, the 'anti-imperialist' objectives they share with the country, and Iran and Syria's tacit approval of their relationship with Pyongyang, it seems likely that certain non-state militias in the Middle East will continue to augment the arms and services they receive from other benefactors with those from North Korea.

In this vein, North Korea may find new opportunities to sell weapons and related services to other non-state actors fighting in regional civil wars. In March 2014, a North Korean-flagged oil tanker was seized by the US Navy after loading oil in a rebel-controlled port in Libya.[192] While North Korea insisted that the *MV Morning Glory* was operated by an Egyptian firm and promptly revoked its use of the North Korean flag, the incident fuelled concerns that Pyongyang may now have relations with rebels loyal to the former Qadhafi regime, one of North Korea's previous political and military partners.[193]

Liberation Tigers of Tamil Eelam

Sri Lanka's civil war lasted twenty-six years, beginning in 1983 and ending with the Sri Lankan military's conclusive defeat of the LTTE in May 2009. During the war, the group established a robust network for raising funds and procuring weapons from abroad. Weapons were sourced from countries as far flung as the US, China and North Korea.

In October 2000, the LTTE sank a Sri Lanka Navy passenger vessel in Trincomalee harbour. The group subsequently released a video of the operation, which was analysed by *Jane's Intelligence Review*. Its assessment confirmed that North Korean weapons were used in the attack. In the video, the rebels are shown firing a wire-guided, twin-barrelled version of a Type 63 107-mm rocket launcher – a design that is unique to North Korea.[194] Jane's also highlighted the possibility that the speedboats used in the attack were designed and produced in North Korea, though this is less certain than the origin of the 107-mm

---

[192] *Guardian*, 'US Sailors Hand Over Control of Captured Oil Tanker to Libyan Forces', 22 March 2014.
[193] *BBC News*, 'North Korea Disowns Libya Oil Tanker', 13 March 2014.
[194] China produces single-barrelled rocket launchers.

rocket launchers.[195] Interviewee C provided photographs to the author, which he claims show a minigun being demonstrated in North Korea to clients 'from Sri Lanka' – plausibly the LTTE – in the early 2000s.[196]

Predictably, North Korea continued to assist the LTTE in its weapons procurement after 2006 and the passage of UN Security Council Resolution 1718. It is widely believed that North Korea transported weapons (including those manufactured beyond its borders) to the LTTE using a 'mothership' or floating-warehouse system. Tamil-owned trawlers or small vessels would go out to the ship stocked with North Korean goods, anchored off the coasts of nearby countries. Colombo confronted Pyongyang directly about these sales in the mid-2000s, but the transfers did not cease.[197]

On 26 September 2007, the Japanese daily *Sankei Shimbun* claimed that the Sri Lanka Navy intercepted three North Korean vessels delivering arms to the LTTE in October 2006, February 2007 and March 2007. It published a few photographs of the weapons said to have been seized during the February 2007 incident.[198] Three more ships (not all North Korean-owned) were sunk by the Sri Lanka Navy in the months thereafter. Furthermore, in 2008, information about the imminent arrival of another two North Korean motherships was raised through official channels between the governments of the US and Sri Lanka.[199] The US believed that the ships were planning to anchor off the coast of India and that LTTE-controlled trawlers would travel to meet them to pick up the wares onboard. The commander of the Sri Lanka Navy agreed that the North Korean vessels would arrive imminently and noted that they had installed trackers on suspected LTTE trawlers to monitor their activity.

North Korean arms traders also seem to have brokered and facilitated the sale of weapons produced in China. In a 2009 meeting with US Assistant Secretary of State for South and Central Asian Affairs Robert Blake, the Sri Lankan defence secretary explained his knowledge of LTTE weapons procurement. Tamil brokers operating outside of the country 'usually married a native [of the foreign country from where they were operating], started a business, and bribed officials to facilitate deals. The shipments

---

[195] Roger Davies, 'Sea Tigers, Stealth Technology and the North Korean Connection', *Jane's Intelligence Review*, March, 2001, available at <http://www.lankalibrary.com/pol/korea.htm>, accessed 20 October 2015.
[196] Author e-mail conversation with Interviewee C, 23 January 2015.
[197] 'Sri Lanka: Procurement of Lethal Military Equipment From North Korea and Iran', Cable #09COLOMBO516, 12 May 2009, accessed via Wikileaks on 27 May 2014.
[198] Kubota Ruriko, 'DPRK Plotted to Export Weapons to Terrorist Organ', *Sankei Shimbun*, 26 September 2007.
[199] 'Request for Sharing of Intelligence on Liberation Tigers of Tamil Eelam Motherships', Cable #08COLOMBO601, 20 June 2008, accessed via Wikileaks on 27 May 2014.

originated in North Korea, and usually contained Chinese-origin goods.'[200] If they did originate in North Korea, it can be reasonably assumed that a North Korean individual or entity will have at some stage been involved in the transaction. Other Sri Lankan government reports around this time implied, though never stated directly, that a Chinese-North Korean network supplied the LTTE.[201] Since the government's own primary weapons supplier was also China, it is not surprising that it would have tried to avoid publicly implicating Beijing in this affair.

Sri Lankan officials have also refrained from offering post-hoc analysis on the arms-procurement networks of the LTTE since the group lost the civil war in 2009. The end of the conflict spelled the end of the North Korea–LTTE relationship and the closure of a North Korean arms market in South Asia. While the above evidence makes it clear that the LTTE and North Korea had dealings in the period since 2006, the lack of more detailed information on their former dealings makes it difficult to assess what sort of weaponry was provided and in what timeframe. Shipments of anything other than heavy weaponry would have been permitted by the UN until the passage of Resolution 1874 in 2009.

The Ties that Bind: The Characteristics of Resilient Customers

This chapter has discussed some of Pyongyang's most committed customers, but not all. In 2014, numerous governments active in non-proliferation démarched over a dozen African nations of concern. The grievance of the day was suspected North Korean arms trade. The targets of the démarches are believed to have included at least some resilient customers about which there is little or no verifiable information in open sources. Angola, Sudan and Zimbabwe are likely amongst them. For instance, Angola is frequently spoken of by Western officials as being of serious concern due to its unspecified involvement in North Korean arms sales in Africa. In June 2015, the *Washington Free Beacon* alleged that Angola had been receiving North Korean training, repair services and spare parts for patrol

---

[200] 'Defense Secretary Defends Sri Lankan Policies With A/S Blake', Cable #09COLOMBO1159, 22 December 2009, accessed via Wikileaks on 27 May 2014. For more details on North Korean diversion of Chinese-origin goods, see also *Small Arms Survey 2008: Risk and Resilience* (Cambridge: Cambridge University Press, 2008), p. 121.

[201] See, for example, an article hosted by the Sri Lankan Ministry of Defence website, which states that North Korea ordered weapons from 'another major arms supplier': Shamindra Fernando, 'Tigers North Korean Link Bared?', Sri Lanka Ministry of Defence, 30 December 2010, <http://www.defence.lk/new.asp?fname= 20070305_07#>, accessed 22 October 2015.

boats since 2009.[202] Similarly, while Sudan is known to have previously had military ties to Pyongyang and is a well-known through-route for Iranian arms, few details are available about its recent dealings with North Korea. A small hint materialised in January 2015, when the US Treasury designated Jang Song-chol, a KOMID representative in Russia 'working with individuals in Sudan who are procuring materials from him'.[203]

In short, it is likely that more resilient clients exist than open sources reveal. Nevertheless, the clients discussed at length in this chapter have common traits that seem to illuminate the characteristics of the 'resilient' group as a whole. Most notably, all appear to be aware of the current sanctions regime and simply choose to defy it. All, excepting Burma, involve military ties dating, unbroken, to the Cold War, when North Korea was an ardent supporter of socialist movements and foreign friends battling 'imperialism' and common enemies. It was willing to show its commitment to these friends however it could. Senior officials in many of the countries analysed in this chapter – from Cuba to Uganda to Syria – have reminisced publicly and fondly about Pyongyang's past contributions to their countries' national defence. Indeed, the history of a country's bilateral relationship with North Korea appears to be a consideration present in most of the cases outlined in this chapter. For some it may serve as a reminder of the desire to maintain the friendship, for others it may be taken as an indicator of dependability, and for others still the historical relationship may simply be synonymous with the personal choices of a particular long-reigning leader.

In a few cases, the bilateral military relationship with North Korea also seems to have a political aspect. For Syria and Uganda, for example, such a relationship with North Korea, once exposed, may serve as a symbol of defiance. Officials of both states have declared that in their ties to Pyongyang, they act entirely independently and defy the wishes of other nations.[204]

In addition, many resilient customers in the post-Cold War era are somewhat isolated from the international community, and are in fact under sanctions themselves. Cuba, Syria, Iran and Burma have few possible sources of weapons-related goods and services, and armed groups in the Middle East may feel they need all the military support they

---

[202] Bill Gertz, 'N. Korea Violating UN Sanctions with Angolan Military Aid', *Washington Free Beacon*, 12 June 2015.
[203] US Department of Treasury, 'Treasury Imposes Sanctions against the Government of the Democratic People's Republic of Korea'.
[204] See, for example, *Syrian Arab News Agency*, 'Parliament Speaker: Syria and DPRK on Same Page against Common Adversaries', 19 June 2014; Among, 'Uganda, Tanzania in Trouble with UN over "Arms Deals"' with North Korea'.

can muster. That North Korea asks few questions may be an important consideration for these isolated clients.

Competitive pricing may also be a factor in the calculations of resilient customers, though few credible details are available to support this conclusion other than the preference of some resilient clients for barter trade. Nevertheless, long-running civil conflicts in countries such as the DRC and Syria may make basic, inexpensive and easily resupplied weapons particularly attractive.

Due to these diverse and complex characteristics, this group of customers is bound to be the most difficult to bring into conformity with UN measures. Chapter VI explores the policy tools that can be deployed in support of efforts to curb demand from these resilient customers. It will emphasise that, despite some shared characteristics, outlined above, sanctions implementers must nevertheless tailor their policy response to any single client carefully, accounting for the substantial differences between them. The international political, domestic political and security situations in Iran vary greatly from those in Burma, which in turn vary from those in Uganda, for example. Similarly, the levers available to the international community or to individual sanctions-active countries differ, and must be used in a way that is appropriate to the context in order to be as effective as possible.

Chapter VI will further show that in some cases, especially those where there are few levers available, a resilient customer may only voluntarily abstain from its dealings with North Korea in the event of a broader change in its political or security situation. The job of the sanctions implementer in the interim is, therefore, to: stay vigilant in order to increase international understanding of the specifics of the client's bilateral trade with North Korea; prevent supply from meeting demand where possible; maintain pressure on the customer; and be prepared to adapt approaches should the opportunity arise, as in Burma.

IV. RELUCTANT CUSTOMERS

Another, smaller group of North Korean customers is made up of countries that are less comfortable with their supplier relationship than those clients discussed in the preceding chapter. Like the resilient customers, the members of this group are aware of the legal restrictions on buying arms and related materiel and services from Pyongyang, primarily because the UN and foreign governments often remind them. These countries have similarly opted to maintain contracts with North Korea despite the sanctions. The essential difference between them and their 'resilient' counterparts is that they seem to have arrived at the decision to continue to buy from Pyongyang with a noteworthy degree of reluctance – a characteristic not observed in the case of countries like Uganda and Syria.

This chapter discusses the considerations that have driven Yemen and Ethiopia, two such reluctant customers, to source from Pyongyang. In both cases, bilateral relations with Pyongyang were once very willingly undertaken. Yet their transition out of the Cold War involved a parallel transition away from strong political and military alignment with North Korea. Their decisions to buy from Pyongyang came to be based primarily on assessments of cost and lack of feasible alternative suppliers for the goods and services required. Yemen coveted missiles and related assistance that few if any countries other than North Korea were willing to sell. Ethiopia found that the help it had received from North Korea with arms production decades earlier had made it partially dependent upon its supply. Had these countries had viable alternative suppliers and sufficient resources to purchase from them, it is reasonable to suggest that both would have preferred to take their custom elsewhere.

As will be demonstrated below, their comparative discomfort is compounded by their respective security partnerships with the US. Washington has increasingly enhanced its co-operation with Sana'a (until the recent civil war and regime change) and Addis Ababa in order to combat regional threats. It has also tried to use the attendant influence in both capitals to pressure them to sever military links with Pyongyang.

Ethiopia's and Yemen's bilateral relationships with North Korea have therefore been a source of tension in other corners of their respective foreign policies, compounding their reluctance in dealing with the DPRK. Both have asked the US for assistance in identifying and facilitating alternative sources of supply. These conversations may have made some headway.

Ethiopia

The Ethiopia–North Korea relationship was once characterised by a strong affinity between their leaders. Kim Il-sung remarked that the country had 'obviously achieved the highest level of consolidation of a Marxist party', and saw Ethiopia as one of his most important African allies.[1] Mengistu Haile Mariam, who was president of Ethiopia from 1977 to 1987, forged close links with the Soviet Union, Cuba, East Germany and North Korea.[2] According to the US Defense Intelligence Agency, North Korea and the Soviet Union co-operated with one another to 'defend [Mengistu's] embattled Marxist government'.[3]

North Korea's contribution to Ethiopian defence development involved hundreds of military advisers,[4] who equipped, trained, and supervised Ethiopian militias and special forces, and participated in the war against Somalia (1977–78). By the end of the Cold War, Ethiopia had also received battle tanks, armoured personnel carriers, and artillery and corresponding munitions from Pyongyang. These systems were paraded through Addis Ababa in 1987.[5]

During the Cold War, the North Korean–Ethiopian partnership was motivated by a range of factors. Ideology and geopolitics were no doubt influential. A civil war (1974–91) and a war against Somalia created substantial need for defence equipment, likely meaning that Addis Ababa was prepared to accept a range of weapons from several of its friends. While the Soviet Union was undoubtedly its most important patron, North Korea was a key supporting actor.

---

[1] Charles K Armstrong, *Tyranny of the Weak: North Korea and the World, 1950–1992* (Ithaca, NY: Cornell University Press, 2013), p. 195.

[2] Mengistu initially approached the US for military and political support in the mid-1970s. When his requests were denied, he promptly turned to Moscow, which became an extremely generous patron.

[3] US Defense Intelligence Agency, 'North Korea: The Foundations for Military Strength', October 1991, available at <https://www.fas.org/irp/dia/product/knfms/knfms_toc.html>, accessed 20 October 2015. See chap. 3 on 'Foreign Policy Goals'.

[4] Armstrong, *Tyranny of the Weak*, p. 196.

[5] Joost Oliemans and Stijn Mitzer, 'North Korea and Ethiopia, Brothers in Arms', *NK News*, 4 September 2014, <http://www.nknews.org/2014/09/north-korean-military-support-for-ethiopia/>, accessed 20 October 2015.

Ethiopia also coveted an indigenous weapons-manufacturing capability. In the 1980s, North Korea was called in to build two weapons factories in the country: one in Ambo and one at Debre Zeyit. These were set up to manufacture rifles and machine guns, light weapons and an assortment of munitions. The Ethiopian Chief of the Defense Staff Samora Yunis more recently explained that at the time that these facilities were built, it was believed they would eventually allow Ethiopia to reduce its dependence upon foreign suppliers.[6] Pyongyang was willing to help Ethiopia realise this goal at low cost, as it was in other states such as Syria, Iran and the Democratic Republic of the Congo (DRC). However, Ethiopia laid the ground poorly for independent production: it did not develop the indigenous scientific and technological base that would allow it to single-handedly maintain and upgrade its facilities in the future (as will be explained in more detail below).

Ethiopia's considerations when purchasing arms and related materiel and services from North Korea in the sanctions era are different. Addis Ababa has distanced itself from an overt Marxist-Leninist alignment and it no longer has an affinity for ideological suppliers. While senior figures in the Ethiopian military hierarchy are sometimes called 'pro-China',[7] the country also regularly co-operates on regional security issues (especially on Somalia) with the US and its allies. Washington helped establish the Ethiopian Defense Command and Staff College, for instance.[8]

While it still has a need for new defence equipment, one of its main considerations now seems to be extending the service lives of some of its existing weaponry. Given the Soviet design heritage of the systems that Ethiopia's military employs, and the government's continuing resource constraints, it is not surprising that North Korea has been asked to help keep those weapons operable. This assistance is believed to have continued even after the arms embargo against Pyongyang was established by the Security Council. According to a leaked US diplomatic cable, 'shortly after UNSCR 1718 banned arms transfers from DPRK in late 2006, the [government of Ethiopia] informed [the US] Embassy of an

---

[6] 'Defense Officials Impose Last-Minute Impediments on Arms Inquiry on North Korea', Cable #08ADDISABABA87, 14 January 2008, accessed via Wikileaks on 27 May 2014.
[7] 'Defense Officials Request More Military Aid', Cable #08ADDISABABA89, 14 January 2008, accessed via Wikileaks on 27 May 2014.
[8] *Ibid.* See also Bernard F Griffard and John F Troxell, 'The Ethiopian Defense Command and Staff College Initiative', Center for Strategic Leadership, US Army War College, Issue Paper 13–09, August 2009, <http://www.dtic.mil/dtic/tr/fulltext/u2/a509094.pdf>, accessed 23 October 2015.

imminent delivery of tank parts and munitions components'.[9] Ethiopian officials told their US counterparts that 'they needed the equipment to sustain their Soviet-era military'.[10] The tank parts were probably for Ethiopia's ageing T-55 tanks, which it has only recently begun to supplement with newer 1970s-designed T-72 models from Yemen and Ukraine.[11] North Korea is unlikely to be called upon by Ethiopia to assist in the repair or servicing of the latter variety, given its comparative lack of familiarity with the newer system. Furthermore, after-sale service contracts have already been awarded to Ukraine. This case is a prime example of the natural erosion of parts of North Korea's conventional defence-export market over time, as discussed further in Chapter VI.

A second consideration for the Ethiopians has been price. According to Ethiopian State Minister of Defense Sultan Mohammed and Prime Minister Meles Zenawi, the aforementioned consignment was worth $3 million and also included lubricants and chemicals for ammunition production.[12] Minister Sultan explained that Ethiopia had initially explored the possibility of purchasing lubricants from China, with which the country has strong and growing military-to-military relations. Upon exploration, North Korean lubricants – even though they contained greater impurities – were found to be sometimes 50 per cent cheaper than those on offer from Beijing. Prime Minister Meles added that Indian and Russian prices for these goods were also much higher than North Korea's, and due to corruption in Russia 'deliveries were either slow or never forthcoming without a good stiff bribe'.[13] These considerations reportedly applied to contracts for some weapons systems and spare parts as well. According to the *New York Times*,

---

[9] 'Ethiopia: Scenesetter for Secretary Rice's December 5 Visit', Cable #07ADDISABABA3430, 30 November 2007, accessed via Wikileaks on 27 May 2014.
[10] Michael R Gordon and Mark Mazzetti, 'North Koreans Arm Ethiopians as US Assents', *New York Times*, 8 April 2007.
[11] The T-55 was designed and first entered service in the 1940s, in contrast to the T-72 main battle tank, which entered service in the 1970s. It is believed that Ethiopia bought an initial consignment of second-hand T-72s from Yemen in 2003, and signed a large contract with Ukraine's state-controlled arms exporter for 200 units with new engines and armour, and upgraded guided weapons in 2011. The Ukrainian firm was also awarded the repair and servicing contracts. See Defence Web, 'Ethiopian Military Receiving T-72s', 1 November 2013, <http://www.defenceweb.co.za/index.php?option=com_content&view=article&id=32486:ethiopian-military-receiving-t-72s&catid=50:Land&Itemid=105>, accessed 23 October 2015.
[12] 'Finding Alternatives to DPRK Trade and Stopping Counterfeiting and Money Laundering', Cable #07ADDISABABA1743, 5 June 2007, accessed via Wikileaks on 27 May 2014; 'Ethiopia: Demarche to Ethiopia Over North Korean Imports', Cable #07ADDISABABA1096, 12 April 2007, accessed via Wikileaks on 27 May 2014.
[13] 'Ethiopia: Demarche to Ethiopia Over North Korean Imports', Cable #07ADDISABABA1096.

which broke the news of the Ethiopian contract after speaking with senior US officials, 'the Ethiopians bought the [weapons] equipment at a bargain price'. Another official quoted said: 'the Ethiopians know they can get the best price in Pyongyang'.[14]

Most of the North Korean consignment never reached Ethiopia, however. Careless use of packaging when shipping the goods led to it catching fire as the vessel transporting it neared Djibouti. As the cargo never made it to its final destination, and to its illegal military end use, the Ethiopians claimed it could therefore not constitute a sanctions violation.[15] Despite this disastrous experience, Addis Ababa continued to buy from Pyongyang. In 2008, it purchased fuel and oxidisers for SA-2 Guideline air-defence missiles from North Korea – another apparent sanctions violation. When démarched by the US, the Ethiopian government requested information on alternative, affordable suppliers.[16]

A final motivation for Ethiopia's recent, possibly sanctions-busting contracts with North Korea is dependence. In the 1980s, in the midst of the country's civil war, Ethiopia's defence leadership set out to develop a domestic weapons-manufacturing capability, particularly in small arms and light weapons. The hope was that domestic arms factories would eventually allow Ethiopia to make its own arms and ammunitions without foreign help. Yet, rather than investing in the creation of an indigenous research-and-development complex – with the requisite scientific and technical expertise that would enable Ethiopia to generate, maintain and in future upgrade this capability independently – the country initially opted, as many did, to outsource. Contracting for weapons-production technology, goods and services from those that already knew how to produce the arms desired would allow Ethiopia to generate the capability more quickly and less expensively. Learning to design and produce one's own weapons is a resource-intensive affair.

Seeking to cut corners on the road to a domestic weapons-production capability, Ethiopia approached North Korea. As will be discussed in greater detail below, Pyongyang assisted with the construction of two arms factories near Ambo and Debre Zeyit in the late 1980s. During this process, Korean technicians would have provided the Ethiopian military with the designs for desired production lines, the machinery and parts to create them, and the training and expertise needed to operate them. However, the age of the North Korean-provided production lines meant that over time, other countries that may have used similar weapon-manufacturing technology moved to more modern designs and equipment. Pyongyang has largely

---

[14] Gordon and Mazzetti, 'North Koreans Arm Ethiopians as US Assents'.
[15] 'Defense Officials Request More Military Aid', Cable #08ADDISABABA89.
[16] 'North Korea: Ethiopia Requests Alternate Supplier Information', Cable #08ADDISABABA952, 7 April 2008, accessed via Wikileaks on 27 May 2014.

not. Ethiopia has therefore needed periodically to buy additional machines and spare parts from Pyongyang to keep its vintage 1980s North Korean-supplied production lines in working order. Similarly, because Ethiopia lacks a sufficient scientific and technological base to upgrade production lines independently to produce newer variants of existing weapons systems, it has had to call in North Korean technicians – and more recently, technicians from Ukraine and China – for those upgrades as well. Ironically, despite the belief that domestic arms factories would allow Ethiopia to make its own arms and ammunitions without foreign help, the opposite has transpired.

As a consequence of these dynamics of dependency, there is credible evidence to suggest that Pyongyang's involvement in arms production in Ethiopia has extended into the sanctions era. However, information regarding the period since the passage of UN Security Council Resolution 1874 (2009) – which forbade North Korean provision of services related to small arms and light weapons – is in shorter supply.

Today, the Ambo and Debre Zeyit factory complexes believed to benefit from North Korean input are known as the Homicho Ammunition Industry[17] and Gafat Armament Industry,[18] respectively. Both are managed by the parastatal Metals and Engineering Corporation (METEC). The Homicho Ammunition Industry was established in 1987 and subsumed under METEC in 2010. Based near Ambo, its production lines include: small, medium and heavy ammunition; tank shells, mortar bombs and grenades; and 120-mm rockets. According to leaked cables, Pyongyang continued to help manufacture rocket-propelled grenades and truck-mounted multiple rocket launchers until at least late 2007.[19]

Around the same time, Ethiopian government officials also began to complain quietly about their dependence on North Korean spare parts and machinery for the factory. As noted above, Homicho's production lines require specific parts and machines for which there are apparently few cost-effective available sources outside of Pyongyang.[20] Costs already sunk into Homicho's existing North Korean-designed and equipped

---

[17]   Also known as the Homicho Ammunition Engineering Industry.
[18]   Also known as the Gafat Armament Engineering Industry.
[19]   'Prime Minister Meles on North Korean Arms Relationship', 13 December 2007, Cable #07ADDISABABA3528, accessed via Wikileaks on 27 May 2014.
[20]   It should be noted that North Korea is not Ethiopia's only source of foreign assistance for the Homicho plant. Homicho's websites indicate that it also has suppliers in India, China, the Czech Republic, Italy and Germany, though what they supply is not specified. METEC, 'Homicho Ammunition Engineering Industry – Fact Sheet', updated 2015, <http://www.metec.gov.et/index.php/en/metec-industries/homicho-ammunition-industry>, accessed 10 June 2014.

production lines may also have increased Ethiopian reluctance to pay for entirely new lines with non-North Korean technology.

Homicho's centrality to the Ethiopia–North Korea relationship since 2006 has made it a subject of scrutiny. Until at least 2009, and probably also thereafter, the US embassy in Addis Ababa repeatedly exerted pressure on senior Ethiopian officials to sever contracts with North Korea, much like the US had previously done with the governments of Yemen, as will be discussed below, and Libya.[21] In November 2008, it appeared that this pressure might finally yield greater co-operation from the Ethiopian Ministry of Defense, which agreed to let the US ambassador and a small team into Homicho. Only a few days before the scheduled visit, Ethiopia's defence minister resigned and US access was abruptly suspended. Officials told the embassy that access would be reconsidered only if an order was given by the president or if 'Ethiopia were to get technology or financial assistance' from the visit.[22] It is believed that access by external inspectors was successfully facilitated thereafter.

In 2014, the UN Panel of Experts on North Korea identified a possible continuing link between North Korea and the Homicho Ammunition Industry. Homicho's official company profile listed the Korea Mineral Trading General Corporation as one of its primary suppliers. This entity does not appear in South Korean company registries.[23] Given the factory's history and its alleged dependence upon North Korean machinery and supplies, it is therefore reasonable to conclude that the company is North Korean. Supporting such a conclusion, METEC swiftly removed reference to the corporation from the Homicho website following the publication of the UN Panel's report (though it forgot to sanitise the corresponding PDF brochure).[24]

---

[21] It is possible that Libya had some dealings with North Korea after the US issued demands that it cease them in the early 2000s. In 2011, at the start of the Libya crisis, North Korea allegedly had hundreds of nationals working in the country – far more than might ordinarily be working in the embassy, media organisations or hospitals. See *NPR*, 'North Korea Doesn't Evacuate its People from Libya', 15 June 2011, <http://www.npr.org/2011/06/15/137192600/north-korea-doesnt-evacuate-its-people-from-libya>, accessed 23 October 2015. Multiple reports at the time also spoke of North Korean-origin weapons being captured by rebel forces in Libya, though this author suspects most, if not all, of them were from Cold War-era contracts. See, for example, *Daily NK*, 'North Korean Weapons Found in Libya', 29 March 2011, <http://www.dailynk.com/english/read.php?num=7511&catald=nk03100>, accessed 23 October 2015.

[22] 'Defense Officials Impose Last-Minute Impediments on Arms Inquiry on North Korea', Cable #08ADDISABABA87.

[23] 'Report of the Panel of Experts Established Pursuant to Resolution 1874 (2009)', S/2014/147, pp. 35–36.

[24] METEC, 'Homicho Ammunition Engineering Industry – A Fact Sheet, Metals and Engineering Corporation', <http://www.metec.gov.et/images/PDF/Homicho%

The second weapons complex to have benefited from North Korean assistance is Gafat Armament Industry, located near Debre Zeyit. Though Gafat's original purpose was to manufacture AK-47s and light machine guns, it now also produces 40-mm grenade launchers, vehicle-mounted automatic weapons and heavy artillery. In addition, it carries out armament maintenance for the Ethiopian National Defense Force. A glance at marketing material for Gafat (see Appendix B) highlights the overlap between the weapons systems that North Korean industry produces and those that Gafat now manufactures. Many of the systems depicted in Appendix B are those that North Korea is known to export. Of course, North Korea originally received or reverse engineered many of these same systems from the Soviet Union or China, and therefore the Gafat designs bear a resemblance to weapons produced by those countries as well. Examples include a twin-barrelled anti-aircraft gun (originally a Soviet design) and a twelve-barrel multiple rocket launcher (originally a Chinese design). Of special note is a tear-gas gun shown in the top right corner of the Gafat brochure. A gun of strikingly similar design was photographed in the hands of North Korea's people's security minister during a 2013 visit to Uganda, which is believed to have recently bought these weapons from Pyongyang.[25] While not conclusive evidence, many of the weapons featured in Gafat's marketing material are also produced by North Korea's defence-industrial complex.

An industrial-engineering study of the Gafat complex's inefficiencies published by Addis Ababa University gives more concrete evidence of North Korean involvement in the site's operations after 2006. It refers specifically to a contract with the Korea Ryong Bong General Corporation, apparently active at the time of the publication's release in 2007, to retool production lines for the AK-47 and a variant of the AK-74.[26] Korea Ryong Bong General Corporation appears to be an alternate romanisation of the Korea Ryonbong General Corporation, a North Korean entity designated

---

20Ammunition%20Engineering%20Industry.pdf>, accessed 23 October 2015. A search using Wayback Machine, an internet tool for retrieving archived versions of web pages, reveals that reference to the Korean entity was removed following the publication of the UN Panel's report.

[25] For the photograph discussed, see Chad O'Carroll, 'Exclusive: North Korean Minister Inspects Ugandan Police Force', *NK News*, 13 June 2013, <http://www.nknews.org/2013/06/exclusive-north-korean-minister-inspects-ugandan-police-force/>, accessed 23 October 2015. For reports of the sale of tear-gas guns to Uganda, see Alex Masereka, 'M7 Nominated for North Korea Top Award', *Red Pepper Uganda*, 17 October 2014, <http://www.redpepper.co.ug/m7-nominated-for-north-korea-top-award/>, accessed 23 October 2015.

[26] Tewodros Rufael, 'Design of Enterprise Resource Planning: Framework and its Implementation', supervised by Subhash Chandra at the School of Graduate Studies of Addis Ababa University, November 2007, pp. 8–9.

by the UN Sanctions Committee pursuant to Resolution 1718 for its repeated involvement in illegal arms sales.[27]

Records of conversations between the Ethiopian Chief of the Defense Staff, General Samora Yunis, and US officials in 2008 refer to what seems to be the same contract. During that conversation, Samora insisted that 'North Koreans have now finished their work and are leaving' Gafat. Despite his adamance, it is difficult to be confident in the claim. Records of numerous conversations highlight the fact that the general's statements regarding the North Korean presence at Ethiopian weapons factories were frequently contradictory. They fluctuated between 'we will continue to source from North Korea', 'we haven't sourced from North Korea in the past year', 'the North Koreans have left' and 'some of the North Koreans may still be around'. It is therefore possible that Pyongyang's involvement in Gafat continued beyond 2008, potentially in breach of the sanctions that were widened under UN Security Council Resolution 1874 (2009).[28]

Indeed, even if bilateral arms co-operation has now ended, modest but growing evidence suggests that sanctions may at some stage have been breached by the Ethiopian government and/or METEC since 2009. The reference to Korea Mineral Trading General Corporation on the Homicho website raises concerns that Ethiopia involved in North Korea in its arms-manufacturing processes until at least 2014, in violation of Resolution 1874. Indeed, Homicho's subsequent, rapid sanitisation of its publicised suppliers list compounds suspicion that interaction between METEC and Pyongyang was illicit and may be continuing. Moreover, North Koreans were acknowledged by Ethiopian officials to still be on the ground at the Gafat site as part of a contract with the Korea Ryong Bong General Corporation only months before Resolution 1874 was adopted, highlighting the possibility that they may have been in breach of the resolution in the immediate wake of its introduction, if not for longer.

US outreach to Ethiopia about its military relationship with North Korea during the sanctions era has ensured that Addis Ababa is fully aware of the risks and consequences of dealing with Pyongyang. However, Ethiopia continues to face security threats that necessitate the prioritisation of equipment for the armed forces and the domestic military industrial complex. It also faces constraints in meeting its equipment requirements: the technology involved in some of its weapon production lines is outdated and of North Korean heritage. Price is also a consistent

---

[27] UN Security Council, 'The List Established and Maintained by the 1718 (2006) Committee', <http://www.un.org/sc/committees/1718/pdf/1718.pdf>, accessed 23 October 2015.
[28] 'Defense Officials Impose Last-Minute Impediments on Arms Inquiry on North Korea', Cable #08ADDISABABA87.

and major consideration in relation to defence projects. Ethiopia's aforementioned contract with North Korea for lubricants with military application demonstrates that it prefers an inferior but cheaper product over a superior but more expensive one.

These factors appear to make Ethiopia something of a reluctant customer. Its officials have been forced to explain, repeatedly and awkwardly, these dealings with Pyongyang. For example, General Yunis told US officials in 2008 that North Korean help at weapons complexes is needed if Ethiopia is to uphold its peacekeeping obligations.[29] Such unsatisfactory explanations have created friction with Ethiopia's other foreign partners, especially the US.

As will be argued in Chapter VI, however, reluctant clients are easier to prise away from North Korean arms and related materiel and services than their resilient counterparts. Ethiopian requests for assistance from the US are a positive indication that Addis Ababa may be willing to move away from North Korea. According to one American official: 'The Ethiopians came to us and said, "Look, we know we need to transition to different [suppliers], but we just can't do that overnight." ... They seem to have the readiness to do the right thing'.[30]

Yemen

Yemen has had warm relations with North Korea since before its unification in 1990.[31] North Korea appears to have entered the market alongside the Soviet Union and Cuba, which were both lending military support to the socialist-oriented People's Democratic Republic of Yemen (also referred to as South Yemen), signing a diplomatic protocol with South Yemen in 1968 as the first shipments of Soviet weapons were arriving there.[32] In the

---

[29] *Ibid.* At the time of Samora's statement in January 2008, Ethiopia was the 14th largest troop-contributing nation to UN missions, with approximately 1,800 deployed. That figure has risen substantially. As of August 2015, the country is now ranked fourth in terms of its contributions, with 7,800 personnel deployed with UN operations in Liberia, Côte d'Ivoire, South Sudan, and the Darfur and Abyei missions in Sudan. Ethiopia also sends its forces to participate in the African Union mission in Somalia. UN Department of Peacekeeping Operations, 'Troop and Police Contributors', <http://www.un.org/en/peacekeeping/resources/statistics/contributors.shtml> , accessed 23 October 2015.

[30] Gordon and Mazzetti, 'North Koreans Arm Ethiopians as US Assents'.

[31] 'KOMID Demarche Delivered', Cable #09SANAA268, 11 February 2009, accessed via Wikileaks on 27 May 2014.

[32] See Daniel Wertz et al., 'DPRK Diplomatic Relations', National Committee on North Korea, last updated 25 March 2014, <http://www.ncnk.org/resources/briefing-papers/all-briefing-papers/dprk-diplomatic-relations>, accessed 23 October 2015. Pyongyang also established a diplomatic representation in North

1970s, Pyongyang helped construct an arms factory at Abyan, which produced small-calibre arms and ammunition,[33] and may have sent military advisers and instructors to the country.

Unified Yemen maintained the relationship, requesting ballistic missiles, naval assistance, continued help with ammunition and small-arms production, and provision of MANPADS. Following a regional trend, Yemen contracted to North Korea for short-range ballistic-missile technology, which was delivered to Sana'a in 1999–2000. Washington imposed unilateral sanctions against North Korea as a consequence of these transactions.[34] A few years later, in December 2002, the Spanish Navy, acting on US intelligence, seized the North Korean vessel *So San*, which was bound for Yemen and whose cargo contained fifteen North Korean-made Scud-B missiles hidden beneath sacks of cement. As ballistic-missile trade of this kind was not illegal at the time, Yemen lodged a formal protest. Its foreign minister insisted that 'the shipment is part of contracts signed some time ago', though the concealment of the cargo beneath cement suggested that it was nevertheless something both supplier and recipient wished to be kept secret.[35] The ship was ultimately released, but the incident was not without consequence. Japan suspended aid to Yemen, and Washington threatened to do the same unless Yemen issued assurances that missile trade with North Korea would swiftly cease.

US diplomats at the time pondered the motivation for Yemen's missile procurement. They noted that the country no longer had any ideological affinity with the DPRK, but liked to buy cheaply. As a result, 'the question of why a country like Yemen – among the world's 25 poorest, with annual per capita income around $400 – would buy a useless weapon system like the SCUD ... is often posed'.[36] Yemeni officials insisted that

---

Yemen in the mid-1970s as part of its campaign to garner greater diplomatic support internationally than its South Korean foe. There has been some unsubstantiated suggestions that DPRK military advisers were also stationed in North Yemen, though it is important to remember that South and North Yemen were not overtly hostile to one another in the way that East and West Germany, or indeed North and South Korea, were. See Guy Hicks, 'North Korea: Exporting Arms and Terror', Heritage Foundation, Asian Backgrounder No. 11, 12 April 1984, <http://www.heritage.org/research/reports/1984/04/north-korea-exporting-arms-and-terror>, accessed 23 October 2015; Derek B Miller, 'Demand, Stockpiles, and Social Controls: Small Arms in Yemen', Small Arms Survey Occasional Paper No. 9, May 2003, p. 10.

[33] 'Yemeni Military Leaders Brief Ambassador on DPRK Contacts', Cable #03SANAA1990, 12 August 2003, accessed via Wikileaks on 15 May 2014.

[34] *BBC News*, 'Legal Maze Over Scud Seizure', 11 December 2002.

[35] *BBC News*, 'Yemen Protests Over Scud Seizure', 11 December 2002.

[36] 'Scenesetter for Under Secretary Bolton's Visit to Yemen', Cable #03SANAA1373, 16 June 2003, accessed via Wikileaks on 15 May 2014.

cost was indeed the driving factor. The atomic-energy adviser to the Yemeni president at the time told then-US Under Secretary of State for Arms Control John Bolton that 'Yemen-DPRK cooperation is purely a question of cost ... The MOD would have no problem working with the U.S. if convinced the U.S. offered affordable, realistic alternatives'.[37] It is difficult to say whether the Yemeni explanation was genuine, given the frequently contradictory comments on the Yemen–North Korea relationship recorded in US diplomatic cables. Yet it is possible that Pyongyang offered attractive financing terms, a factor that was decisive in an agreement with North Korea for a naval facility that was reached around the same time, which will be explained in greater detail below.

Following the *So San* incident, Yemen privately forswore new missile co-operation with North Korea or any other country, in order to avoid the application of penalties under US laws restricting missile trade.[38] However, it noted that the consignment of Scud-Bs that it had received in December 2002 was 'defective'. North Korea would not offer a refund for the missiles, but instead agreed to provide repair services. Yemeni officials explained to their US counterparts that North Korean repair workers would therefore continue to visit Yemen until the defective Scuds were operational.[39] The US initially accepted this explanation and the pledged imminent cessation of missile procurement, but continued to monitor interaction. As a result, it detected payments made in January 2003 by the Yemen Commercial Bank to the Yemen-based representatives of the Tosong Technology Trading Corporation – another name for the former third bureau of the designated entity Korea Mining Development Trading Corporation (KOMID), North Korea's primary overseas arms dealer. These were believed to be related to a string of missile-related contracts.[40] Because those transactions involved new payments, it is implausible that they merely included the repair services that North Korea was said to have 'owed' Yemen after initially shipping defective weapons. Addressing these suspicions, Yemen's foreign minister at the time, Abu Bakr Al-Qirbi, explained that the country had also placed orders with North Korea for spare parts for artillery and radar systems, but reiterated that these

---

[37] *Ibid.*
[38] 'Continuing Cooperation between North Korea's KOMID and Yemen', Cable #09STATE50258, 15 May 2009, accessed via Wikileaks on 27 May 2014.
[39] 'Demarche to Yemeni FM Qirbi on DPRK Military Contacts', Cable #03SANAA2769, 23 November 2003, accessed via Wikileaks on 15 May 2014.
[40] 'E.O. 13382 Entities – Examples of Proliferation', Cable #06STATE152914, 14 September 2006, accessed via Wikileaks on 27 May 2014.

contracts would be the last with Pyongyang.[41] The revelation about the supply of spare parts for other conventional weapons systems suggests that the need to inexpensively extend the life of certain military platforms was another consideration for Yemen at the time.

Shortly thereafter, in a May 2003 conversation with officials from the US embassy in Sana'a, then-Defense Minister Abdullah Ali Aliwa acknowledged that Yemen had signed a contract with North Korea to have the latter build a naval facility near the port of Hodeidah. In response, the US urged the Romanians to make the Yemeni navy a competitively priced offer for the same in order to undercut the North Koreans.[42] Doing so proved difficult, as North Korea had offered highly attractive financing terms, allowing Yemen to repay the total cost over more than ten years.[43] Instead, the then Yemeni Chief of the General Staff Mohammed Al-Qasimi suggested that the US, Japan and its own Gulf neighbours offer financing assistance to permit Yemen to facilitate a contract with another supplier.[44] It appears that the facility described was never built by North Korea in the end,[45] making it possible that this request was somehow fulfilled.

When then-US Under Secretary of State John Bolton visited Yemen the following month, in June 2003, Yemeni President Ali Abdullah Saleh informed him that a team of North Koreans were present at the same small-arms factory that Pyongyang had helped to build in the 1970s, 'were making munitions for Kalashnikovs', and had in fact been there for over a year.[46]

North Korea may still have been selling Yemen MANPADS around this time as well. The US was working with the government in Sana'a to arrange a programme to buy back 'loose' MANPADS at a pre-agreed price. However, there was concern that dishonest Yemeni officials would see this as an opportunity to buy more weapons at a discount from North Korea, claim them to be recovered loose weapons, and sell them at a profit to the US. The conversation between US embassy and Yemeni officials, as recorded,

---

[41] 'Meeting with Yemen FM Qirbi: Discussion on Scuds, Diplomatic Pouch, USAID, CT, and Military Cooperation', Cable #03SANAA154, 20 January 2003, accessed via Wikileaks on 27 May 2014.
[42] 'Scenesetter for Under Secretary Bolton's Visit to Yemen', Cable #03SANAA1373.
[43] 'Yemeni Military Leaders Brief Ambassador on DPRK Contacts', Cable #03SANAA1990, 12 August 2003, accessed via Wikileaks on 27 May 2014.
[44] *Ibid.*
[45] Based on numerous non-attributable interviews with officials and experts familiar with military affairs in Yemen.
[46] 'U/S Bolton's Visit to Yemen: President Saleh on the DPRK', Cable #03SANAA1454_a, 24 June 2003, accessed via Wikileaks on 15 May 2014.

implies a belief that trade between North Korea and Yemen in MANPADS was occurring.[47]

Yemen's pledge to forswear North Korean assistance was seriously called into doubt again some years later, in 2009. That year, the director of the Americas office in the Yemeni Foreign Ministry refused to discuss 'sensitive' US allegations that Yemen's military had signed new contracts with North Korea for spare parts and repair services for Scud missiles. The wording of leaked diplomatic cables detailing these allegations suggests there may have been a lull in discernible military co-operation between North Korea and Yemen in the preceding years. Missile-focused projects are believed to have resumed in May 2008, despite the clear prohibition of such co-operation under UN Security Council Resolution 1718 (2006). Around that time, a Yemeni delegation visited North Korea to meet with KOMID. In February and March 2009, three KOMID delegations travelled in the opposite direction. Members of these delegations were known to have previously assisted with missile repair work in Yemen, and US diplomats reasonably suspected that their travel to Yemen on this occasion was for similar purposes.[48] That April, Washington confronted Sana'a with intelligence pointing to KOMID efforts to procure engines for MAZ-543 vehicles usable as transporter-erector-launchers for Scud missiles, as well as Scud ground-support equipment. KOMID was formally designated by the UN Security Council Sanctions Committee the same month.[49]

In addition to ballistic missiles, a Yemeni military source suggested North Korea also provided weapons-related services for 'air defence missiles' and anti-ship missiles, though timeframes were unclear and these assertions cannot be corroborated.[50] It is also unclear as to which anti-ship missiles these are in reference to, though one possibility is the North Korean indigenous version of the Chinese CSS-C-3 Seersucker coastal-defence cruise missile.

Documentation detailing the results of repeated US démarches and political pressure is unfortunately unavailable. Conversations with government and military sources, including Yemeni sources, however,

---

[47] See 'President Saleh to A/S Bloomfield: No New MANPADS', Cable #04SANAA2346, 2 September 2004, accessed via Wikileaks on 15 May 2014. See also 'Scenesetter for Visit of A/S Bloomfield to Yemen', Cable #04SANAA2055, 24 August 2004, accessed via Wikileaks on 15 May 2014.
[48] 'Continuing Cooperation between North Korea's KOMID and Yemen', Cable #09STATE50258.
[49] UN, 'Security Council Committee Determines Items, Designates Entities Subject to Measures Imposed in Resolution 1718 (2006)', press release, 24 April 2009, <http://www.un.org/press/en/2009/sc9642.doc.htm>, accessed 23 October 2015.
[50] Author conversations with Interviewees F and G, conducted by e-mail in July and August 2014.

indicate the relationship was likely wound down in about 2010.[51] These sources confirmed that the military-controlled, North Korean-constructed arms factory in Abyan governorate had been mothballed and subsequently destroyed. Its destruction may have been unplanned, however. Media reports cite a deadly Al-Qa'ida-organised explosion at a munitions factory near Ja'ar (in Abyan) in 2011, which demolished that facility. When operational, the facility had produced reconditioned AK-47 rifles and corresponding rounds, a description that fits that of the North Korean-built plant.[52]

This history suggests that Yemen's military relationship with North Korea was peppered with hesitation. Evidently, any pull towards Pyongyang existed partly as a result of the pricing of its goods and services (especially spare parts), offers of attractive repayment terms, and willingness to provide Sana'a with ballistic-missile technology that others would be reticent to offer. Some level of dependence on North Korea to service previously bought Scud missiles may also have been influential. Sana'a has affirmed that these factors outweigh the low quality of the goods and services in Pyongyang's catalogue. Importantly, Washington has had some success in wooing Sana'a away from North Korea in the past, at least temporarily.

However, at the time of writing Yemen is in the midst of a new civil war, with Houthi insurgents supported by Iran fighting for political and territorial control against Saudi Arabia-backed Sunni groups. The situation could yet unfold in a way that results in fresh market opportunities for North Korea – whether that is because of urgent need for new weaponry, Iranian endorsement of the provision of weaponry to the Houthis by others, a more definitive change in governance, or indeed a wider fracturing of the country. The current situation in Yemen is an important reminder of the fact that while broader changes to a country's political and security situation can aid sanctions implementation, as in Burma, it can also undo its progress.

At Arm's Length

Neither Ethiopia nor Yemen is ignorant of the illegality of continuing to buy weapons and related goods and services from North Korea. However, since the advent of sanctions, both have selectively chosen to disobey these rules.

---

[51] Author conversations with Interviewees F and G, conducted by e-mail in July and August 2014. This view was echoed by Interviewees H and I during e-mail exchanges with the author in July 2014.

[52] Michael Horton, 'Al-Qaeda in the Arabian Peninsula: Challenges and Opportunities in Revolutionary Yemen', *Terrorism Monitor* (Vol. 9, No. 16, April 2011).

This choice comes not from politics or ideology, but is based upon affordable prices, ageing weaponry and lack of alternative supply. In some cases, such as Ethiopia's arms factories and Yemen's Scud arsenal, lack of alternatives has created a dependence that is difficult to overcome.

Importantly, these customers have recently complained about their respective supplier arrangements and have not sought to defend them in public. Ethiopia lamented its reliance on North Korean machines, spare parts and some services crucial for the operation of its arms factories. It has continually expressed a desire to retool them and diversify suppliers, but has reportedly encountered difficulties mustering the funds to accomplish this goal. Yemen's government expressed dismay at the quality of the goods and services it received from Pyongyang, not to mention the carelessness with which they were packaged and transported.

Adding to their apparent desire to buy elsewhere are their respective security partnerships with the US. Military contracts with North Korea create notable friction in those relationships, and Washington has repeatedly emphasised that continued defiance of UN sanctions will erode its patience and generosity. The result is that, to an extent, Yemen and Ethiopia have had to weigh tactical relations with North Korea against strategic relations with the US. Drivers and constraints in the procurement decisions of reluctant customers such as these may make it easier to prise them away from North Korea – a policy opportunity that will be explored further in Chapter VI.

V. AD HOC CUSTOMERS

For as long as North Korea has exported weapons and military services, it has earned revenue from sporadic or one-off customers. During the Cold War, numerous state and non-state buyers showed fleeting interest. Peru purchased 100,000 AK-47s, as the price offered was allegedly 80 per cent lower than the closest offer.[1] In 1982, after hosting the young Kim Jong-il for English-language training, the Labour government in Malta secretly signed two back-to-back deals with Pyongyang that stipulated that the latter would 'free of charge, provide weapons and ammunitions'.[2]

Between 1990 and 2005, other countries showed similar tendencies towards sporadic purchasing. Cambodia bought what appeared to be a single ammunition consignment in 1996.[3] Vietnam bought 100 man-portable air-defence systems.[4] Michael Ranger, a British arms dealer who marketed Pyongyang's wares before being caught by UK authorities

---

[1] US Defense Intelligence Agency, 'North Korea: The Foundations for Military Strength', October 1991, available at <https://www.fas.org/irp/dia/product/knfms/knfms_toc.html>, accessed 20 October 2015. See chap. 3 on 'Foreign Policy Goals'.
[2] In exchange, the Maltese government had to provide one-way tickets for the North Korean instructors, who were sent to train their Maltese counterparts in the use of the gifted weapons. In addition, Malta covered their 'subsistence expenditure during the flight and expenses for lodging, meals, medical treatment, transport means (including the driver) and salaries during their stay in Malta, and training equipment needed in the education of the Maltese military personnel'. See *Malta Independent*, '1982 Labour Government "Secret" Agreement with North Korea', 7 February 2010, <http://www.independent.com.mt/articles/2010-02-07/news/1982-labour-government-secret-agreement-with-north-korea-times-change-alex-sceberras-trigona-270034/>, accessed 23 October 2015.
[3] 'Blue Lantern Check on Denied License Application 050128842', Cable #09STATE81473_a, 5 August 2009, accessed via Wikileaks on 27 May 2014.
[4] Michael Ashkenazi and Jan Grebe, 'Chapter 3: MANPAD Transfers' in Michael Ashkenazi et al., 'MANPADS: A Terrorist Threat to Civil Aviation?', Bonn International Center for Conversion, Brief No. 47, February 2013, p. 48, <https://www.bicc.de/publications/publicationpage/publication/manpads-a-terrorist-threat-to-civilian-aviation-382/>, accessed 23 October 2015.

in 2011, reached advanced stages of negotiations for the sale of weapons to Azerbaijan and was pursuing a deal with Kazakhstan as well.[5]

Ballistic missiles were also a hot-ticket item that won Pyongyang a handful of contracts it may not otherwise have secured. The United Arab Emirates (UAE) and North Korea concluded two agreements for ballistic missiles. The first was in 1988, which included the sale of between eighteen and twenty-four Scud-B missiles,[6] artillery, multiple rocket launchers and related munitions.[7] Transfers of this materiel are believed to have taken place into the early 1990s. Abu Dhabi was apparently dissatisfied with the quality of the Scud-Bs it received, and quickly consigned them to storage. They were allegedly never made operational.[8] Perhaps to replace or augment the original consignment, the UAE and North Korea negotiated a second shipment, this time of longer-range Scud-C missiles, which was delivered to the UAE in 1999.[9] The fact that the UAE has twice turned to Pyongyang suggests they may do so again in the future.

North Korea's ability to offer off-the-shelf ballistic missiles swayed Iraq as well. Baghdad decided to overlook North Korea's longstanding military ties with Iran in order to procure its own batch of longer-range Nodong missiles. A 2001 US National Intelligence Estimate on ballistic-missile proliferation asserted that following the first Gulf War and the significant erosion of Iraq's military capabilities that the conflict entailed, Saddam Hussein's near-term priority would be to reconstitute the country's ability to carry out regional strikes.[10] In 2003, following the US-led invasion, members of the Iraq Survey Group (ISG) investigated possible WMD and missile programmes in the country. In the process they uncovered a wealth of evidence pointing to 'clandestine attempts between late 1999 and 2002 to obtain from North Korea technology related to 1,300-km-range ballistic missiles – probably the No Dong – 300-km-range anti-ship

---

[5] For information on the Azerbaijan case see Margaret Davis, 'Man Jailed for Azerbaijan Arms Bid', *Independent*, 20 July 2012.

[6] Director of Central Intelligence, National Intelligence Estimate, 'Prospects for Special Weapons Proliferation and Control', NIE 5-91C, Vol. II: Annex A (Country Studies), July 1991, p. 6, available at <http://digitalarchive.wilsoncenter.org/document/116907>, accessed 23 October 2015.

[7] Joseph S Bermudez, Jr, 'A History of Ballistic Missile Development in the DPRK', Center for Nonproliferation Studies Occasional Paper No. 2, 1999, p. 12.

[8] *Ibid.*

[9] 'August 2008 Visit to North Korea by a UAE Delegation for Meetings with KOMID', Cable #08STATE123035, 19 November 2008, accessed via Wikileaks on 2 November 2014.

[10] National Intelligence Council, 'Foreign Missile Developments and Ballistic Missile Threats through 2015', unclassified summary of National Intelligence Estimate, December 2001, p. 10.

cruise missiles, and other prohibited military equipment'.[11] Technology to construct a domestic production line was allegedly also requested.[12]

According to ISG-acquired transcripts of conversations between Iraqi and North Korean officials, Iraq paid a $10 million deposit on the contract. However, frustrations began to arise when substantial delays were experienced in delivery, which Pyongyang blamed on US scrutiny of Iraq. Baghdad demanded its money back, but appeared unsuccessful in securing repayment before the US-led invasion. Reflecting upon the evidence uncovered, one of the ISG members said: 'we've learned this much: that Kim Jong-il took Saddam to the cleaners.'[13]

Since 2006, a portion of North Korea's clients appear similarly to regard their relationships with Pyongyang as transactional and transient. Admittedly, as taboos and regulations against North Korean arms trade have strengthened over time, the number of ad hoc customers has shrunk. From open sources, it seems that in the sanctions period only the Republic of the Congo (RoC), Tanzania and Eritrea can be placed in this category. These clients seem to have been largely motivated by the need to keep certain types of ageing weapons systems or production technology in service, and North Korean willingness to provide that assistance economically.

They also differ from the two other categories of clients – those that are 'resilient' and 'reluctant' – in terms of their sensitivity to external criticism. In the RoC and Tanzania, and perhaps Eritrea as well, it is probable that relevant decision-makers may have been genuinely unaware that their deals constituted sanctions violations. With the UN having since singled them out for precisely this offence, it is thus possible that their brief interaction will come to a rapid end.

Republic of the Congo

In contrast to the longstanding custom of the Democratic Republic of the Congo, neighbouring RoC's contracts with North Korea only span the 2008–09 period. In fact, the RoC case speaks to the fact that, for some, North Korea is merely a supplier of last resort. For Brazzaville, the problem was that its aged Soviet-made T-54, T-55 and T-62 tanks, its armoured vehicles, and its 122-mm and 107-mm multiple rocket launchers

---

[11] 'Text of David Kay's Unclassified Statement', *CNN*, 3 October 2003, <http://edition.cnn.com/2003/ALLPOLITICS/10/02/kay.report/>, accessed 23 October 2015.
[12] *Ibid*.
[13] David E Sanger and Thom Shanker, 'A Region Inflamed: For the Iraqis, A Missile Deal that Went Sour; Files Tell of Talks with North Korea', *New York Times*, 1 December 2003.

desperately needed repairs if they were to be kept in service. Other possible suppliers of spare parts and maintenance services for these systems approached by the Congolese were allegedly either unwilling to provide them or were notably more costly. Buying new systems was also out of the question.[14]

North Korea, said to be aggressively marketing its wares across the African continent through regional offices of the Korea Mining Development Trading Corporation, stepped in. The two sides agreed an initial contract, valued at nearly €2 million, for eight months of refurbishment work and associated technical manuals and training. As mentioned in Chapter II, repairs for B-12 107-mm multiple rocket launchers were charged at approximately €1,220 per unit, while repairs for BM-21 122-mm multiple rocket launchers were charged at €5,520 per unit – substantially cheaper than prices charged by Ukrainian defence firms for similar repairs.[15] North Korean technicians are believed to have arrived in Brazzaville in June 2008. Between then and September the same year, Congo received five shipments from North Korea that were confirmed or suspected to contain items related to the contract and the technicians' work (see Table 2).

In the first three incidents outlined in Table 2, the consignee was a North Korean-owned company (DGE Corporation) operating in the RoC. Furthermore, in the case of the *Hong Tai 1* shipment, the bill of lading was filled out to the attention of the counsellor at the North Korean embassy in Brazzaville. Dispelling any doubt about the nature of the arrangement, the UN Panel of Experts on North Korea acquired an invoice for the refurbishment services provided by approximately forty North Korean technicians, which was submitted by the same diplomatic representative.[16] All five of these shipments in 2008 and the accompanying service contract were in firm violation of UN sanctions at the time they took place, given the involvement of heavy conventional weapons systems.

The following year, the final consignment related to the contract was seized in Durban port on its way to the RoC.[17] Hidden behind sacks of rice

---

[14] Author interview with Interviewee E, conducted in May 2014. Corroborated by Interviewee D via e-mail in January 2015.

[15] Prices have been adjusted for inflation.

[16] See 'Report of the Panel of Experts Established Pursuant to Resolution 1874 (2009)', S/2013/337, Annex XVII, p. 40 for the number of North Korean technicians. See p. 112 for the related contract.

[17] There has been some suspicion that the *MV Westerhever's* arms-laden containers were in fact bound for end users in neighbouring Democratic Republic of the Congo. Indeed, the 2010 report to South Africa's parliament submitted by its National Prosecuting Authority claims the same. However, this detail did not feature in

Table 2: North Korean Weapons-Related Shipments to the Republic of the Congo in 2008–09.

Date of Arrival in the RoC	Mode of Transport	Destination	Cargo	Weight (tonnes)	Consignee
25/06/2008	Ethiopian Airlines charter flight from Beijing	Brazzaville, ROC	Tank engines, armoured vehicles	5	DGE Corp
23/07/2008	Hong Tai 1, sailing from Guangzhou, China	Pointe-Noire, ROC	Declared as including 'tyre, steel ring of tyre, lathe, drill press, milling machine, dynamotor'	7.5	DGE Corp
25/08/2008	Otello, sailing from Dalian, China	Pointe-Noire, ROC	Declared as 'spare parts of bulldozer' – a classic North Korean mislabelling technique for tank parts	45	DGE Corp (incorrectly declared as DGA Corp on bill of lading)
09/2008	Charter flight from Pyongyang	Brazzaville, ROC	Motors for T-55 and T-62 tanks, motors for BTR-60 (Soviet) armoured personnel carriers, spare parts for armoured light vehicles	Unknown	Unspecified
15/09/2008	Sea shipment (vessel unknown)	Unspecified (presumably Pointe-Noire)	Over 130 types of item, including engines, radiators, and shock absorbers for tanks and armoured vehicles	Unknown (3 containers full)	Unspecified
11/2009	MV Westerhever, seized in Durban, South Africa	Pointe-Noire, ROC	Components for T54/55 tanks, including communication equipment, gun sights, tank tracks, and periscopes	Unknown	North Korean company in RoC

Source: *'Report of the Panel of Experts Established Pursuant to Resolution 1874 (2009)', S/2013/337, Annex XVII, pp. 108–11.*

aboard the *MV Westerhever*, South African authorities discovered spare parts for T-54 and T-55 tanks, including gun sights, periscopes and tracks. Amongst other things, the cargo also included communications equipment, protective headgear and searchlights for tank crews. The cargo's estimated value was approximately €550,000.[18]

As a result of the backlash against the contract, the RoC expelled the North Korean technicians in April 2010, despite the fact that they had yet to complete about a quarter of their work. It also cancelled a second, smaller contract valued at just over €1.5 million for additional refurbishment of similar weapons systems.[19] No corrupt pay-offs seem to have been involved on either side of the deal.

Brazzaville has since co-operated with the UN, sharing details and documents related to its contract with Pyongyang, as evidenced by the volume of information contained in reports by the UN Panel of Experts on North Korea. This behaviour highlights the fact that the RoC was unlikely to have been a frequent customer of North Korea's, and harboured no special affinity for it as a supplier.

Tanzania

Tanzania appears to have been another of North Korea's one-off or sporadic customers. *Africa Confidential*, known for its investigative journalism, published a report in August 2013 alleging that eighteen military technicians from Pyongyang were helping the Tanzanian air force to refurbish F-7 fighter jets at the Mwanza air base.[20] In response, Tanzania's minister of foreign affairs instructed critics 'to carefully read the UN resolution in question to see if hiring technicians from North Korea to

---

South Africa's report to the UN, and the vast majority of analysis subsequently published by the Panel of Experts on North Korea and others does not concur that the intended recipient was anyone other than the RoC government. See National Prosecuting Authority of South Africa, 'Annual Report of the National Prosecuting Authority 2009/2010', 2010, p. 22, <http://www.npa.gov.za/UploadedFiles/Sub-Programme1%20Public%20Prosecutions_2010.pdf>, accessed 23 October 2015.

[18] Joe Lauria, Gordon Fairclough and Peter Wonacott, 'Pretoria Seized North Korean Weapons', *Wall Street Journal*, 26 February 2010. Original figure provided was $750,000. This figure has been converted to euros using sensitivity-tested historical rates and adjusted for inflation.

[19] Interviews with experts familiar with the deal.

[20] *Africa Confidential*, 'The Dar Leader' (Vol. 54, No. 16, August 2013), <http://www.africa-confidential.com/article-preview/id/5002/The_Dar_leader>, accessed 23 October 2015. F-7s are Chinese upgrades of the Soviet MiG-21, which forms the backbone of North Korea's air force. While North Korea would not likely be able to provide all of the spare parts for these jets, as they differ slightly from the variants it deploys, the country's technicians would be familiar enough with most of the technology to offer repair services, for example.

repair warplanes amounts to violating sanctions'.[21] The misguided implication that such activity would not in fact be in breach of UN Security Council Resolution 1874 points to ignorance within at least some parts of the Tanzanian government about the boundaries of the current sanctions regime.

The UN Panel of Experts on North Korea continues to investigate the allegation. It has confirmed that 'the Tanzanian People's Defence Force Air Wing has around 10 F-7 fighter jet aircraft based at Mwanza Air Force Base and that new facilities to store these aircraft had recently been constructed, a strong indication that the aircraft are operationally maintained'.[22] However, the Tanzanian government had still not responded to the Panel's requests for further information at the time that its 2014 or 2015 reports were published, and the Panel was therefore unable to conclude that there had been North Korean involvement in F-7 maintenance and repair.[23] *Africa Confidential* subsequently alleged that pressure from the US had persuaded Tanzania to expel the North Korean technicians present in the country.[24]

Eritrea

Adding to North Korea's list of African clients is Eritrea. An East African country informed the UN that in May 2011 it had inspected the Singapore-flagged *MV Kota Karim* bound for Eritrea, acting on information that North Korea was involved in the consignment. The vessel contained a radial drilling machine and vertical milling machine, equipment that is commonly used for forming metal, but that was declared as having an agricultural application.[25] Having found no persuasive evidence at the time that the machines were destined for a military end use, the cargo was released by port authorities one week later.

However, upon examination of the evidence, the UN's Somalia and Eritrea Monitoring Group concluded that the equipment may have indeed

---

[21] *East African*, 'Tanzania Denies Presence of North Korean Army Experts', 14 August 2013.
[22] 'Report of the Panel of Experts Established Pursuant to Resolution 1874 (2009)', S/2014/147, p. 35.
[23] 'Report of the Panel of Experts Established Pursuant to Resolution 1874 (2009)', S/2015/131, 23 February 2015, p. 79.
[24] *Africa Confidential*, 'The MiGs of Mwanza' (Vol. 55, No. 10, 16 May 2014), <http://www.africa-confidential.com/article-preview/id/5628/The_MIGs_of_Mwanza>, accessed 23 October 2015.
[25] The container had been loaded onto the *MV Kota Karim* in Shanghai, having arrived there on the *MV Monrovia*, presumably from the DPRK. 'Report of the Monitoring Group on Somalia and Eritrea Pursuant to Security Council Resolution 2060 (2012)', S/2013/440, p. 27.

been part of a North Korean programme to repair and maintain Eritrean weapons systems. According to the Monitoring Group's interviews with Ethiopian military defectors, that programme has been active since 2010. At that time, a meeting allegedly took place between: officials from the Department of Governmental Garages, responsible for the maintenance of Eritrea's tanks, armoured vehicles and mobile missile launchers, the refurbishment of weapons and ammunition, and the modification of weapons systems; Eritrean President Isaias Afwerki; and representatives of the Green Pine Associated Corporation, a designated North Korean arms-trading entity (see Chapter II). Throughout 2010, Green Pine technicians were present at department facilities, namely those in Asha Golgol and Gash-Barka.[26]

The May 2011 shipment thus appears to have been part of this contract. The ship's manifest declared the consignee to have been the Public Technical Services Centre, an alternative but lesser-known name for the Department of Governmental Garages.[27] Further supporting the conclusion of the consignment's military application, defectors identified the machine tools inspected and photographed as being the same as those used in the weapons-repair facility at Asha Golgol.[28]

Open-source information, which documents only a single contract with North Korea, tends to place Eritrea in the 'ad hoc' rather than 'resilient' or 'reluctant' camps. Eritrea may merely have purchased replacement machines for its arms-repair facilities, and had North Korean technicians assist with their installation and the actual repair work. It is possible that the contract has now been fulfilled and international attention to it has eroded any prospect of a new one being signed. That said, it is also possible that beneath the surface, their dealings are more regular and entrenched than implied by Eritrea's inclusion in this chapter. Admittedly, Eritrean groups, prior to independence from Ethiopia in 1991, had known dealings with North Korea in the distant past. In 1980, for instance, Ethiopia criticised the North Korean government for supporting Eritrean forces.[29] More recently, North Korean commercial vessels have repeatedly stopped in Eritrea en route to Al-Shabaab-controlled ports in Somalia, raising the possibility of concerning interaction in this space.

---

[26] *Ibid.*
[27] 'Report of the Panel of Experts Established Pursuant to Resolution 1874 (2009)', S/2014/147, p. 34.
[28] *Ibid.*
[29] 'Hungarian Embassy in Ethiopia, Telegram, 25 November 1980. Subject: DPRK-Ethiopian Relations', 25 November 1980, History and Public Policy Program Digital Archive, MOL, XIX-J-1-j Korea, 1980, 84. doboz, 81-10, 00884/1980. Translated for NKIDP by Balázs Szalontai; available at <http://digitalarchive.wilsoncenter.org/document/115823>, accessed 23 October 2015.

However, none of these suspicions can be confirmed using open-source information. Should more information come to light, it may be prudent to place Eritrea in another category.

A Small and Shrinking Group

Countries with limited resources, external or internal insecurity, and aged weapons systems and production lines designed long ago in the Soviet Union or China face a dilemma. Soviet-designed systems are still in use by many countries that received assistance from Moscow during the Cold War, the RoC being a prime example. The T-54 and T-55 tanks for which Brazzaville asked Pyongyang to provide spare parts and services were designed in the Soviet Union in the late 1940s. Their technology is thus over half a century old. Former Chinese beneficiaries such as Tanzania, which deploy Chinese-adapted versions of Soviet aircraft technology, similarly face the need for life-extension programmes.

Indeed, the pressure on such countries to keep their arsenals operational is high, given their domestic and regional security environments. Their resources available for defence procurement are, however, limited. In many cases, the complete replacement of a class of weapons system with a newer and pricier variant is unpalatable, if not impossible. Instead, a country may assess that it is more cost-effective to continue to repair and maintain smaller segments of a particular category of weapons (or in Eritrea's case, weapons-refurbishment equipment), allowing cost to be spread over a longer period of time and avoiding any need to pay to train forces to use a new system. As the case of the RoC shows, the original manufacturers of the goods in question are either unable or unwilling to help with life-extension programmes for goods that are many decades old, or cannot do so cost-effectively. North Korea has in that respect been the supplier of last resort for the RoC, and possibly for Tanzania and Eritrea as well.

In this respect, the customers described above share some degree of the 'reluctance' of those described in the preceding chapter; their choice of North Korea reflects a relative lack of options. Yet, according to open sources, they appear to be less regular buyers, and in some cases even one-off ones. The value of their military trade with North Korea is therefore substantially less than in the case of the resilient customers, and for the most part probably less than the reluctant ones as well. From a North Korean perspective, this makes them an entry or growth market, rather than an established one.

Crucially, while there is evidence to conclude that all of the resilient customers discussed in Chapter III were well aware of the boundaries of sanctions against North Korea, this cannot be said confidently about the

RoC, Tanzania or Eritrea at the time that their deals were concluded. As a matter of fact, there is reason to suspect that at least RoC and Tanzania were genuinely unaware that co-operation with North Korea in repairing large weapons systems would constitute a sanctions violation. Their behaviour after they were accused of contracting with Pyongyang suggests that they were unwilling to stomach international criticism in order to allow North Korean military technicians to keep working in-country.

Of the three categories of customers described in this Whitehall Paper, it is the 'ad hoc' group that demonstrates the least affinity for North Korea as a supplier, and is more receptive to normative arguments to curtail any such relations. Though new, potentially ignorant ad hoc customers may continue to emerge periodically, on the whole they represent a small and shrinking proportion of North Korea's arms clientele.

VI. KNOW YOUR CUSTOMER

The previous chapters highlight the fact that a notable share of Pyongyang's contemporary global military market consists of supplying spare parts for or servicing 'antique' systems designed and sold decades ago. Many of North Korea's clients were previous beneficiaries of communist bloc generosity, but today struggle to keep portions of their arsenals operational. Yet systems designed in the early or mid-Cold War cannot be kept in service forever. Over time those weapons must be replaced by newer technology, because of their declining functionality, their lack of likely effectiveness against enemy forces, or both. North Korea's uphill battle in marketing weapons and related services is therefore on the cusp of becoming even steeper.

One of the greatest contributions of the UN sanctions regime has been to deny North Korea the ability to keep pace with its competitors. As a result of UN Security Council Resolution 1874 (2009), countries are no longer permitted to sell any military designs, equipment or production technology to North Korea, except small arms and light weapons.[1] Despite this loophole, there are only two confirmed instances of UN member states selling small arms and light weapons to North Korea since 2009: Switzerland reported $174,000 of exports in this category in 2012,[2] and China declared 3 tons of exports of 'bombs, grenades, ammunition and parts' in 2012 and 2014.[3]

This arms embargo has made it extremely difficult for North Korea to obtain new weapons designs or technology that it can produce under licence. In addition, reverse engineering from single units (which are easier to import clandestinely) without the help of others is usually a slow

---

[1] It is unclear whether services related to small arms and light weapons are included in the exemption.

[2] 'Report of the Panel of Experts Submitted Pursuant to Resolution 2050 (2012)', S/2013/337.

[3] *NK News*, 'China Exports Shotgun Ammo to North Korea without Notifying UN', 1 December 2014, <http://www.nknews.org/2014/12/china-exports-shotgun-ammo-to-north-korea-without-notifying-un/>, accessed 23 October 2015.

and difficult process. As outlined in Chapter II, while North Korea has fielded some new products in the sanctions era, it has done so rarely. Instead, its 'new' offerings tend more frequently to involve modifications to old designs. The base technology behind the majority of North Korea's weapons catalogue therefore still dates to the mid-Cold War period. In all likelihood, North Korea's defence-export offerings will continue to fall behind the competition.

This trend could, over time, significantly influence demand for North Korean weapons and repair and maintenance services, especially when it comes to customers that are presently, or may in the future be, in the 'reluctant' or 'ad hoc' categories. As argued above, countries that currently possess Cold War-era weaponry will eventually remove them from service. When they do, they will no longer need repair or maintenance services for weaponry of that age and heritage, which is one of Pyongyang's contemporary specialisations. If North Korea does not have newer wares to offer or if it can no longer boast expertise in repairing or servicing, Pyongyang may find itself unable to identify new conventional markets or retain existing ones. Examples of this dynamic already exist. Though Ethiopia still has dealings with North Korea, it has begun to phase in T-72 main battle tanks designed nearly thirty years after the T-54 and T-55 models that North Korea is most comfortable manufacturing and repairing. Addis Ababa's contracts for tanks and related parts and services are thus now going to countries like Ukraine, rather than to North Korea.

Over the long term, those eager to shrink North Korea's arms-export revenue and military customer base should place an emphasis on continuing to deny Pyongyang advanced weapons technology. Yet at the same time, they should also work actively to accelerate a decline in demand for North Korean products. In doing so, a 'one-size-fits-all' strategy should be avoided, as indicated by the diversity of the customers presented in this study. Rather, it is essential to tailor policy approaches to take account of the motivations that propel state and non-state groups to buy from North Korea in the sanctions era. This chapter will consider the policy tools presented at the beginning of this study and offer guidelines regarding those that are most likely to dissuade customers in the 'resilient', 'reluctant' and 'ad hoc' categories, bearing in mind that this Whitehall Paper cannot comprehensively address the unique complexities of each client.

It addresses the 'resilient' category first, given that it is now the largest in terms of numbers of clients and that it probably also accounts for the bulk of North Korea's revenue from arms-related sales. These customers represent both the highest priority and the greatest challenge for those seeking to improve sanctions implementation. Most of these clients now take a defiant attitude towards the international expectation that they curb their enthusiasm for Pyongyang's military products and services.

Yet the reluctant and ad hoc customers must not be forgotten either. Reluctant customers still offer North Korea a regular market if unchecked. Similarly, if their purchasing decisions go unmonitored, ad hoc customers may provide repeat or expanded business for Pyongyang in the future. Had the *MV Westerhever* not been seized in 2009, it is likely that the Republic of the Congo (RoC) would have commenced its second planned contract with North Korea. The fact that a second contract was negotiated after the start of work on the first suggests that Brazzaville's initial experience was sufficiently positive. It is also therefore reasonable to conclude that the RoC could have continued to give North Korea business, perhaps indefinitely, had their co-operation not been detected by foreign governments.

This author acknowledges that treating sanctions violators differently, as this chapter suggests, is a normatively significant decision. Imposing harsh, publicly visible penalties on those in breach of UN sanctions resolutions, while pressuring others behind closed doors, may be seen as both unfair and a harmful precedent. Yet as many scholars examining the use of sanctions have recognised, sanctions serve a higher purpose.[4] UN measures pertaining to North Korea's arms sales are no exception. They seek to restrict North Korea's access to revenue through this stream by inhibiting supply from meeting demand, and by reducing that very demand. If sanctions implementers are to increase their chance of inducing behavioural change on the part of North Korea's military customers, they must recognise that those customers respond to pressures and incentives differently.

Equally, the nature of the sanctions implementer applying any policy instrument must be considered: the United Nations Security Council and 1718 Committee, national governments, and other actors each have different roles, powers and policy priorities. Policy tools that are appropriate and feasible for one may not be for another. Consequently, the suggestions presented below are intended as general frameworks, rather than complete prescriptions for policy approaches.

Eroding the Demand from Resilient Customers

Chapter III outlined the characteristics of resilient customers. They are generally aware of the existence of sanctions and realise that their co-operation with North Korea either approaches the grey areas of the

---

[4] Brendan Taylor, *Sanctions as Grand Strategy*, Adelphi series (Abingdon: Routledge for IISS, 2010), p. 12.

Table 3: Possible Policy Tools by Client Type.

	Intelligence Sharing	Interdiction/ Overflight Denial	Normative Pressure (Private)	Normative Pressure (Public)	Threats of Penalties	Penalties/ Withholding Engagement	Conditional Incentives	Facilitate Alternative Supply	Sanctions-Regime Education
Resilient	X	X	X	X	X	X	X		
Reluctant	X	X	X		X			X	
Ad Hoc	X	X	X	X					X

current sanctions regime or directly violates it. Their ties to North Korea run deep, extending back decades. In some cases, North Korea is remembered as having responded in a time of severe and genuine need. Relatedly, resilient clients may face internal or external security threats, or both. They are often isolated internationally – a trait they share with Pyongyang, and one that restricts the types and sources of arms available to them. The significance, value, volume and regularity of their trade with North Korea is probably higher than in the cases of reluctant or ad hoc customers.

Compelling these countries to refrain from contracting with North Korea for arms and related materiel and services is thus extraordinarily difficult. Normative pressure alone is unlikely to be effective. Uganda – which, of the resilient clients, arguably has the best relationship with the West – has flatly rejected any effort to shame it out of contracts with Pyongyang, as discussed in Chapter III. It has reminded those that have tried to do so that its foreign relations are purely its own business. Others exhibit even dimmer prospects of bending under the weight of normative arguments. Syrian President Bashar Al-Assad's reputation is already so badly tarnished by his violent and repressive behaviour within Syria that any criticisms of his illegal trade with North Korea would fall on deaf ears. Similarly, normative pressure would be ineffective against armed non-state groups in Gaza or Lebanon.

Similarly, loud reminders of the illegality of missile-related contracts with North Korea have, unsurprisingly, proven unpersuasive to Iran's leaders. Today, key members of the international community also appear to be grappling with the risk that yelling loudly about any continued military ties between Iran and North Korea could jeopardise the fragile, recently concluded nuclear deal with Tehran. Rather than make ties to North Korea a major feature of talks on the implementation phase of the deal, the preferred strategy of the Western governments active on counter-proliferation seems to be to remind the regime periodically, through UN reports and designations of entities and individuals, that its illicit trade is still being watched, and will be disrupted whenever possible.[5]

Trade or financial penalties imposed either nationally or multilaterally, or the threat of such penalties, are unlikely to be effective in changing supplier decisions either. Most of the resilient customers described above – perhaps excepting Uganda – are already isolated from the international community, partly as a consequence of penalties previously imposed on them for other behaviour. They are largely accustomed to the reality that

---

[5] US Department of Treasury, 'Treasury Imposes Sanctions against the Government of the Democratic People's Republic of Korea', 2 January 2015, <http://www.treasury.gov/press-center/press-releases/Pages/jl9733.aspx>, accessed 20 October 2015.

they will face difficulties in their military procurement, and many are keen to show themselves unmoved by external opposition. Assad's frequent publicised meetings with North Korean delegations seem to declare both states' defiance of the measures imposed against them. Further penalties specifically relating to a resilient client's ties to North Korea are unlikely to sway the calculations of decision-makers. While it is important not to allow sanctioned entities and individuals to operate unencumbered, these measures cannot be expected to bring about the end of ties to North Korea on their own.

Specific, visible actions such as interdictions of prohibited cargoes offer better insight into a client's illicit relationship with Pyongyang, as demonstrated by the seizure in 2013 of the *Chong Chon Gang* sailing from Cuba, and make it more costly and difficult for these transactions to continue. However, unless they reveal a previously unknown attempt to transfer a particularly destabilising military capability, their significance is liable to be modest. In fact, they may simply increase the client's determination to outwit those with prying eyes.

The opposite approach – employing carrots rather than sticks – can be useful when applied to encourage a broader political or security change by the client, which may involve severing ties to North Korea. As mentioned in Chapter I, conditional incentives were a feature of the approach taken by the US and UK in securing agreement by the Qadhafi government in 2003–04 that it would no longer pursue WMD programmes or co-operation with North Korea. Promised improvements in relations and the ability to buy arms more openly from other sources were likely attractive to the Libyan regime. In most cases of resilient clientele, however, incentives alone are probably insufficient to convince customers to cease trade with Pyongyang.

Moreover, offering incentives to the types of regimes or groups that make up the resilient client base would be unpalatable from the perspective of the governments most active against North Korean arms sales. It is unlikely that the US or other Western governments would offer such incentives to Syria, Iran, Hamas or Hizbullah to sever ties with North Korea in the current political circumstances, especially as the North Korea dimension is unlikely to be viewed as the priority issue in relation to those actors. Armed groups residing on national lists of terrorist organisations, certainly, are considered illegitimate and irreconcilable enemies, while states listed as sponsors of terrorism occupy a category only somewhat less attractive in relation to offering incentives. Uganda stands out as an exception, as a resilient customer not affected by these difficulties. So far, however, Kampala has not shown much openness to reconsidering its service contracts with North Korea.

On their own, none of the aforementioned tools offer much hope of bringing about an end to a resilient client's military ties to North Korea. Yet, as the cases of Libya and Burma show, success, or at least significant progress, can be achieved when tools are combined and folded into a broader campaign to reintegrate the client into the international community. High-profile verbal pressure, combined with interdictions, financial penalties on entities and individuals, the lifting of general US and EU sanctions in the event of good behaviour, and the other 'carrots' of tourism and foreign direct investment, is a recipe which seems to have convinced these governments to take steps towards the international community and away from Pyongyang. It may be hoped that Washington's recent decision to relax restrictions against Cuba might lead to a wider détente that encourages Havana to choose alternative military suppliers.

However, as Chapter III showed, even the intensive approach pursued with Burma has not yet succeeded in bringing about the complete severing of contracts with North Korea. US Treasury designations in the past several years point to the likelihood of continuing, residual illegal activity.[6] While progress has been made in driving Burma and North Korea apart, the remaining distance may be particularly hard to travel. If arms procurement from North Korea is now driven by Burmese military officials and organisations at the sub-state level, they are less likely to feel burdened with foreign-policy considerations. On the other hand, if dealings with North Korea are still undertaken with the knowledge or acquiescence of the civilian government, then the current state of affairs would suggest that Burma has cleverly found a way to have it both ways.

In either scenario, high-visibility normative pressure over illicit North Korean interactions has in practice been removed from the policy toolbox in relation to Burma. The US seems to have recognised that continued public shaming would hinder, not encourage, the country's further progress down the path of reform and opening. When designating new Burmese individuals or entities, the US Treasury has explicitly clarified that these measures are not being posed against the government of Burma itself.

---

[6] US Department of the Treasury, 'Treasury Designates Burmese LT. General Thein Htay, Chief of Directorate of Defense Industries', 2 July 2013, <http://www.treasury. gov/press-center/press-releases/Pages/jl1998.aspx>, accessed 20 October 2015. See also 'US Department of the Treasury, 'Treasury Designates Burmese Companies and an Individual with Ties to the Directorate of Defense Industries', 17 December 2013, <http://www.treasury.gov/press-center/press-releases/Pages/jl2247.aspx>, accessed 20 October 2015.

Indeed, the Burma case exemplifies the difficulties of weaning resilient customers off North Korean supply in the short and medium term. Only after the country transitioned to civilian government, implemented initial policy reforms, and actively pursued a détente in its relations with the West did a partial relaxation of its strong bonds with Pyongyang occur. It could thus be argued that the history of resilient clients shows that the catalysts for compliance might include the change in nature (or in effective existence, in the case of the Liberation Tigers of Tamil Eelam) of the customer, the renouncement of a military ambition in which Pyongyang had a role, significant improvement in the client's security situation, or a wider political rapprochement with the international community and the West in particular. Unless Syria's Assad eventually falls, a lasting political settlement involving armed non-state actors in the Middle East is reached, and the new nuclear deal with Iran ushers in an era of broader détente with the West, it is difficult to foresee bilateral relations between these countries and North Korea dying off. Among resilient customers, sanctions-implementation progress is hostage to broader political and security issues.

Eroding demand from resilient customers is therefore likely to be a long game. This applies to strategies that would undermine the attractiveness of North Korea's military offerings as well. Resilient customers interested in rarer big-ticket items such as missiles or WMD-related technology will likely always view Pyongyang as a potential supplier for such items, as their options for purchasing them elsewhere are highly limited. However, at least some resilient government clients, such as the Democratic Republic of the Congo, are interested only in North Korea's conventional weapons and related services. As highlighted above, North Korea's catalogue for such weaponry is sliding out of date. This trend can be cemented if the international community continues to block Pyongyang's access to advanced conventional weapons technology as part of an arms embargo. Should it succeed, at least some resilient customers are likely to stop turning to Pyongyang in the long term. Political and historical ties are less likely to have a binding effect in a relationship if the wares North Korea can offer are of no use to the customer, or if North Korea cannot repair the weaponry that the client has in service. As with other approaches, a longer-term denial-of-technology strategy relies to some extent on broader international participation in the arms embargo.

Eroding the Demand from Reluctant Customers

While a long-term effort to deny North Korea advanced military technology could also eventually help to curb demand from reluctant and ad hoc customers, other policy tools that may be appropriate in deterring resilient customers may not necessarily be effective towards reluctant ones.

These governments choose to buy from North Korea because cost considerations put other suppliers out of budget; because other countries are *unable* to provide the specific goods or services desired, perhaps due to the age of the technology; or because other suppliers are *unwilling*, as in the case of Scud repairs in Yemen. Ethiopia's 1980s-designed North Korean small-arms production lines are an example of the consequences of a lack of alternative suppliers, which has bred a degree of dependency that partially explains that relationship. As the discussion in Chapter IV suggests, Yemen and Ethiopia would probably prefer to have higher-quality goods and services from suppliers other than Pyongyang. This reluctance should be taken into account when devising and implementing a dissuasion strategy.

For those reluctant customers where the primary issue is one of cost, strategies to increase the actual and perceived cost of buying from North Korea can be helpful. Here, there is evident value in interdicting suspect cargo and denying overflight permission to sanctions-busting flights. However, this type of visible action must be balanced against the possible long-term benefits of confining pressure to more private channels. Widely publicised penalties and overt shaming may push these countries into greater isolation, and make them believe they have even less to lose from continuing to do business with Pyongyang. At the same time, it may also reduce the influence of security partners like the US – a broadly positive influence in the area of non-proliferation. In other words, policy tools should be selected and applied in a way that does not diminish these clients' reluctance, but instead exploits it for the benefit of sanctions implementation.

It may therefore be preferable in the event of repeated sanctions violations to allow the threat of future unilateral penalties to hang over private discussions, while reserving the actual application of those penalties as a last resort. In the case of reluctant customers, policy-makers should expect a slow and somewhat strained process of changing the client's cost calculations. Yet the prospect of success makes that patience worthwhile, as both Ethiopia's and Yemen's openness to co-operation demonstrates.

For clients such as Ethiopia, that buy from North Korea as a result of the collision of at least two of the factors mentioned above – namely, cost and lack of viable alternative suppliers for outdated goods – positive incentives may also be offered in parallel. Assisting the client with finding alternative suppliers might be particularly worthwhile. For example, it may be possible to identify countries that could help retool Ethiopian production lines affordably away from North Korean machines and designs. For this strategy to be viable, it may be necessary to work with identified alternative suppliers to arrange financing terms for any initial upgrade projects. In short, the approach with the highest chances of eroding demand on the part of reluctant clients probably involves a mixture of carrots and sticks, discretion and patience.

Eroding the Demand from Ad Hoc Customers

In theory, the least challenging clients to turn away from Pyongyang are those whose dealings with the state have been infrequent. While they presumably do not represent the greatest share of the value of North Korea's overseas arms contracts, ad hoc customers are nevertheless important to detect and confront. If left unchecked, they have the potential to become growth markets for Pyongyang.

As outlined in the previous chapter, this group of countries exhibits unique characteristics. Most notably, it is likely that they are comparatively ignorant of the specific restrictions on military trade with North Korea contained within UN Security Council resolutions. Careful monitoring of North Korean entities and individuals known to be involved in the proliferation of weapons and related goods, as well as the provision of related services, is therefore essential to identify any new or resurgent customer relationships. So too is the interdiction of suspicious cargo.

Once a new client relationship is suspected, the logical first order of business is to share information with the possible customer government in question, and clarify the provisions of relevant UN resolutions. This can be done by the UN Sanctions Committee established pursuant to Resolution 1718, by concerned foreign diplomats, or preferably both. Doing so can ensure that senior government figures are fully aware of the dealings of North Korean entities being undertaken by their nationals or on their territory – of particular importance where contracts with Pyongyang are agreed at the sub-state level (for instance, by one branch of the armed forces). Equally, this approach can eliminate any ignorance of the sanctions regime on the part of customer governments and make those governments aware of the fact that their dealings with North Korea are being, and will continue to be, monitored.

Thereafter, the application of a degree of public and private pressure on buyers to change suppliers may be worthwhile. There are two reasons for this, both relating to the nature of ad hoc customers. First, by virtue of being new or sporadic clients, these countries have no apparent political or military affinity for Pyongyang. In fact, one such ad hoc customer, Eritrea, could be argued to have strong disincentives for doing business with North Korea, given its history with rival (and reluctant customer) Ethiopia. That this circumstance has not noticeably affected either country's contracts with Pyongyang only seems to confirm that their motivations for continued dealings are practical – and not ideological – in character. Ad hoc clients' contractual relationships with Pyongyang tend to be, furthermore, at a much earlier stage. As a result, the sanctions-implementation exercise is less one of breaking habits than preventing them.

Second, this client group is made up primarily of those countries that are trying to keep antique and ageing systems in service, or replace portions of aged stock. North Korea's contracts with countries like the RoC, Eritrea and possibly Tanzania demonstrate that those governments have chosen to extend the service lives of their existing systems and arms production lines, rather than acquire newer ones. It is therefore reasonable to assume that cost is a major consideration in these decisions. A tailored pressure strategy would therefore capitalise on the infancy of the relationship with Pyongyang to raise the financial cost of any potential future contracts. These financial costs could include the denial of contracts or aid to the client by other foreign governments (especially those active in the non-proliferation arena) or, if future illicit consignments are intercepted by foreign governments while in transport, the client could face additional costs associated with having to replace seized cargo.

The cases of the RoC and Tanzania, apparent ad hoc customers of North Korea, highlight the merits of this particular package of measures. Both seemed to be ignorant of the illegal nature of their dealings with Pyongyang, came under public and private fire because of it, and have allegedly expelled North Korean technicians and ended their contracts.

Yet the possibility nevertheless exists that countries currently in this category, or those that join it in future, will not be quickly dissuaded. Should it become apparent that these customers are increasingly regular, it may be necessary to pursue an approach more akin to that adopted *vis-à-vis* the 'resilient' or 'reluctant' categories.

A Long Road Ahead

International efforts to strengthen the legal and normative regime against the North Korean arms trade, sever supply from demand, and dissuade North Korea's clients from returning have had some success. The advent of the arms embargo itself has already helped make it more difficult for Pyongyang to maintain the appeal of its defence-export catalogue to potential customers, especially foreign governments. This is a crucial contribution that receives too little attention in discussions over whether sanctions have 'worked'. Member states should continue to strengthen implementation of the arms embargo, to ensure that North Korea's conventional defence exports are rendered obsolete in the longer term, and thereby to reduce the likelihood that resilient, reluctant and ad hoc customers alike find North Korea's offerings attractive.

Despite the positive effect of the sanctions regime so far, the comparative size of each of the categories of clients outlined above demonstrates that much hard work remains ahead. Resilient customers are several in number, highly valuable to North Korea and notoriously difficult for those supportive of the sanctions regime to influence. Dissuasion strategies focusing on resilient customers should involve a mixture of different policy tools, including interdiction, public pressure and sanctions. Yet in many cases, their custom may only truly evaporate, or even reduce, in the event of a broader change in their political or security situation. For this reason, approaches towards resilient customers must also be agile. They must be able to react to new opportunities to harness any emerging rapprochement, in order to curb demand for North Korean military goods and services.

Resilient customers may be the top priority over the long run, but efforts to counter their illegal trade should not come at the expense of efforts relating to customers in other categories. All three varieties deserve attention, tailored to their unique circumstances. Reluctant customers may require dissuasion strategies that centre primarily on threats of penalties, private pressure, conditional incentives and assistance in finding alternative supply. Ethiopia appears to be on the right track in terms of sanctions implementation, and should be encouraged further in that direction using these tools. The same could have been said of Yemen prior to the outbreak of the current civil war. Ad hoc customers must also be informed of the specific restrictions encompassed by the arms embargo, and swiftly pressured to adhere to them. In addition, their trade must continue to be closely monitored to ensure their custom is not repeated thereafter.

The approaches outlined in this chapter can serve as a general framework for dissuading resilient, reluctant and ad hoc clients from continuing their sanctions-busting trade. This framework can assist sanctions implementers in closing North Korea's existing revenue streams from weapons-related imports. However, a general strengthening of the norm against North Korean defence exports is needed in order to prevent new, lucrative relationships with Pyongyang from forming. Raising awareness amongst the numerous governments that are still ignorant of the current sanctions regime, or pay it little attention, is similarly important. This can mitigate the prospect that new ad hoc customers arise in the way that the RoC did in 2008, when it went searching for suppliers to repair and provide spare parts for its ageing armoured vehicles and artillery. A broad range of actors can become engaged in awareness-raising activities, including the UN Panel of Experts, foreign governments and even civil-society representatives. Yet it is the use of some of the aforementioned tools *vis-à-vis* existing customers that is likely to have a greater impact in entrenching the norm against weapons-related trade with North Korea. Cargo interdictions, individual and entity designations, and broadcasted verbal condemnations issued in the process of confronting some of North Korea's current clientele can demonstrate the reputational cost of doing defence business with Pyongyang to a wider audience.

CONCLUSION: REMAINING SEIZED OF THE MATTER

Until 2007, Syrian President Bashar Al-Assad was pursuing a nuclear capability with North Korean help. The plutonium-production reactor at Al-Kibar was nearing operational readiness when it was bombed by Israel. Had the reactor become operational before being detected, the Middle East might look quite different today. North Korea had already assisted Syria in acquiring its own ballistic-missile arsenal and production capability.

WMD- and missile-related items may be the most concerning articles in North Korea's defence export catalogue, but its conventional wares and weapons-related services have larger available markets and are problematic in their own right. Pyongyang has been known to sell conventional weapons to violent non-state groups in the Middle East and South Asia, for example, giving those groups a source of replenishment stocks that allows them to continue fighting. Moreover, the revenue generated through the sale of such arms and related materiel and services may flow into the same coffers that are used to facilitate North Korea's procurement for, and development of, its own missile and nuclear programmes. North Korea's defence exports may not rival that of its competitors in terms of volume or value, but they can still have a disproportionate effect on the international security environment.

Several factors have helped to ensure that fewer potential customers take interest in North Korea's wares. Changes in the global arms market, compounded by North Korea's inability to keep pace with technological developments, have meant that appetite for its weapons systems has subsided. Sales of off-the-shelf ballistic missiles or related production technology, once a major earner for Pyongyang, have largely saturated the demand for those particular goods. Pyongyang's primary competitive edge is therefore its familiarity with antiquated systems and its ability to help with life extension of Cold War-era equipment or production lines. For customers on a budget, bargain prices for conventional weapons and services may also offset the higher-quality offerings from other countries, including China, Russia and Ukraine. Despite Pyongyang's retention of certain corners of the market, an analysis of its client list – which had dwindled from sixty-two members during the Cold War[1] to a fraction of that by the time sanctions were enacted in 2006, and even fewer after almost a decade of sanctions – shows that it is fighting an uphill battle.

The development of norms against the proliferation of WMD and delivery-vehicle technology, and against North Korea as a defence supplier, has made marketing arms even harder for Pyongyang. The UN arms embargo has cemented North Korea's illegitimacy as a defence exporter. Consequently, it has helped to compel some states to cease buying Korean weapons and services – as appears to have been the case after the Republic of the Congo's (RoC) 2008–09 contracts for repairs and spare parts for its tanks, armoured vehicles and artillery (see Chapter V) – and to encourage others to co-operate in ensuring that supply does not meet any lingering demand.

However, much more work remains. Pyongyang may yet find new defence markets where customers are either ignorant of the sanctions regime or willing to circumvent it. Progress made by the international community in implementing sanctions can be reversed by political or security changes in former or current customer states. Furthermore, as the previous chapters have shown, despite the presence of sanctions, a number of customers continue to buy from North Korea. No single factor explains their persistence, contrary to the frequently heard blanket assertion that 'the reason for importing North Korean military equipment is because of the cheap prices for which they're offered on the international market'.[2] Price is important for some customers, but rarely constitutes the whole picture.

Whether resilient, reluctant or ad hoc, all types of customers merit appropriately 'tailored' attention from active sanctions implementers. Resilient customers, such as Syria, Iran, Burma and Uganda, are arguably the most important, since they are greatest in number and probably account for the bulk of North Korea's defence-export revenue, but they may be the most difficult to peel away from Pyongyang. Reluctant customers like Ethiopia are less challenging to woo, but if neglected by counter-proliferators they will continue to provide a relatively stable income stream for North Korea. Of all of the categories, ad hoc customers, which have included the RoC and Eritrea, have the weakest ties to North Korea. Yet if left unchecked they could become growth markets for Pyongyang.

---

[1] Andrea Matles Savada (ed.), *North Korea: A Country Study* (Washington, DC: GPO for Library of Congress, 1994).

[2] Joost Oliemans and Stijn Mitzer, 'North Korea and Ethiopia, Brothers in Arms', *NK News*, 4 September 2014, <http://www.nknews.org/2014/09/north-korean-military-support-for-ethiopia/>, accessed 20 October 2015.

Realistically, the preferred policy approach will depend on who is seeking to apply it. National governments, especially the US, will inevitably balance their need to bring the targeted country into compliance with sanctions against the DPRK with other bilateral political or security considerations. In the case of Ethiopia, for example, Washington will be mindful that alienating decision-makers in Addis Ababa could render them less supportive partners on counter-terrorism and regional security.

The selection of tools should also take into account the type of client. For example, public pressure may be more appropriately deployed against resilient or ad hoc clients than against reluctant ones, that merit a quieter form of outreach. Offering incentives such as financing assistance to the customer in question would be unthinkable if that customer is resilient, but may be necessary if it is reluctant. Interdiction, on the other hand, is useful across the board. For customers less wedded to Pyongyang, it can have a role in changing the client's cost-benefit calculation. While interdictions of illicit cargoes cannot be expected to reduce the determination of resilient customers, they can shed light on the nature of illegal transactions and help to raise awareness of the sanctions regime. In short, policy approaches to eroding the demand for North Korean military goods and services must be as varied as the sources of that demand.

On the day that the UN Security Council enacted a complete arms embargo against North Korea in response to its testing of a second nuclear device, members of the Council were resolute: Pyongyang 'should shun provocations and proliferation.' However, for now, they added, 'its choices have led it to face markedly stronger sanctions from the international community.'[3] After years of sanctions being in place, it is clear that North Korea remains determined to sell its technology and knowledge abroad.

Hopes of improving implementation of the arms embargo centre on the demand side of the equation. The old adage 'know your customer' takes on new meaning in this context: it is the nuances that differentiate North Korea's customers that the sanctions implementers must understand and consider when formulating appropriate dissuasion strategies. Conditional incentives, facilitation of alternative supply, public or private condemnation of the customer, threats of penalties, and cargo seizures can all have a role to play in compelling decision-makers to quit Pyongyang. Yet above all else, the most important policy from a sanctions-compliance perspective is seizure of a different nature, as spelled out in the final line of each UN Security Council resolution: the international community must remain actively seized of the matter.

---

[3] Statement by Ambassador DiCarlo of the United States of America, 6141st meeting of the UN Security Council, S/PV.614112 June 2009, New York.

APPENDIX A: NORTH KOREAN BROCHURE FOR AT-4 ANTI-TANK MISSILE

This is intended to destroy AFVs such as stopped or moving hostile tanks, pillboxes.

CHARACTERISTICS

Max. range:	2500m
Min. range:	75m
Armour penetration:	460mm
Average flying speed:	180m/s
Launcher caliber:	120mm
Missile/loaded missile length:	863/1093mm
Missile/loaded missile mass:	7.8/13kg
Control mode:	Semiauto laser beam guidance
Laser wave length:	0.85~0.92μm
Laser beam diameter:	∅6±0.5m
Power consumption of laser beam indicator:	30W or less
Sight magnification:	x10
Sight field of view:	5°
Aiming angle: Traversing angle	0~360°
Elevating angle	−20°~+20°
Launch guidance device mass:	22kg
Firing rounds per minute:	2rds
Launch guidance device size: in portable position	530x495x390 mm
in combat position	1110x770x800 mm

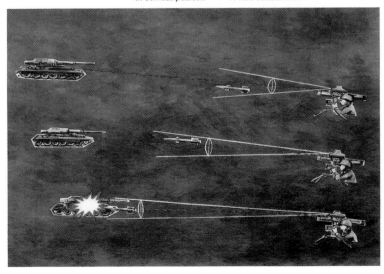

COMPONENTS OF WEAPON SYSTEM

This weapon system is largely composed of loaded missile, launch guidance device, missile test equipment and launch guidance device test equipment.

Launch guidance device is composed of laser beam indicator, control apparatus and launching device.

In laser beam indicator are built laser oscillator, modulator, zoom optic system and sight. Control apparatus operates laser beam indicator and incorporates built-in electronic circuit which controls the launching of missile.

Power is fed to launch guidance device for operation from ground thermal battery built in launching tube of loaded missile.

Loaded missile consists of missile, launching tube and launching booster.

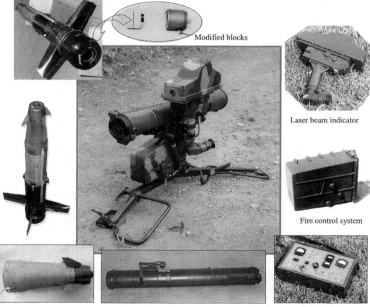

Modified blocks

Laser beam indicator

Fire control system

Test device

OPERATING PRINCIPLES OF WEAPON SYSTEM

Missile is controlled by the principle of 3-point guidance.

i. e. if operator continues to aim at the target even after missile is fired, missile will be guided to target, it's deviation from sight line between target and operator being steadily reduced to minimum.

To this end, zoom optic system of laser beam indicator on launch guidance device emits a laser beam from 60m to 2500m (laser beam diameter: 6m) on the basis of flying distance variation law of missile. This laser beam is specially encrypted.

If the operator pulls the trigger, PS (power source) is fed to launch guidance device and missile is launched.

When the operator aims reticule of sight at center of target, missile will automatically pick up its deviation from sighting line and make up a command for realization of control towards target.

As soon as target is killed, launch guidance device is converted over to next launching readying position.

ADVANTAGES OF WEAPON SYSTEM

Superiority of this weapon system to IR wire-guided missile

- No hostile jamming at all thanks to existence of laser light sensor on missile tail part.
- No effect by water surface, valley, shrubs, etc. because there is no control wire.
- Inherent advantage of laser beam system leads to a minor missile guidance error to aiming axis.

Operators with modified missile and laser designator

APPENDIX B: BROCHURE FOR GAFAT ARMAMENT INDUSTRY

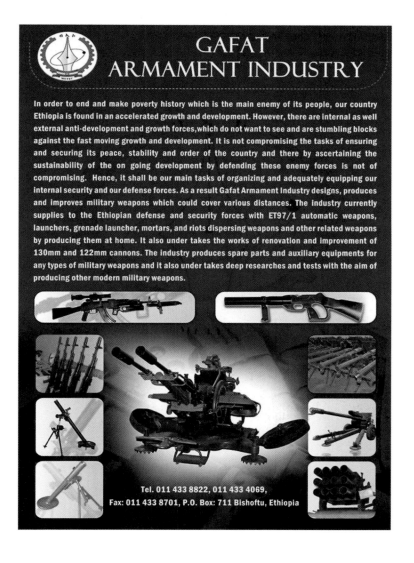

About Whitehall Papers

The Whitehall Paper series provides in-depth studies of specific developments, issues or themes in the field of national and international defence and security. Published occasionally throughout the year, Whitehall Papers reflect the highest standards of original research and analysis, and are invaluable background material for specialists and policy-makers alike.

About RUSI

The Royal United Services Institute is the UK's leading independent think-tank on international defence and security. Its mission is to be an analytical research-led global forum for informing, influencing and enhancing public debate on a safer and more stable world.

Since its foundation in 1831, RUSI has relied on its members to support its activities. Annual membership subscriptions and donations are a key source of funding for the Institute; together with the revenue from publications and conferences, RUSI has sustained its political independence for over 180 years.

London | Brussels | Nairobi | Doha | Tokyo | Washington, DC